Rational egoism

It is often thought that the rational thing to do must be to pursue one's own self-interest. This position is rational egoism. This book is the first extensive history and evaluation of rational egoism.

The author focuses on Hobbes and Sidgwick. They are, after the ancients, the foremost exponents of rational egoism. He also considers other figures – Grotius, Samuel Clarke, John Clarke, Butler, Hume, Reid, Kant, Paley, and Bentham – and a related position: the instrumental theory of rationality. Robert Shaver's conclusion is that none of the arguments for rational egoism or the instrumental theory are cogent.

This is an important book not just for historians of philosophy but for all readers in philosophy or the social sciences interested in theories of morality and rationality.

Robert Shaver is Associate Professor of Philosophy at the University of Manitoba.

Rational egoism

A selective and critical history

ROBERT SHAVER

CAMBRIDGE
UNIVERSITY PRESS

PUBLISHED BY THE PRESS SYNDICATE OF THE UNIVERSITY OF CAMBRIDGE
The Pitt Building, Trumpington Street, Cambridge CB2 1RP, United Kingdom

CAMBRIDGE UNIVERSITY PRESS
The Edinburgh Building, Cambridge CB2 2RU, UK   http://www.cup.cam.ac.uk
40 West 20th Street, New York, NY 10011-4211, USA   http://www.cup.org
10 Stamford Road, Oakleigh, Melbourne 3166, Australia

First published 1999

Printed in the United States of America

Typeface Palatino 10/12.5 pt.   System MagnaType™ 3.52 [AG]

A catalog record for this book is available from
the British Library.

Library of Congress Cataloging-in-Publication Data
Shaver, Robert William, 1961–
Rational egoism : a selective and critical history / Robert
William Shaver.
p. cm.
Includes bibliographical references.
ISBN 0-521-63253-6
1. Egoism, 2. Hobbes, Thomas, 1588–1679 – Ethics. 3. Sidgwick,
Henry, 1838–1900 – Ethics. I. Title.
BJ1474.S43   1998
171'.9 – dc21   98-17212
                                                            CIP

ISBN 0 521 632536 hardback

To my parents

Contents

Acknowledgments

I wish to thank Carl Matheson and Karyn Freedman, for a winter of discussions of the instrumental theory; Sigrún Svavarsdóttir, for comments on a version of 2.2, and 4.5 read at the 1995 A.P.A. Central Division meetings; Anne Jaap Jacobson, for comments on a version of 4.5; the University of Manitoba Institute for the Humanities, for a fellowship during the winter of 1996; audiences at Manitoba that heard versions of Chapters 1, 2.2, and 4.5; an audience at the 1994 Hume Conference in Rome that heard a version of 4.5; two anonymous referees for Cambridge University Press; and most of all, Joyce Jenkins, for the appropriate mix of support and stubborn resistance throughout the project.

I also wish to thank the University of Chicago Press, for permission to reprint part of "Sidgwick's False Friends," ETHICS 107, 1997, pp. 314–20; the University of Calgary Press, for permission to reprint part of "Hume's Self-Interest Requirement," *Canadian Journal of Philosophy* 17, 1994, pp. 1–17; and Pennsylvania State University Press, for permission to reprint part of "Mr. Hobbes Could Have Said No More" (co-written with Joyce Jenkins), forthcoming in the Hume volume of the *Rereading the Canon* series, edited by Anne Jaap Jacobson.

Abbreviations

Hobbes, Chapter 1

B   *Behemoth.* Edited by Stephen Holmes. Chicago: University of Chicago Press, 1990.

DC   *De Cive,* in *Man and Citizen.* Edited by Bernard Gert. Garden City, NY: Anchor, 1972.

DH   *De Homine,* in *Man and Citizen.*

EL   *The Elements of Law,* second edition. Edited by F. Tonnies. London: Frank Cass, 1969.

EW   *English Works.* Edited by Sir William Molesworth. London: 1839–45. References are to volume and page.

L   *Leviathan.* Edited by C. B. Macpherson. Harmondsworth: Penguin Books, 1968. References are to chapter and page.

Sidgwick, Chapters 3 and 4

BB   "Bentham and Benthamism," in *Miscellaneous Essays and Addresses.* Edited by Eleanor Mildred Sidgwick and Arthur Sidgwick. London: Macmillan, 1904.

EP   "The Establishment of Ethical First Principles." *Mind* 4, 1879, pp. 106–11.

FC   "Some Fundamental Ethical Controversies." *Mind* 14, 1889, pp. 473–87.

GG   Review of Green and Grose's edition of Hume's *Treatise. Academy* 5, 1874, pp. 608–10.

LE   *Lectures on the Ethics of T. H. Green, Mr. H. Spencer, and J. Martineau.* Edited by E. E. Constance Jones. London: Macmillan, 1902.

LK   *Lectures on the Philosophy of Kant and Other Philosophical Lectures and Essays.* Edited by James Ward. London: Macmillan, 1905.

M   *Henry Sidgwick: A Memoir,* by Arthur Sidgwick and Eleanor Mildred Sidgwick. London: Macmillan, 1906.

ME   *The Methods of Ethics,* seventh edition. Indianapolis: Hackett, 1981. References to the first and third editions (London: Macmillan, 1874, 1884) take the form *"ME (1)"* or *"ME (3)."*

O   *Outlines of the History of Ethics,* fourth edition. London: Macmillan, 1896.

PC   "Professor Calderwood on Intuitionism in Morals." *Mind* 1, 1876, pp. 563–6.

PE   *Practical Ethics,* first edition. London: Swan Sonnenschein, 1898.

PSR   *Philosophy, Its Scope and Relations.* Edited by James Ward. London: Macmillan, 1902.

SE   "Mr. Barratt on 'The Suppression of Egoism.'" *Mind* 2, 1877, pp. 411–12.

UG   "Hedonism and Ultimate Good." *Mind* 2, 1877, pp. 27–38.

VB   "Verification of Beliefs." *Contemporary Review* 17, 1871, pp. 582–90.

Introduction

SIDGWICK writes that there is "preponderant assent" to rational egoism in "the common sense of mankind" and "the history of ethical thought in England."[1] It is, he thinks, "hardly going too far to say that common sense assumes that 'interested' actions, tending to promote the agent's happiness, are *prima facie* reasonable: and that the *onus probandi* lies with those who maintain that disinterested conduct, as such, is reasonable."[2] A century later, many agree that rational egoism is and has been the "default view" that any rival normative theory must defeat.[3]

This book is a selective history of rational egoism.[4] I consider Hobbes and Sidgwick in detail. I concentrate on them because they are, after the ancients, the foremost champions of rational egoism. Hobbes is the textbook example.[5] Arguments in favour of rational egoism culled from him remain very attractive today. Sidgwick is less influential but more squarely focussed on the case for rational egoism. (He is also, to my mind, the most astute moral philosopher.) I argue that neither Hobbes nor Sidgwick provides good arguments for rational egoism and that

1 Henry Sidgwick, "Some Fundamental Ethical Controversies," *Mind* 14, 1889, p. 483.
2 Henry Sidgwick, *The Methods of Ethics* (Indianapolis: Hackett, 1981), p. 120.
3 See, for example, David Brink, "Rational Egoism, Self, and Others," in *Identity, Character and Morality*, ed. O. Flanagan and A. Rorty (Cambridge, MA: MIT Press, 1990), p. 341; Stephen Darwall, *The British Moralists and the Internal "Ought": 1640–1740* (New York: Cambridge University Press, 1995), p. 3.
4 For two fine and relevant papers, see W. K. Frankena, "Concepts of Rational Action in the History of Ethics," *Social Theory and Practice* 9, 1983, pp. 165–97, and "Sidgwick and the History of Ethical Dualism," in *Essays on Henry Sidgwick*, ed. Bart Schultz (New York: Cambridge University Press, 1992), pp. 175–98. Henry Sidgwick's *Outlines of the History of Ethics* (London: Macmillan, 1896) is also very helpful.
5 Thus he is the one rational egoist supplied by Kurt Baier, "Egoism," in *A Companion to Ethics*, ed. Peter Singer (Oxford: Blackwell Publisher, 1991), p. 201.

Sidgwick suggests good arguments against it. My aims are both interpretive and critical.

I shall, throughout, use some technical terms.

Two sorts of descriptive, non-normative egoism should be distinguished. *Psychological* egoism needs no introduction: It holds that one can pursue only what one takes to be in one's self-interest.[6] *Predominant* egoism holds that altruism overcomes self-interest only in a small number of people and situations, and then typically where the sacrifice is small and the gain to others is large or where those benefiting are friends, family, or favourite causes.[7]

Some account is also required of what, following Sidgwick, I call "rational egoism."[8] Rational egoism is a normative rather than descriptive position. A rational egoist claims that it is necessary and sufficient, for an action to be rational, that it contribute to the well-being of the agent. Distinct positions are produced with specific accounts of contribution (maximising, satisfying) and well-being (pleasure, perfection, the satisfaction of self-regarding desires), and one might take rules or dispositions rather than actions as the objects of evaluation. (The same holds, where appropriate, for the normative positions below.) I shall usually not distinguish between these formulations of rational egoism, since I am concerned with arguments for any one of them.

I shall also occasionally consider two other normative positions. The first position claims it is necessary (but not sufficient), for an action to be rational, that it contribute to the well-being of the agent. Call this position "veto egoism." Veto egoism captures those, like Samuel Clarke, Reid, and (perhaps) Butler, who admit reasons grounded in something other than self-interest, yet give self-interest a veto over these reasons.

The second position is the instrumental theory of practical reason. According to the instrumental theory, it is necessary and sufficient, for an action to be rational, that it best contribute to the satisfaction of the agent's desires. The instrumental theory will differ, in its verdicts, from the self-regarding desire version of rational egoism whenever the agent's desires are not all self-regarding. It will differ from the perfectionist or hedonist versions of rational egoism whenever the agent's desires are not all for her own perfection or pleasure. Since, on the

---

6 For an excellent discussion, highlighting the problems afflicting explications of "self-interest," see Gregory Kavka, *Hobbesian Moral and Political Theory* (Princeton, NJ: Princeton University Press, 1986), pp. 35–64.

7 See Kavka, *Theory*, pp. 64–5.

8 See, for example, Sidgwick, *Methods*, pp. xix, 89, 170, 173, 386, 420.

instrumental view, practical reason is limited to discovering how desires can be satisfied, (non-instrumental) desires that fail to be self-regarding, or fail to aim at one's perfection or pleasure, cannot be criticised on the basis of practical reason. The instrumental theory, then, is not a form of rational egoism. Nonetheless I consider it, for two reasons: It is suggested by Hobbes, and so must be considered as an interpretation of him; and it provides a popular challenge to moral demands that resembles the challenge posed by rational egoism, in that judgements of the rationality of an action depend solely on the concerns of the agent.

In outline, the argument runs as follows.

Hobbes is a rational egoist. When asked why, he gives several answers. Some of these answers depend on psychological or predominant egoism. Since we must pursue our self-interest, Hobbes suggests, it is pointless to require that we do otherwise. Another Hobbesian answer relies on the normative claim that we think self-defence is justified.

These arguments fail. Even if Hobbes's descriptive claims are true, it does not follow that contribution to self-interest is necessary or sufficient for rational action. One might merely conclude instead, with Bentham, that adequate sanctions are needed to make duty and self-interest coincide. This is a concession to motivation, irrelevant to rationality. In the case of self-defence, we do not, with Hobbes, believe that *anything* is permitted. Many think, for example, that large numbers of innocents cannot be harmed in self-defence.

Hobbes also suggests a different defence, relying on the instrumental theory of rationality. However, he assumes, rather than proves, that practical reason can only be instrumental. Since many think that, for example, we have reason, regardless of our desires, to relieve suffering when we can do so with little effort or cost, Hobbes requires an argument here.

Instrumentalists after Hobbes, such as Larry Laudan, John Mackie, and David Gauthier, have not provided the needed argument. Hume, the classic instrumentalist, is better read as suggesting an argument against instrumentalism. For Hume, both the instrumental theory and its rivals rest on our judgements concerning particular cases; the instrumental theory is but one normative theory among many.

Sidgwick suggests various arguments in favour of rational egoism. At times, he suggests that rational egoism is self-evident. He also argues that rational egoism is supported by common-sense prudential beliefs and by the distinction between one person and another.

Again, these arguments do not convince. At best, considerations of self-evidence establish that the time at which some good comes is, in itself, irrelevant. Common-sense beliefs about cases in which prudence and duty conflict do not support prudence. And the distinction between persons, while defeating one argument against rational egoism, does not thereby establish rational egoism.

Sidgwick also argues that the historical agreement of thoughtful people on rational or veto egoism provides some reason to believe them. But the historical record does not support his claim. Some of those whom Sidgwick cites as rational or veto egoists probably hold neither position (Butler, Hume, Kant, Bentham). Others who do perhaps hold one of these positions give arguments that neither we nor Sidgwick should endorse, and so also fail to provide significant historical support (Samuel Clarke, John Clarke, Reid, Paley).

After Sidgwick, rational and veto egoism find somewhat less favour. One reason is that most follow Sidgwick in giving God no role. Apart from Hobbes, almost everyone Sidgwick cites as supporting rational or veto egoism deploys God and His design either to ensure that duty pays or to infer, from our largely self-interested nature, that we *ought* to be self-interested. Many, such as Butler and Reid, give God both roles. Without God, it becomes costly for duty to say that we ought to pursue our self-interest, and the appeal to our nature loses its normative upshot. In this way, surprisingly, the "death of God" hurts rather than helps normative egoism.

There are some topics and figures to which I give little attention.

I assume that morality and self-interest do not completely coincide in their dictates.

I say little about rival theories of the good, such as hedonism, desire-satisfaction, or perfectionism. I assume that hedonism or desire-satisfaction is the correct view, but my arguments would not be changed substantially by adopting a perfectionist or "objective list" theory, provided the list did not ensure that morality and self-interest completely coincide.[9]

I do not discuss Spinoza, Pufendorf, Cumberland, Locke, Shaftesbury, Hutcheson, or the ancients. All merit serious treatment in a more complete history.

I do not consider ethical egoism or whether rational egoism counts as a moral theory.[10] Like Sidgwick, I consider rational egoism to be a

---

9 For an excellent taxonomy and discussion, see Derek Parfit, *Reasons and Persons* (New York: Oxford University Press, 1984), pp. 493–502.
10 For a sample discussion, see Kavka, *Theory*, pp. 365–78.

theory of reasons for action that competes with traditional moral theories, and which deserves attention in its own right.

I leave some normative positions undiscussed. One might hold that contribution to the well-being of the agent is neither necessary nor sufficient for rational action, but that such contribution sometimes excuses an action. One might hold versions of the instrumental theory on which, for an action to be rational, it is necessary (but not sufficient), or sufficient (but not necessary), that it contribute to the satisfaction of the agent's desires. Or one might hold that contribution to the agent's well-being is sufficient (but not necessary) for rational action. I leave aside the first position because excusing conditions seem to require wholly separate treatment; they typically concern responsibility rather than justification. I leave aside the variations on the instrumental theory since few endorse them – no doubt because the arguments supporting the instrumental theory are supposed, if successful, to establish desire-satisfaction as both necessary and sufficient for rational action.

More needs to be said about the view that contribution to the agent's well-being is sufficient (but not necessary). Again, few hold this position – though it is a potential gloss on the claim, made by Butler and Reid, that concern for one's own good has "authority" or is a "governing" principle. It could also find support from considerations of self-defence: One might find action in self-defence rational but optional. I shall mention this position on occasion. I omit detailed treatment for two reasons: this position poses less of a threat to morality than rational or veto egoism; and, more importantly, some of the objections I consider to rational egoism serve as objections here. For example, concerns of arbitrariness or common-sense beliefs about limits on prudence or self-defence cut against the sufficiency claim.

There are, on the other hand, some issues outside of those noted in the summary to which I do pay attention. I try to clarify Sidgwick's controversial methodology in 3.1. I examine, albeit quickly, Sidgwick's arguments for utilitarianism in 3.3 and 3.4. And in various places, I consider (though too briefly) figures other than Hobbes and Sidgwick: Bentham in 1.1 and 4.9; Grotius in 1.2; Samuel Clarke, John Clarke, Butler, Reid, and Paley in 4.2, 4.3, 4.4, 4.6, and 4.8. I consider Kant's argument for the hypothetical imperative in 2.1, Hume's instrumentalism in 2.2, and the supposed veto egoism of each in 4.5 and 4.7. Throughout, even readers without special interest in rational egoism should, I hope, profit from the interpretations presented.

Chapter 1

Hobbes

THERE is a recent enthusiasm for Hobbes's moral theory. Hobbes is "the greatest of English moral philosophers," offering a moral theory uniquely suitable to our sceptical age. "Kant, Locke, Marx, and the Classical Utilitarians all have their current defenders and are taken seriously"; Hobbes should join this group, since "his insights on morals and politics are as profound, as systematic, and as close to be being true as those of any philosopher."[1]

In this enthusiasm for Hobbes, there is widespread agreement that he is a rational egoist.[2] At times, Hobbes claims only that reason does

---

1   David Gauthier, "Thomas Hobbes: Moral Theorist," *Journal of Philosophy* 76, 1979, p. 547; Richard Tuck, *Hobbes* (New York: Oxford University Press, 1989), pp. 115–16; Kavka, *Theory*, p. xii.

2   See, for example, Kurt Baier, "Egoism," p. 201; Kavka, *Theory*, ch. 9; Jean Hampton, *Hobbes and the Social Contract Tradition* (New York: Cambridge University Press, 1986), pp. 50, 56–7, 92–4; David Gauthier, "Taming Leviathan," *Philosophy and Public Affairs* 16, 1987, pp. 285–8; Tom Sorell, *Hobbes* (London: Routledge & Kegan Paul, 1986), pp. 100–10; David Boonin-Vail, *Thomas Hobbes and the Science of Moral Virtue* (New York: Cambridge University Press, 1994), pp. 83–4, 92, 107, 113–14, 198–201; Edwin Curley, "Reflections on Hobbes: Recent Work on his Moral and Political Philosophy," *Journal of Philosophical Research* 15, 1990, pp. 192–3. Tuck holds that Hobbes's rational egoism is limited to self-preservation (see references in 1.2). For a similar view, see Johann P. Sommerville, *Thomas Hobbes: Political Ideas in Historical Context* (New York: St. Martin's, 1992), pp. 3, 33, 43, 46, 49, 74–5, 78–9, 162–4. Earlier statements of a rational egoist interpretation include Thomas Nagel, "Hobbes's Concept of Obligation," *Philosophical Review* 68, 1959, pp. 68–83; M. M. Goldsmith, *Hobbes's Science of Politics* (New York: Columbia University Press, 1966), pp. 93–4, 113–17; J. W. N. Watkins, *Hobbes's System of Ideas* (London: Hutchinson, 1973), pp. 56–7; and Stanley Moore, "Hobbes on Obligation, Moral and Political," *Journal of the History of Philosophy* 9, 1971, pp. 43–62. Skinner argues that this interpretation has the advantage of making sense of the reactions of Hobbes's contemporaries. See Quentin Skinner, "The Ideological Context of Hobbes's Political Thought," *Historical Journal* 9, 1966, pp. 313–17. I shall not spend much time defending the rational egoist interpretation against its chief rival, the

not forbid the pursuit of self-interest. Where peace cannot be obtained, one can "use all helps, and advantages of Warre." (*EL* I.15.1, *DC* 2.2, *L* 14/190) No one is obliged to let others kill, hurt, or imprison them. (*EL* I.17.2, *DC* 2.18–19, 5.7, 6.13, *L* 14/192, 14/199, 21/268–70, 27/337, 343, 345–6, *B* 50) Where following the laws of nature is not necessary for self-preservation, because of one's superior power, one is not obliged to follow them. (*EL* I.14.13, *DC* 15.5, *L* 31/397) This position is not quite rational egoism. On it, contribution to self-interest permits an action, or perhaps is sufficient to make an action rational, but is not necessary for an action to be rational. But elsewhere Hobbes implies that contribution to self-interest is indeed necessary to make an action rational, and so seems to embrace rational egoism. In the state of nature "*jus* and *utile*, right and profit, is the same thing." (*EL* I.14.10; *DC* 1.10). The laws of nature tell people what to do to preserve themselves: "A Law of Nature . . . is a Precept, or general Rule, found out by Reason, by which a man is forbidden to do, that, which is destructive of his life, or taketh away the means of preserving the same; and to omit, that, by which he thinketh it may be best preserved." (*L* 14/189; also 15/216–17, *EL* I.15.1, I.17.14, *DC* 2.1–2, 3.26, 3.27n, 3.31–2) "[P]rudence [is] the same with virtue in general." (*EL* I.17.14) In this rational egoism, Hobbes differs from Kant, Marx, and the utilitarians; it is a distinctive Hobbesian thesis.

One expects, then, an extended defence of rational egoism. In 1.1 through 1.3, I consider arguments offered by Hobbes's recent admirers, highlighting Gregory Kavka, Richard Tuck, Jean Hampton, David Gauthier, and Stephen Darwall. The arguments rely on the practicality of morality (1.1); intuitions concerning self-defence (1.2); and the instrumental theory of practical reason (1.3). I find none persuasive, and some textually unsupported. In 1.4, I suggest why Hobbes is not a good source for arguments in favour of rational egoism.

One preliminary is needed. The argument from practicality is most

divine-command or "Taylor-Warrender" thesis. Almost all of the works noted above attack A. E. Taylor or Howard Warrender; for a summary of the objections, see Curley, "Reflections," p. 190. For Taylor and Warrender, see A. E. Taylor, "The Ethical Doctrine of Hobbes," *Philosophy* 13, 1938, pp. 406–24; and Howard Warrender, *The Political Philosophy of Hobbes* (Oxford: Oxford University Press [Clarendon], 1957). Recently, A. P. Martinich has argued that Hobbes makes divine command and conduciveness to self-preservation individually necessary and jointly sufficient for obligation. Since his arguments for the role of divine command do not differ much from Warrender, I leave him aside. See A. P. Martinich, *The Two Gods of Leviathan* (New York: Cambridge University Press, 1992), p. 73.

plausibly read as showing that contribution to self-interest is necessary for rational action (veto egoism). The argument from self-defence is most plausibly read as showing that contribution to self-interest (or self-preservation) is sufficient for rational action. Neither argument alone seems to secure rational egoism, which sets out necessary and sufficient conditions. I shall pass up criticism that turns on this point. Victory by this means is cheap, since both the necessity and (to a lesser extent) the sufficiency claims are significant individually. I shall, then, contend that neither argument secures even its more modest and plausible conclusion.

1.1

In reply to the question of why the laws of nature are "grounded in considerations of prudence," Kavka writes that

> for Hobbes . . . if moral systems are to be *practical* their requirements must link up in appropriate ways with people's motivational capacities. Rules of conduct grounded in prudence . . . connect with [one] of the most ubiquitous and reliable of human motivations: rational self-interest. . . . They are therefore much less likely to enmesh moral theory in problems concerning motivation than are principles requiring unilateral action or impartial concern for the welfare of all.[3]

An insistence that morality must be practical, combined with psychological or predominant egoism, yields rational egoism.

There is a problem with this argument. It holds whether one is a predominant or psychological egoist.

The problem is that the argument does not support rational egoism more than it supports some rival theories. For example, Bentham admits that morality must be practical. He is also a predominant egoist: "[I]n the general tenor of life, in every human breast, self-regarding

---

3   Kavka, *Theory* p. 310. See also Kavka, *Theory*, pp. xi, 338, 364, 383; Watkins, *System*, pp. 56–7; Frankena, "Concepts of Rational Action," p. 169. For a similar argument in Spinoza, see Edwin Curley, "Spinoza's Moral Philosophy," in *Spinoza: A Collection of Critical Essays*, ed. Marjorie Grene (Garden City, NY: Anchor, 1973), pp. 366–9. The other reliable motivation Kavka notes, "a sense of reciprocity or fair play," may not lead to rational egoism at all, if "fair play" is taken to demand, for example, uncompensated sacrifices by those lucky enough to be well-off. For the tension between self-interest and (some versions of) fairness, see Brian Barry, *Theories of Justice* vol. 1 (Berkeley and Los Angeles: University of California Press, 1989), pts. 2 and 3.

interest is predominant over all other interests put together."[4] He holds, however, that a system of sanctions is needed that will promote, not each individual's welfare, but total welfare. From the conjunction of predominant egoism and practicality, he concludes with the "*Duty and Interest* junction principle," which demands that one "make it each man's *interest* to observe on every occasion that conduct which it is his *duty* to observe." He proposes, for instance, that the income of those running jails, orphanages, and poorhouses vary inversely with the death rate and proportionately with the productivity of the inhabitants; management of these institutions should be by contract rather than salary; tax collectors should be paid a percentage of their collection; and anyone in any position of power should be exposed to complete publicity, to provide incentives against abuse of power.[5] He does not add, as the rational egoist does, that the self-interest of the agent is relevant to the grounds of the duty or of what one has reason to do.[6]

Kavka assumes that, to link up with motivation, a duty must lie in one's self-interest. Bentham agrees. But it does not follow that the course of action must lie in one's *initial* self-interest. Sanctions aside, extra solicitude is not in the self-interest of the orphanage governor. But with sanctions in place, solicitude may well be in his self-interest, provided (say) another job is not more attractive and death rates cannot be falsified. Predominant egoism and practicality tell Bentham what sanctions are needed. They do not tell him to become a rational egoist.

One might object that separating motive and justification "carries the inherent danger of instability."[7] The orphanage governor would attempt to evade Bentham's sanctions. This would not be to build on a foundation "as passion not mistrusting, may not seek to displace." (*EL* ded. xvi) There are two replies.

First, one can reply, with Mill, that the instability should decrease

4 For reference and discussion, see John Dinwiddy, *Bentham* (New York: Oxford University Press, 1989), pp. 22–5 and Ross Harrison, *Bentham* (London: Routledge & Kegan Paul, 1983), ch. 6. The quotation comes from Jeremy Bentham, *Constitutional Code*, in *Works*, ed. John Bowring (New York: Russell & Russell, 1962), vol. 9, p. 5.

5 See Harrison, *Bentham*, ch. 5. The quotation comes from Bentham, *Pauper Management Improved*, in Bowring, *Works*, vol. 8, p. 380.

6 I am supposing that Bentham's "private ethics," which explains to each individual how best to pursue his or her happiness, represents an attempt to encourage, in the absence of legislation, actions the utilitarian demands, rather than a surprise conversion from utilitarianism to rational egoism. I discuss this further in 4.9.

7 Thomas Nagel, *Equality and Partiality* (New York: Oxford University Press, 1991), p. 56.

over time. Increasing equality forces more and more people to consider
the interests of others; in time, we come to satisfy the interests of others
not only instrumentally, but also because we care for the interests themselves.[8] Hobbes should be sympathetic. He supposes that our innate
desires are few; the vast majority "proceed from Experience." (*L* 6/119–
20; also *DH* 13) The minds of the people, "unlesse they be tainted with
dependence on the potent, or scribbled over with the opinions of their
Doctors, are like clean paper, fit to receive whatsoever by Publique
Authority shall be imprinted in them." (*L* 30/379; also *EL* II.9.8) His
programme can be adopted, should it be taught in the universities. (*EL*
II.9.8, *L* 30/383–5, 31/408, R&C/728, *EW* iv 438–9, *B* 39–40, 56, 58–9,
71, 148) He often emphasises more general forms of education. (e.g. *DC*
pref., 1.2n, *DH* 13.7, *B* 159–60)

Kavka is much less sanguine. In part, this is because he takes the
failure of various socialist governments as evidence that predominant
egoism cannot be overcome.[9] This dubious claim aside, he does admit
that people may be much less selfish given high levels of welfare.[10]
Elsewhere, he argues that "dominators" – those who value power over
others for its own sake – are needed to ensure conflict in the state of
nature, and that dominators are produced by a process of ends–means
reversal: Power over others starts as a means and becomes an end.[11]
This mechanism is the very one Rousseau and Mill rely on to reduce
selfishness: Mill's argument, for example, is that satisfying the interests
of others starts as a means and becomes an end.[12] Kavka admits, then,
the resources that could overcome predominant egoism.

Second, there is instability even given Kavka's preferred scheme. In
the face of predominant egoism, Kavka tries to show how obeying
moral demands lies in the (pre-sanction) self-interest of each agent. He
admits, however, that his reconciliation of morality and self-interest

8 John Stuart Mill; *Utilitarianism*, in *Collected Works* vol. 10, ed. J. M. Robson (Toronto: University of Toronto Press, 1969), pp. 231–3; and *The Subjection of Women*, in *Collected Works* vol. 21, pp. 288–9, 324–6.
9 Kavka, *Theory*, pp. 76–7.
10 Ibid., pp. 66–7, 78.
11 Ibid., pp. 104–7, 115. To illustrate the reversal, Kavka cites the example of the miser, also cited by Mill (and John Gay) (115). See Mill, *Utilitarianism*, pp. 235–6; and Gay, *Concerning the Fundamental Principle of Virtue or Morality*, in *British Moralists*, ed. L. A. Selby-Bigge (Oxford: Oxford Univeristy Press [Clarendon], 1897) vol. 2 pp. 283–4.
12 For this process in Rousseau, see my "Paris and Patriotism," *History of Political Thought* 12, 1991, pp. 627–46.

applies to ways of life rather than particular actions. . . . It succeeds with respect to most people and groups in actual social circumstances, but not with respect to all people and groups in all actual or possible circumstances. It may not convince the sceptical immoralist to change his ways, but it provides good reasons for moral people not to regret (or abandon) their way of life.

He asks "Am I confessing, then, that we are helpless in the face of the immoralist? No, we are not helpless in the practical sense, for we can use external sanctions to restrain immoralists."[13] For both Bentham and Kavka, there will be occasions on which individuals will lack motivation to be moral.

Kavka might reply that more will feel the lack more often where extensive sanctions are needed. But even if this is so, it is wrong to use this difference of degree to ground the choice between rational egoism and (say) utilitarianism. It may be a requirement on any moral theory that agents can be motivated to follow its dictates. But one moral theory does not defeat another simply because it more easily motivates. If this were so, the "moral theory" telling us to follow our present inclinations would win. To prevent this, the rational egoist must say that high compliance is only one, non-decisive virtue. But if so, high compliance cannot decide between rational egoism and utilitarianism.

Kavka sometimes puts his point in terms of "ought implies can" rather than practicality.

When conjoined with Psychological Egoism . . . this doctrine implies that moral ought-principles can require of an individual only conduct consistent with his self-interest (or believed by him to be so consistent). For the individual would be motivationally incapable of performing acts known to be against his interests. This strict implication does not hold . . . wher[e] Psychological Egoism has been replaced by Predominant Egoism. Even here, however, compliance with the theory's ought-principles

13 Gregory Kavka, "The Reconciliation Project," in *Morality, Reason, and Truth*, ed. David Copp and David Zimmerman (Totowa: Rowman and Allanheld, 1984), pp. 315, 307; also see *Theory*, pp. 381–2. For arguments to show the need for these concessions, see Sidgwick, *Methods*, pp. 166–75; Moore, "Hobbes on Obligation," pp. 50–1; Alan H. Goldman, *Moral Knowledge* (London: Routledge & Kegan Paul, 1988), pp. 34–41; and much of the critical literature on Gauthier's *Morals by Agreement* (Oxford: Oxford University Press [Clarendon], 1986), such as Geoffrey Sayre-McCord, "Deception and Reasons to Be Moral," in *Contractarianism and Rational Choice*, ed. Peter Vallentyne (New York: Cambridge University Press, 1991), pp. 181–95.

must generally be compatible with the agent's interests, or else these principles will often be impossible to follow and hence nonapplicable.[14]

This makes the appeal to practicality more precise, and Hobbes clearly subscribes to "ought implies can."[15]

With his argument put this way, Kavka must address those who deploy "ought implies can" by first arguing that we ought to do some action, and then concluding that we must be capable of said action.[16] He must address objections to "ought implies can" that treat it as merely a conversational convention, irrelevant to the truth of any ought-claim.[17] He must address objections – decisive ones, I think – to "ought implies can" in any form, which cite uses of "ought" to state ideals, or to reduce future failures to do what ought to be done, or to point to a continuing obligation, or to register moral despair.[18] And, even if "ought implies can" is accepted and is understood as restricting the set of true ought-claims, the point made on behalf of Bentham and Mill can be repeated: Unless Kavka restricts the "can" to what an agent can do at the moment of acting, "ought implies can" should merely direct the moralist to supply motives.

Kavka himself sees a problem for restricting the "can" to the moment of acting. He notes that culpable incapacity does not cancel an ought-claim. "We do not, for example, withdraw our judgement that the watchman ought to have stopped the midnight robbery when he points out that he was unable to do so because he was sound asleep at the time."[19] He then worries that this modification to "ought implies can" is inconsistent with "the most plausible justification of the doctrine itself," which is that "ought-judgements are by their nature action-guiding." Kavka replies that ought-judgements can remain action-guiding, since

14 Kavka, *Theory*, pp. 310–11; also pp. 291–2, 329.
15 For evidence and discussion, see Warrender, *Political Philosophy*, pp. 32–3.
16 Thomas Nagel, *The Possibility of Altruism* (Princeton, NJ: Princeton University Press, 1970), pp. 11–14.
17 See W. K. Frankena, "Obligation and Motivation in Recent Moral Philosophy," in *Perspectives on Morality*, ed. K. E. Goodpaster (Notre Dame, IN: University of Notre Dame, 1976), p. 61; and Walter Sinnott-Armstrong, "'Ought' Conversationally Implies 'Can,'" *Philosophical Review* 93, 1984, pp. 249–61.
18 See Sidgwick, *Methods*, p. 33; Sinnott-Armstrong, "'Ought' Conversationally Implies 'Can,'" p. 259; and, especially, Joseph Margolis, "One Last Time: 'Ought' Implies 'Can,'" *The Personalist* 48, 1967, pp. 33–41.
19 Kavka, *Theory*, p. 311. Kavka finds evidence that Hobbes agrees; see *Theory*, pp. 311–12. Similar cases are noted by Sinnott-Armstrong, "'Ought' Conversationally Implies 'Can,'" pp. 252–4; and Margolis, "One Last Time," p. 39.

they direct people to avoid the incapacitating actions. "[S]uch judgements rendered earlier may motivate the agent to avoid the . . . incapacity (e.g., the guard either resigns or drinks coffee to stay awake), and those rendered at the time of action or later may usefully instruct the agent and others as regards similar future situations."[20]

This is plausible. But if so, Bentham and Mill can claim that they, too, issue action-guiding ought-judgements. Ought-judgements made before the action may motivate the agent to avoid incapacities to perform what utilitarianism demands; ought-judgements made during or after the action may instruct the agent and others as to what is acceptable, on utilitarian grounds, in similar future situations. Once the action-guiding character of ought-judgements is broadened to permit cases where the agent cannot obey, rational egoism is no longer favoured.

Kavka might note a difference. He might stress that he allows only *culpable* incapacities. The utilitarian, primarily concerned with the effects of keeping the ought-judgement in force on others, may be less concerned with culpability. But it is unclear why Kavka should insist on culpable incapacities, given that he sees effects on others as important to recognising the action-guiding character of ought-judgements, and that it is this character that motivates accepting "ought implies can" in the first place. One suspects Kavka might reject incapacities for which the agent is not culpable on grounds of fairness. But considerations of fairness cannot play this sort of foundational role in an argument for rational egoism against utilitarianism. This would be both question-begging and suicidal – the latter since considerations of fairness will very probably rule out rational egoism.

One might still, unlike Kavka, restrict the "can" to the moment of acting. This, however, does not help rational egoism. For in cases of weakness of will, we find ourselves unable to pursue our self-interest. A "can" restricted to the moment of acting rules out rational egoism just as it rules out utilitarianism and any traditional deontological theory. Since we sometimes find ourselves unable even to act on what we judge to be our most important present desires, it also rules out the maximising version of the instrumental theory. At best, "ought implies can" supports a minimal version of the instrumental theory. Suppose we can only act on the basis of our desires. Then, if we ought to do anything, we ought to act on the basis of these desires. Where the "can" is restricted to the moment of acting, all normative theories are ruled out, other than a version of the instrumental theory according to which an action is

20   Kavka, *Theory*, pp. 312–13.

rational if, and only if, it serves at least one of our present desires. This, however, looks more like a reductio on restricting the "can" to the moment of acting than an argument for a version of the instrumental theory.

The distinction between a "can" restricted and not restricted to the moment of acting helps in dealing with a further objection. I argue that the appeal to practicality does not favour rational egoism over, say, utilitarianism, since the utilitarian can motivate even psychological egoists to do their (utilitarian) duty by imposing sanctions. One might object that the act of imposing sanctions is excluded by psychological egoism. For it seems unlikely that imposing sanctions forcing the pursuit of the general happiness lies in the interest of anyone.

One reply is to note that imposing utilitarian sanctions may lie in the interest of some people. Hobbes argues that the sovereign will be motivated to apply his sanctions because the sanctions are needed for the health of the nation, and the sovereign's interest lies in a healthy nation. (L 18/238, 19/241–2, 30/388) Hume argues that, initially, property conventions will be enforced by those who are well-off and so have great interest in having them enforced.[21] Other policies a utilitarian would plausibly support, such as those found in a welfare state, seem to lie in the interest of those who are now badly off. Kavka suggests that they may also lie in the interest of those who are well-off, as revolution preventatives or insurance programmes.[22] Thus even if everyone pursues their self-interest, sanctions aimed at the general happiness might arise, provided those with power see the sanctions as in their interest.

The story becomes more plausible where predominant replaces psychological egoism. We then sometimes care about the welfare of others directly. Provided we do so at important moments, utilitarian sanctions could arise. Thus Brian Barry, for example, finds it sufficient that when one votes – particularly on issues that do not affect one's interest – one considers the interests of others, although when one acts as an economic agent, one is self-interested. In voting, one puts into place a system of sanctions that make it in one's self-interest to help others.[23]

One might object that it is not, right now, in the interest of many people to impose utilitarian sanctions. If "ought implies can" is accepted, it follows that it is not the case that these people ought to

21 David Hume, *A Treatise of Human Nature*, ed. L. A. Selby-Bigge and P. H. Nidditch (New York: Oxford University Press, 1978), p. 537.
22 Kavka, *Theory*, pp. 441–6.
23 Barry, *Theories*, pp. 366, 393–400.

support imposing these sanctions. But this falls prey to the objection given above, directed at relativising the "can" to the moment of acting. If imposing utilitarian sanctions is ruled out for some because it is not something they can do, then many of the actions required by rational egoism must also be ruled out for some, since these actions, too, are not actions they can do, given their weakness of will. The rational egoist can reply that the actions need be possible only in some wider sense. But the utilitarian can then note that the actions utilitarianism requires are also possible in this wider sense.

Before leaving the argument from practicality, two historical points should be made.

First, Bentham's separation of motive and justification is common. Barry writes that "[b]ecause of the practical nature of justice, a theory of the motivation for being just must at the same time be a theory of what justice is."[24] Unhappy with Hobbesian morality, he is led to search for an alternative motive to self-interest. But no such search is demanded by the practical nature of justice. Most modern natural lawyers and early utilitarians hold that "what justice is" is set by non-egoistic considerations such as God's will or our sociability, but suppose the main (and sometimes only) motive to be just is self-interest. Barbeyrac is particularly clear. To confound the *"Motive"* and *"Foundation"* of obligation is

> to reduce every Thing to our own *Utility*, to confound what is *just* with what is *profitable*, and, by that Means, give Room to dangerous Mistakes. Besides, the Motive of *Utility* may cease, and the Duty remain.[25]

> [C]onfounding the *honest* with the *useful*, by that Means destroy[s] all Ideas of Virtue and Vice, all *Natural Law*, and all Morality. . . . [I]t is in no way precisely on account of . . . Utility, that we should actually conform ourselves to the Will of God: But rather, because we acknowledge our Dependance, and hereby shew, that we think it good and honest to obey him; and that even tho' he should require of us what is useless. . . . In short, it is to confound Ideas, and make the Accessory the Principal to establish this Utility, (however real or universal) as the Foundation of moral Honesty and *Obligation*, properly so call'd.[26]

Utility "is only the *Motive* which leads us to the Observation of our Duty."[27] Our duties toward others are founded on the "Principle of

24 Ibid., p. 359.
25 Jean Barbeyrac, "Notes to Samuel Pufendorf," *The Law of Nature and Nations*, trans. Basil Kennet (London, 1749), p. 58n5.
26 Ibid., p. 126n2.
27 Ibid., p. 139n3; also see p. 135n1.

Sociableness," which, along with our duties toward God and ourselves, rests on "our natural dependence on the supream Authority of God."[28]

Second, it is often objected, against interpretations of Hobbes that fail to make him a rational egoist, that his psychological or predominant egoism makes any other interpretation otiose. Howard Warrender supposes that the laws of nature are founded on God's will and that egoistic claims about motivation are merely "validating conditions" for these laws. The critics reply that, since the validating conditions rule out any action contrary to self-interest, the ground of the laws of nature may as well be prudence. God plays no role.[29] The argument above shows that Warrender's critics are mistaken (on this point). For one must distinguish pre-sanction and post-sanction self-interest. Ruling out actions contrary to self-interest does not determine what actions will be performed. Some further consideration is needed, to see what (if any) sanctions should be erected. There is room for God, or general happiness, or individual prudence to provide the foundation of the laws of nature, even if we cannot act against our self-interest.

1.2

Given the problems of moving from psychological or predominant egoism to a normative position, one might try another tack. Hampton claims that "Hobbes's central insight about ethics was that it should not be understood to require that we make ourselves a prey for others." Those who disagree "have the burden of proof of showing why Hobbes is wrong to believe that morality should never demand of us that we make ourselves [such] 'prey.'"[30] Kavka finds the right of nature "a normative *postulate* of Hobbes's moral theory," for which "[n]o argument is ever offered."[31] Tuck writes that "[t]here is one thing on which even in a state of nature we can all agree, and that is that other people have a right to defend themselves against attack."[32] There are dif-

---

28 Ibid., pp. 135n1, 64n3.
29 Warrender, *Political Philosophy* pp. 91–3, 212–13, 220, 257–8, 263–4; Nagel, "Hobbes's Concept"; Hampton, *Tradition*, pp. 31–2; Watkins, *System*, pp. 60–3.
30 Jean Hampton, "Two Faces of Contractarian Thought," in *Contractarianism*, p. 53, *Tradition*, p. 94. For Hobbes on "prey," see EL I.17.10, II.1.5, DC 3.27, L 13/184, 185, 14/190, 15/215, 27/345; and Kavka, *Theory*, p. 344.
31 Kavka, *Theory*, p. 315. Arguments are offered outside *Leviathan*: See EL I.14.6 and DC 1.7, noted in 1.4, which rely on psychological egoism. I consider what may count as an argument at L 17/224 below.
32 Tuck, *Hobbes*, p. 58.

ferences between these positions. But they are united in defending Hobbes, not by appealing to claims about motivation, but by making a foundational moral claim.

This interpretation has one great textual strength. Hobbes's normative claims explicitly allow only self-defence, not the general pursuit of self-interest.[33]

[I]f any man pretend somewhat to tend necessarily to his preservation, which yet he himself doth not confidently believe so, he may offend against the laws of nature. (*DC* 1.10n)

[I]f any man will contend . . . for superfluities, by his default there will arise a war; because that on him alone there lay no necessity of contending; he therefore acts against the fundamental law of nature. (*DC* 3.9; also *L* 15/210)

[T]here are certain natural laws, whose exercise ceaseth not even in the time of war itself. For I cannot understand what drunkenness or cruelty, that is revenge which respects not the future good, can advance toward peace, or the preservation of any man. (*DC* 3.27n; also 3.11, *EL* I.16.10, I.19.2, *L* 15/210)

It is a proverbial saying, *inter arma silent leges.* . . . Yet thus much the law of nature commandeth in war: . . . nothing but fear can justify the taking away of another's life. (*EL* I.19.2)[34]

[N]ot every Fear justifies the Action it produceth, but the fear onely of corporeall hurt, which we call *Bodily Fear,* and from which a man cannot see how to be delivered, but by the action. (*L* 27/343)

---

33 This is often noted. See Richard Tuck, *Hobbes*, pp. 60–1, 107–9, "Optics and Sceptics: The Philosophical Foundations of Hobbes's Political Thought," in *Conscience and Casuistry in Early Modern Europe*, ed. Edmund Leites (New York: Cambridge University Press, 1988), pp. 260–1, *Natural Rights Theories* (New York: Cambridge University Press, 1979), pp. 125, 129, *Philosophy and Government 1572-1651* (New York: Cambridge University Press, 1993), p. 306; A. G. Wernham, in Benedict de Spinoza, *The Political Works* (New York: Oxford University Press, 1958), pp. 13–14; Warrender, *Political Philosophy*, pp. 59–63; R. E. Ewin, *Virtues and Rights* (Boulder, CO: Westview Press, 1991), p. 65; Edwin Curley, "Reflections," p. 192, "The State of Nature and Its Law in Hobbes and Spinoza," *Philosophical Topics* 19, 1991, pp. 98–9.

34 *DC* 5.2 *seems* to make the same claim: "It is a fond saying, that all laws are silent in the time of war, and it is a true one . . . provided [the laws of nature] be referred not to the mind, but to the actions of men, by chap. iii art. 27." *DC* 3.27 distinguishes between being prepared to follow the laws of nature and acting on them. One who kills on a basis other than fear shows that he is not prepared to follow the laws of nature. The law is not silent here. But the law is silent about the action of killing, without reference to any motive.

But this strength is also a weakness. At best, Hobbes will establish only that self-preservation, not self-interest in general, can or ought to be pursued. In cases where I do not take my preservation to be at issue, I would have no right to pursue my interest. This is considerably less than rational egoists want. Indeed, where an aggressive action maximises my self-interest but is not one I see as needed for self-preservation, the maximising form of rational egoism requires what Hobbes forbids.

Those who offer a rational egoist interpretation of Hobbes have two replies.

First, Hobbes writes of self-preservation rather than self-defence. The two might be distinguished: Self-defence justifies defence against an immediate threat; self-preservation justifies whatever one believes is needed to maximize one's lifespan. Self-preservation requires many of the actions a rational egoist would endorse, and which an appeal to self-defence would not. One "cannot assure the power and means to live well, which he hath at present, without the acquisition of more." (*L* 11/161) One's "own conservation" requires "[a]nticipation; that is, by force, or wiles, to master the persons of all men he can, so long, till he see no other power great enough to endanger him." (*L* 13/184; also *EL* I.14.13) Those who would not "by invasion increase their power . . . would not be able, long time, by standing only on their defence, to subsist." (*L* 13/185) Hobbes can still condemn pursuing superfluities and practicing wanton violence. But little might count as superfluous or wanton, given the need to attack and accumulate as a means to self-preservation. This position is not quite rational egoism, since it is possible that some action might be in one's interest but not justified by appeal to self-preservation. Yet Hobbes might find few such actions. In the important cases, where my action causes conflict, Hobbes might even deny that it is ever in my interest to so act: The bad consequences of bringing conflict always outweigh the good consequences of satisfying my desire, say, for some superfluity. That is, Hobbes could deny the existence of cases where an aggressive action maximises my self-interest without contributing to my self-preservation. An aggressive action must either maximise my self-interest by contributing to my self-preservation or fail to maximise my self-interest by causing avoidable conflict.[35]

---

35 The point can also be made without separating self-defence and self-preservation. Hobbes sees fear as "a certain foresight of future evil." (*DC* 1.2n) Fear then justifies

Second, in various places, Hobbes gives a generous gloss to the right in question. Anticipation is needed to "live well." (*L* 11/161) The right of nature retained after leaving the state of nature includes a right "to governe their own bodies; enjoy aire, water, motion, waies to go from place to place; and all things else without which a man cannot live, *or not live well*." (*L* 15/212, italics added)[36] It also includes a right to decline any "dishonourable Office." (*L* 21/269; also *DC* 6.13) Similarly,

> a man cannot lay down the right of resisting them, that assault him by force, to take away his life; because he cannot be understood to ayme thereby, at any Good to himselfe. The same may be said of Wounds, and Chayns, and Imprisonment; both because there is no benefit consequent to such patience; . . . as *also* because a man cannot tell, when he seeth men proceed against him by violence, whether they intend his death or not. And lastly the motive, and end for which this renouncing, and tranferring of Right is introduced, is nothing else but the security of a mans person, in his life, and in the means of so preserving life, *as not to be weary of it.* (*L* 14/192, italics added; also 199, *DC* 2.18)

The point of leaving the state of nature is "not the sole preservation of life in what condition soever, but in order to its happiness," that is, to "live delightfully." The sovereign "would sin against the law of nature" if he failed to furnish his subjects "not only with the good things belonging to life, but also with those which advance to delectation." (*DC* 13.4; also 10.1, *EL* II.5.1, II.9.1, *L* 15/216, 17/223, 227, 30/376)

To this, one can add that Hobbes's arguments support the pursuit of self-interest just as well as they support self-preservation. In his arguments in favour of an egoist position (to be noted in 1.4), Hobbes appeals to the "necessity of nature" that

> maketh men to will and desire . . . that which is good for themselves, and to avoid that which is hurtful; but most of all . . . death. (*EL* I.14.6)

> [E]very man is desirous of what is good for him, and shuns what is evil, but chiefly . . . death; and this he doth by a certain impulsion of nature. (*DC* 1.7)

---

not only defence against an immediate attack, but also the anticipation and acquisition noted.

36 *DC* 3.14 and *EL* I.17.2 are slightly different. In *De Cive,* after a similar list, Hobbes writes "and all necessaries for life." There is no mention of living well. The *Elements* is the same as *De Cive,* except that Hobbes adds that "[n]or doth the law of nature command any divesting of other rights, than of those only which cannot be retained without the loss of peace."

The same appeal to necessity appears where Hobbes argues that the right of self-defence is inalienable. By natural necessity we shun death, "or wounds, or some other bodily hurts"; in *Leviathan,* the argument for inalienability starts from a premise that does not distinguish between self-preservation and self-interest: "[O]f the voluntary acts of every man, the object is some *Good to himselfe.*" (*DC* 2.18; *L* 14/192) Since we must pursue our interest, just as we must pursue our preservation, both pursuits are justified.

It may not be possible to reconcile these passages with the explicit restriction of the right of nature to self-preservation. But one can offer a position that captures most of what Hobbes says: Our right is limited to what we take to be needed for living a decent life. In this the right reflects our diminishing desperation as we move from avoiding death, wounds, or imprisonment down to avoiding a small drop in "delectation." This is still not quite the usual version of rational egoism, but it looks like an egoist position, and so is worth examining. (In what follows, I shall call the right in question a right to self-defence, intending to cover both self-preservation and the more liberal right specified here.)

Hampton, Kavka, and Tuck suggest that Hobbes defends this position by making a foundational moral claim: Each has a right to self-defence. But this by itself may not establish an egoist position at all, for utilitarians such as Sidgwick also endorse a right to self-defence.[37] To see whether the right does support an egoist position, one must see how the right is interpreted. The question is whether the right is constrained by, for example, consideration of the common good or the status of the agent. I shall argue that Hobbes does not constrain his right to self-defence in these ways, and so arguments in favour of the right as he understands it would, if successful, support an egoist position. If these arguments fail, one is left without, at least, a purely egoist position. Depending on the nature of the constraints, this may be a non-egoist position, such as utilitarianism, or, more likely, a mixed position, allowing the agent to give special weight to himself within limits set by utilitarian or deontological constraints. I leave discussion of these alternatives to 3.4; my concern here is with arguments for a purely egoist position.

Since Tuck gives the most developed version of the argument for a right to self-defence, I focus on him. I shall consider both the plausibility

37 Sidgwick, *Methods,* p. 457, *Practical Ethics* (first edition) (London: Swan Sonnenschein, 1898), pp. 71–82, *Elements of Politics* (fourth edition) (London: Macmillan, 1919), p. 263.

of his interpretation and the cogency of the argument he attributes to Hobbes.

Tuck does not see Hobbes as simply starting from the claim that we have such a right. Instead, he sees our agreement on this right as providing an argument for it. His interpretation proceeds by placing Hobbes in a particular historical setting. Montaigne claims that "the only likely sign by which [one] can argue certain laws to be natural is universality of approval."[38] Montaigne then notes that no moral law receives universal approval. Grotius replies that Montaigne is wrong: All agree that everyone has the right to self-defence. Tuck claims that Hobbes simply follows Grotius. Both offer a sceptic-proof moral theory that appeals to agreement.[39]

Tuck's interpretation faces two problems as an interpretation and one problem as an argument for rational egoism.

The first interpretive problem concerns the role of agreement. It is plausible to see Grotius as relying on agreement. Universal consent – or at least the agreement of those "more advanced" – is one way in which the law of nature is discovered, and so, to defend the right to self-

---

38 Montaigne, *Essays*, trans. Donald M. Frame (Stanford, CA: Stanford University Press, 1957) II:12, p. 437.

39 Tuck repeats his interpretation in a number of places. For this view of Grotius, see Richard Tuck, "Grotius, Carneades, and Hobbes," *Grotiana* (n.s.) 4, 1983, pp. 51–3, "Optics," pp. 242–3, 245, 258, "Rights and Pluralism," in *Philosophy in an Age of Pluralism*, ed. James Tully (New York: Cambridge University Press, 1994), pp. 164–7, "The 'Modern' Theory of Natural Law," in *The Languages of Political Theory in Early-Modern Europe*, ed. Anthony Pagden (New York: Cambridge University Press, 1987), pp. 110–17, "Grotius and Selden," in *The Cambridge History of Political Thought*, ed. J. Burns (New York: Cambridge University Press, 1991), pp. 499, 506, 509, 512, 516, 525, *Hobbes*, pp. 20–1, 51–2, *Government*, pp. xvi, 173–4, 176, 185, 188, 347. For this view of Hobbes, see Tuck, "Grotius," p. 60, "Optics" pp. 259–61, "Rights," p. 168, "Modern," pp. 114–15, *Hobbes*, pp. 52, 58–9, 61, 93–4, *Government*, pp. xvii, 304–6, 347. In places, Tuck adds that Hobbes goes beyond Grotius in providing a "theoretical foundation" by means of "psychological arguments." (Tuck, *Hobbes*, p. 94, "Grotius," p. 60) He quotes *EL* I.14.6 (which I discuss in 1.4). (Tuck, "Optics," p. 260, *Hobbes*, pp. 61–2, *Government*, p. 305) If such passages are emphasised, however, it is unclear whether the appeal to universal agreement has any role to play, and so unclear whether Hobbes owes anything to Grotius. In this section, I shall ignore this "foundation" and read Tuck as relying on universal agreement to a moral claim. For worries about Tuck's interpretation of Grotius, see my "Grotius on Scepticism and Self-Interest," *Archiv für Geschichte der Philosophie* 78, 1996, pp. 27–47. For worries about Tuck's interpretation of Hobbes as replying to Montaigne, see Tom Sorell, "Hobbes Without Doubt," *History of Philosophy Quarterly* 10, 1993, pp. 123–5 and Sommerville, *Context*, p. 168n7.

defence, Grotius invokes his characteristic swarm of authorities.[40] It is implausible to see Hobbes as also relying on agreement. Hobbes cites almost no other writers, other than Scripture. When he explicitly discusses agreement, he scorns it. To discover the law of nature,

> [t]he method . . . wherein we begin from definitions and exclusion of all equivocation, is only proper to them who leave no place for contrary disputes. For the rest, if any man say that somewhat is done against the law of nature, one proves it hence; because it was done against the general agreement of all the most wise and learned nations: but this declares not who shall be the judge of the wisdom and learning of all nations. Another hence, that it was done against the general consent of all mankind; which definition is by no means to be admitted. For then it were impossible for any but children and fools, to offend against such a law; for sure, under the notion of mankind, they comprehend all men actually endued with reason. These therefore either do nought against it, or if they do aught, it is without their joint accord, and therefore ought to be excused. But to receive the laws of nature from the consents of them who oftener break than observe them, is in truth unreasonable. Besides, men condemn the same things in others, which they approve in themselves; on the other side, they publicly commend what they privately condemn; and they deliver their opinions more by hearsay, than any speculation of their own; and they accord more through hatred of some object, through fear, hope, love, or some other perturbation of mind, than true reason. (*DC* 2.1; also *EL* I.13.3, I.15.1)[41]

In *Leviathan*, Hobbes notes that he has "neglected the Ornament of quoting ancient Poets, Orators, and Philosophers, contrary to the custom of late time." He gives eight reasons for this: Two are that "all Truth of Doctrine dependeth either upon *Reason*, or upon *Scripture*," and that "the matters in question are not of *Fact*, but of *Right*, wherein there is no place for *Witnesses*." (*L* R&C/727) Given this attitude, it is unlikely that Hobbes would feel threatened by an appeal to moral disagreement or would seek to resolve this disagreement by finding some point of agreement. It is no surprise that the *Elements* and *De Cive* chapters "confirming" the laws of nature by appeal to Scripture disappear in *Leviathan*. (*EL* I.18, *DC* 4)

The second interpretive problem concerns the historical context.

40 Hugo Grotius, *De Jure Belli ac Pacis*, trans. F. W. Kelsey (Indianapolis: Bobbs-Merrill, 1962), I.I.XII; also prol. 40, 46; I.II.I.4, 6, I.II.III.1, I.III.II.2.
41 This is also noted against Tuck by Curley; see Curley, "Reflections," p. 220n52.

Suppose Hobbes did, like Grotius, appeal to agreement. The claim that everyone agrees on the right to self-defence in the sense Hobbes intends – and the sense that is needed if some form of a purely egoist position is to be supported – is incorrect. The right of nature is a right "of doing any thing, which [one] in his own Judgement and Reason, hee shall conceive to be the aptest means" to preservation. (*L* 14/189) It is a right to "all the means," to use "all the power he hath." (*DC* 1.10n; *EL* I.14.7; *EL* I.14.6) One can, for example, "invade a suspected neighbour, by way of prevention." (*L* 27/335) "[A]ugmentation of dominion over men," over "all men [one] can" and "against whom he thought fit," whether the men are innocent or aggressive, "ought to be allowed." (*L* 13/184, 185; *DC* 1.10) The same disregard for innocence goes for wars between or within nations:

> [T]he infliction of what evill soever, on an Innocent man, that is not a Subject, if it be for the benefit of the Common-wealth, and without violation of any former Covenant, is no breach of the Law of Nature. . . . [A]gainst Enemies . . . it is lawfull by the originall Right of Nature to make warre; wherein the Sword Judgeth not, nor doth the Victor make distinction of Nocent, and Innocent. . . . And upon this ground it is, that also in Subjects, who deliberately deny the Authority of the Common-wealth established, the vengeance is lawfully extended, not only to the Fathers, but also to the third and fourth generation not yet in being. (*L* 28/360)

The right of nature forbids only actions the agent does not believe "tend" (or even "may tend") to his preservation. (*EL* I.14.10, I.19.2, *DC* 1.10n, 3.27n) Within this constraint, "every man has a Right to every thing," a right "to use all the means, and do all the actions, without which he cannot preserve himself." (*L* 14/190; 28/354, *EL* I.14.10, *DC* 1.10; *DC* 1.8, italics eliminated) The laws of nature "forbi[d] [one] to omit, that, by which he thinketh [his life] may be best preserved." (*L* 14/189) Thus Hobbes puts no limit on what one can do in the name of self-preservation; neither consideration of the common good nor the distinction between aggressors and bystanders nor the restriction of war to a last resort has any place. Nor does the past action of the agent: As noted above, Hobbes holds that the right to self-defence is inalienable, and so both justly convicted criminals and rebels retain it. (*EL* I.17.2, *DC* 2.18, 3.14, 6.3, 6.13, *L* 15/192, 199, 212, 21/268–70, 272, 27/343, 345–6, 28/353)

This goes far beyond the right to self-defence that most of Hobbes's contemporaries would grant – particularly where the right to "self-defence" is extended into a right to a decent life.[42] Thus Grotius finds it necessary to respond to those, such as Augustine and Erasmus, who forbid self-defence altogether.[43] Grotius himself differs from Hobbes in various respects. Since Grotius is a careful representative of common opinion here, and so these differences also suggest why the appeal to agreement does not give Hobbes a good argument for rational egoism, they are worth detailing.[44]

First, Grotius emphasises that killing assailants in self-defence is permitted only if "no other way of escape is open."[45] (Hobbes agrees in cases where a sovereign exists and cannot provide immediate defence. (*L* 27/343) But where there is no sovereign, he does not require "last resort.")

Second, Grotius supposes that one is obliged to give oneself up, or fail to resist attack, where self-defence would be calamitous for one's society. It is a "duty . . . that a person should value the lives of a very large number of innocent persons above his own life."[46]

> Defence is sometimes not permissible against a person useful to the state because at variance with the law of love. . . . [T]his is true, not only according to divine law . . . but also by the law of nature.

> At times the circumstances of the case are such that to refrain from the exercise of one's right is not merely praiseworthy but even obligatory, by reason of the love we owe even to men who are our enemies, whether this be viewed in itself or as the most sacred law of the Gospel demands. . . . [T]here are some persons for whose safety we ought to desire to die, even

---

42 The claim that we agree on a right to self-defence of the sort Hobbes wants should be distinguished from the claim that we agree on when it is appropriate to implement this right. Hobbes claims that I can implement the right whenever I believe I am threatened; whether I am *really* threatened is irrelevant. Tuck recognises that not everyone agrees with Hobbes here. My point concerns not the implementation of the right, but the right itself. Suppose I believe that I can best protect myself by killing many innocents. One might, unlike Hobbes, require that my belief be true, and admit that it is true, without agreeing that I have a right to kill them. See Tuck, *Hobbes*, pp. 59, 63–4, *Government*, pp. 306–7, 348, "Optics," pp. 261–3, "Grotius," p. 61.

43 Grotius, *De Jure*, prol. 29, I.II.

44 For a similar case for the unpopularity of Hobbes's position, see Suzanne Uniacke, *Permissible Killing: The Self-Defence Justification of Homicide* (New York: Cambridge University Press, 1994), pp. 58–87.

45 Grotius, *De Jure*, II.I.III; also II.I.IV.2, II.I.V.2, III.XI.II.

46 Ibid., II.XXV.III.3. Grotius is also sensitive to the numbers in the case of guilty persons: It is "right," or at least "the part of mercy," to "spare those who are guilty, if their number is very great." (III.XI.XVII)

24

if they should restrain us, because we know that they are necessary, or extremely useful, to mankind in general.[47]

Self-defence against the state "in case of extreme and imminent peril" is permitted unless it "could not be made without a very great disturbance in the state, and without the destruction of a great many innocent people," or provided one does not "abandon consideration of the common good."[48]

Third, Grotius gives bystanders a special status: "[E]xcept for reasons that are weighty and will affect the safety of many, no action should be attempted whereby innocent persons may be threatened," "even by accident."[49] Grotius follows this with an enumeration of typical bystanders: children, women, old men, priests, scholars, farmers, merchants, and all whose life "is foreign to arms."[50] There is no right of

---

47 Ibid., II.I.IX.1, italics eliminated; II.XXIV.II.3.

48 Ibid., I.IV.VII.1, 2, 4. Almost everyone agreed that the right to self-defence was overridden by concern for "greater evils . . . for the community." For a brief survey, see Sommerville, *Context,* pp. 33–7. The quotation comes from the English royalist Thomas Preston. Consideration of the community is common: For example, Aquinas holds that one can resist evil rulers only if a "serious disturbance" is unlikely. (S.T. II-II qu. 69 a. 4; in Aquinas, *St. Thomas Aquinas on Politics and Ethics,* ed. and trans. Paul E. Sigmund [New York: Norton, 1988]) The Oxford condemnation of Hobbes listed as one of its grounds the view that "[s]elf-preservation is the fundamental law of nature, and supersedes the obligation of all others whenever they stand in competition with it." See "The Judgement and Decree of the University of Oxford," in *Divine Right and Democracy,* ed. David Wootton (Harmondsworth: Penguin Books, 1986), p. 122. Sommerville notes that for some the prohibition on murder ruled out suicide and so required self-defence. (p. 35) In these cases, the rationale for self-defence itself sets limits on what one can do in self-defence.

49 Grotius, *De Jure,* III.XI.VIII. "Bystanders" is preferable to "innocent persons" here, because Grotius holds that "innocent aggressors" can be attacked: See II.I.III.

50 Ibid., III.XI.IX–XII. Grotius sometimes makes much more Hobbesian claims. But these almost always occur in III.I and III.IV, where he is explaining not what is "right" or "free from fault" but rather what can be "done with impunity" – that is, what "among men . . . is not liable to punishment." For the distinction, see prol. 35, III.IV.II, III.IV.XV.1, III.X.I. Two exceptions are II.I.IV.1 and II.XXVI.VI.1. In the former, Grotius writes that "[i]t is a disputed question whether innocent persons can be cut down or trampled upon when by getting in the way they hinder the defence or flight by which alone death can be averted." Grotius does not, there, resolve the dispute: The section is entitled "War in defence of life is permissible only against an actual assailant," and II.I.IV.2 follows with a statement of the doctrine of double effect. In the latter passage, Grotius writes that innocents cannot be killed "unless either as a necessary defensive measure or as a result and apart from [one's] purpose." This is laxer than III.XI.VIII – though both passages are stricter than Hobbes, for whom this is not a "disputed question."

war against neutral parties: Their property can be involved only if "the necessity [is] extreme" and the owner is not faced with "an equal necessity;" the property must be retained, used, or consumed according to what is strictly necessary, and if consumed, "the value of the thing must then be repaid."[51]

Fourth, Grotius does not permit self-defence given prior violation of the law. He has no doubt that convicted criminals lose their right to resist.[52]

Hobbes, then, could not hold that "all agree" on the right to self-defence in the intended sense.

It is true that Hobbes is sympathetic to some of the Grotian restrictions. The laws of nature condemn actions that are harmful to others and unnecessary for self-preservation, such as pointless revenge, wanton violence, and the taking of superfluities. Like Grotius, Hobbes demands the confident belief that a preemptive strike is needed for self-defence, and he has reservations about *inter arma silent leges*.

Yet there is still a large disagreement between Grotius and Hobbes. Hobbes denies the Grotian restrictions that call for giving up the right to self-defence. He has no equivalent to the law of love. (He does speak of a "law of honour," more stringent than the law of nature. (*EL* I.19.2, *DC* 5.2, *L* 17/224) But the law of honour demands mere abstention from killing and taking *all* the goods of those one invades, and its point is not to help others, but to increase one's glory by not showing fear.) Even where Grotius and Hobbes are closest, they differ. Thus in the case of preemptive strikes, Grotius demands more than confident belief and excludes most "anticipation." He asks that one have "the degree of certainty required . . . which is accepted in morals" that one faces "immediate and imminent" danger.[53] Preemptive strikes are forbidden "if the danger can in any other way be avoided, or if it is not altogether certain that the danger cannot be otherwise avoided."[54] It is not right "to take up arms in order to weaken a growing power which, if it

---

51 Grotius, *De Jure*, III.XVII.I; also II.II.X.
52 Ibid., II.I.XVIII.1. On this point, Hobbes's critics – even parliamentarians otherwise fond of resistance – were quick to agree with Grotius. This was, for example, one of the grounds of the (royalist) Oxford condemnation: See "Judgement," p. 123. For brief surveys of opinion, see Hampton, *Tradition*, pp. 198–202; Sommerville, *Context*, pp. 34–7; Ewin, *Virtues*, p. 69; and Mark Goldie, "The Reception of Hobbes," in Burns, *Cambridge History*, pp. 603–4.
53 Grotius, *De Jure*, II.XXII.V.1; II.I.V.1.
54 Ibid., II.I.V.2.

become too great, may be a source of danger."[55] More importantly, Hobbes places no limits on what one can do in the name of self-preservation.

The disagreement between Grotius and Hobbes should not be surprising, even to Tuck. Hobbes says what one expects a rational egoist to say; thus he usually justifies his restrictions on, say, wanton violence, by noting that the actions condemned do not aid the self-preservation of the agent. Similarly, the restrictions Grotius imposes stem from his basic position. As Tuck notes, it is plausible to see Grotius as justifying self-defence on the ground that no society could survive without granting this right to its members.[56] Taking the survival of the society as one's foundation justifies the restrictions on self-defence that Grotius adds, and Hobbes does not.

As suggested, the disagreement between Grotius and Hobbes is not simply a point about opinion at the time, counting simply against the plausibility of Tuck's interpretation. Many *today* disagree with Hobbes, for largely Grotian reasons. This undercuts the defence of Hobbes that relies on agreement. Consider the current literature on the morality of war. In this literature, Hobbes is sometimes seen as a "realist" – one who denies moral constraints on starting and waging war. His sympathy for some of the Grotian restrictions shows that this is a false picture.[57] Nonetheless, Hobbes holds an unpopular position. Suppose "just war theory" is taken to codify our intuitions.[58] According to just war theory, there are constraints on whether a war can be fought: The war must be authorised by a competent authority, have a just cause, be motivated by right intentions, and be forecast not to cause harms out of proportion to the benefits to be obtained. Since the concern here is war between individuals, set aside competent authority. Hobbes agrees with the need for right intention; one's motives must at least include self-defence. Hobbes also agrees with the need for just cause – self-defence again – although, given his relaxed view of when preemptive

---

55 Ibid., II.I.XVII; also II.XXII.V.1–2.
56 Tuck, "Rights," p. 165, "Modern," p. 112.
57 This point is made by Curley, "State," p. 115n5, against Michael Walzer, *Just and Unjust Wars* (New York: Basic, 1977), pp. 4, 7.
58 For a short introduction to just war theory, see Douglas P. Lackey, *The Ethics of War and Peace* (Englewood Cliffs, NJ: Prentice-Hall, 1989), chs. 3–4. Kavka sees just war theory as "the only developed moral theory of warfare that we have," and so he should admit that viewing Hobbes in light of just war theory is a plausible test of how much we agree with Hobbes. See Gregory Kavka, "Was the Gulf War a Just War?" *Journal of Social Philosophy* 22, 1991, p. 20.

strikes are permitted, he disagrees with contemporary just war theory over what self-defence allows. Most importantly, however, Hobbes has no proportionality constraint: Unlike just war theorists, he counts only harms and benefits to the agent, and so permits the destruction of many for the benefit of one.

Hobbes also disagrees with just war theorists over the constraints under which a war can be prosecuted. Just war theory requires that a particular operation be necessary, that it be forecast not to cause harms out of proportion to its benefits, and that noncombatants not be attacked. Hobbes agrees with the need for necessity, given his ban on wanton violence. As above, he does not agree with proportionality. And he draws no distinction between combatants and noncombatants: If attacking noncombatants were the "aptest" strategy, Hobbes would have no complaint.[59]

59 Other war theorists are closer to Hobbes. Kavka writes that "philosophers as divergent as utilitarians, nonutilitarian rights theorists, and libertarians are reluctant to come down unambiguously on the side of restraint" where self-defence must be conducted at the expense of bystanders. (*Theory*, p. 319) It is true that utilitarians cannot endorse a strict constraint against killing bystanders – although Sidgwick does come close. (See Sidgwick, *Elements of Politics*, p. 269; and Walzer, *Just and Unjust Wars*, pp. 129–37. Sidgwick is even stricter concerning neutral parties: See *Elements of Politics*, p. 274.) But this does not support a Hobbesian right of nature, given the very different restrictions utilitarians have in mind. The same holds for Kavka's other support. He notes John Hospers, Robert Nozick, and Michael Walzer. Hospers does fail to endorse a strict constraint against killing bystanders. (He does not reject such a constraint either – he merely notes disagreement over the libertarian principle that force can be used only against those who have already used force.) Unlike Hobbes, however, he does not seem to doubt that *guilty* parties cannot use force against bystanders. (Hospers, "Some Problems About Punishment and the Retaliatory Use of Force II," *Reason*, 1973, pp. 19–20) Nozick might permit killing innocent threats, and perhaps even "innocent shields of threats" – for example, innocents strapped on to the front of an aggressor's tank – but he does not seem to permit killing innocents who, but for the actions of the defender, would stand outside the causal process. (Robert Nozick, *Anarchy, State, and Utopia* (New York: Basic, 1974), p. 35) Walzer is also a dubious ally. Walzer does hold that one can kill innocents provided doing so is the only means of self-defence. But he holds this "not without hesitation and worry," describes it as "blasphemy against our deepest moral commitments," and restricts permission to political communities rather than individuals. His argument rests on our intuitions about specific cases: For example, many think British bombers in 1940–1 could kill innocents. But this intuition does not show that *any* political community can kill innocents in self-defence. Many would deny this right to Germany in 1945. If so, Walzer's argument may show that we think innocents can be killed to avoid catastrophes such as the triumph of Naz-

The point that Hobbes would not elicit general agreement can also be made by reference to the literature on individual self-defence. Again, in this literature, few think one has a right to defend oneself at the expense of a bystander. What *is* debated is, for example, the doctrine of double effect, or whether the innocence or numerical size of the threat matters.[60]

I do not deny that Hobbes occasionally appeals to agreement, with some success. Perhaps the best evidence for Tuck's interpretation comes when Hobbes tries, at one point, to support his claim that in the state of nature "every man will and may lawfully rely on his own strength and art, for caution against all other men."

[I]n all places, where men have lived by small Families, to robbe and spoyle one another, has been . . . so farre from being reputed against the Law of Nature, that the greater spoyles they gained, the greater was their honour; and men observed no other Lawes therein, but the Lawes of Honour; that is, to abstain from cruelty. [Similarly] Cities and Kingdomes . . . upon all pretences of danger, and fear of Invasion, or assistance that may be given to Invaders, endeavour as much as they can, to subdue, or weaken their neighbours, by open force, and secret arts, for want of other Caution, justly; and are remembered for it in after ages with honour. (*L* 17/224)

ism, but not to avoid just any national defeat. (See Walzer, *Just and Unjust Wars*, pp. 227–8, 231–2, 241, 247–50, 259–260, 262, 266, 268, and esp. pp. 254–5. For [perhaps] the suggestion that only justified political communities can kill innocents in self-defence, see pp. 259–60.) On other purported cases of necessity – the German invasion of Belgium in 1914, German submarine warfare in the Second World War, British violation of Norwegian neutrality, British terror bombing of German cities later in the war, American use of the atomic bomb – Walzer clearly denies the right of nature. As with Grotius, then, apparent agreement with Hobbes diminishes upon closer inspection.

60 Some theories of self-defence do agree with Hobbes that many can be destroyed by one. This is a consequence, for example, of Judith Jarvis Thomson's claim that self-defence is permitted, even against an innocent threat, because a threat to my life will violate my right that the threat not kill me, and so the threat lacks the right not to be killed by me. Presumably I can exercise my right repeatedly, or against many simultaneous innocent threats, until many innocent threats are dead. But here, where Thomson agrees with Hobbes, is where her theory seems counter-intuitive, and so appeal to it may not help Hobbes much. For a sample of the debate, see Judith Jarvis Thomson, "Self-Defense," *Philosophy and Public Affairs* 20, 1991, pp. 283–310; Michael Otsuka, "Killing the Innocent in Self-Defense," *Philosophy and Public Affairs* 23, 1994, pp. 74–94; and Jeff McMahan, "Self-Defence and the Problem of the Innocent Attacker," *Ethics* 104, 1994, pp. 252–90.

We approve of aggressive self-defence in the state of nature, provided cruelty is avoided.[61]

It would be odd to view this passage, coming well after the discussion of the state of nature and the right of nature, as Hobbes's main argument. But suppose it is – the passage does state what Hampton, Kavka, and Tuck take to be crucial. In reply, two cases should be distinguished. In one case, I allow myself to be made prey when there is no justification for my loss. These are the cases Hobbes and Hampton present: Kings are attacked by ambitious priests or parliamentarians (*B* 94, 118); one is attacked in the state of nature by someone bent on self-preservation, domination, or glory; a woman is exploited by her family.[62] Here most will agree with Hobbes: There is no objection to self-defence, and in many cases self-defence will be honoured.

In another case, I allow myself to be made prey (or increase my chance of being prey) when there is some justification for the loss. Suppose the most effective strategy for self-defence requires preemptive strikes or killing far more bystanders than an alternative strategy would.[63] Here many, like Grotius, will object to self-defence, and more will refuse to honour it. Consider, for example, the post-war dishonouring of Arthur Harris, head of Bomber Command.[64] Hobbes is wrong to think that all instances of self-defence are remembered with honour.

These worries about the right of nature also tell against those who simply assert the right of nature, without Tuck's claim that all agree to it. That we have a right to self-defence is not (too) controversial. That we have a right as Hobbes understands it, and in the sense needed as a basis for a purely egoist position, is very controversial. It is not the sort of claim that can be made without argument, nor is the burden of proof on anyone who opposes it.

---

61 There are other stray appeals to agreement. For example, anticipation in self-defence is "generally allowed." (*L* 13/184) But typically, Hobbes does not note agreement here. Instead he simply claims that anticipation "being necessary to a mans conservation, it ought to be allowed him" or that "no man is bound" to "expose himselfe to Prey." (*L* 13/185, 14/190)
62 For the latter, see Hampton, "Two Faces," p. 54.
63 As an example of the latter, Walzer gives the Vemork raid, where commandos were initially chosen over an air attack. A commando attack was less likely to succeed, but also less likely to kill civilians. See Walzer, *Just and Unjust Wars*, pp. 157–8.
64 Ibid., pp. 323–5.

1.3

There is a more general worry about beginning with an undefended right of nature. Some see Hobbes as attractive because they suppose he starts with no moral assumptions at all. This might appeal because one does not want to rely on trading moral intuitions, such as those concerning self-defence. Or it might appeal because one wants an explanation, in non-moral (though not non-normative) terms, of the authority of morality. Or, most ambitiously, it might appeal because one wants a non-normative explanation of normativity itself.[65] Those who read Hobbes in this way see him as claiming that practical reason can only be instrumental reason. If one adds psychological egoism, one may seem to get rational egoism. And even if one does not add psychological egoism, the instrumental theory is still worth discussing, since this position will declare irrational duties that many moralists want to consider rational, particularly if predominant egoism is true.

There is no doubt that Hobbes holds the instrumental theory. The calculation of consequences is the task of reason. (*EW* i 3, *EL* I.5.11, *L* 4/106–7, 5/110–11, 113, 115) When it comes to applying reason to action, Hobbes assumes that the relevant consequences concern the welfare of the agent deliberating. (*L* 6/129)[66] Thoughts "are to the Desires, as Scouts, and Spies, to range abroad, and find the way to the things Desired." (*L* 8/139) Thus an action is "not against Reason, when it conduce[s] to ones benefit," and "those actions are most Reasonable, that conduce most to [one's] ends." To be "against reason" is to be "against . . . benefit." (*L* 15/203–4; also *DC* 14.16, *DH* 12.1)[67]

Hobbes does not, however, defend these claims. Hampton and Darwall suggest a "naturalistic" motive for them. Consider the view that practical reasoning is means–ends calculation; practical reasoning can-

---

65 For the first and second appeals, see Gauthier, "Why Contractarianism?" (in Vallentyne, *Contractarianism*), and *Morals by Agreement*, p. 269. For the third, see Jean Hampton, "Hobbes and Ethical Naturalism," *Philosophical Perspectives* 6, 1992, pp. 333–53; Stephen Darwall, "Motive and Obligation in the British Moralists," *Social Philosophy and Policy* 7, 1989, pp. 140–1, "Internalism and Agency," *Philosophical Perspectives* 6, 1992, pp. 162–3, and *Internal*, ch. 3.

66 At one point, he also supposes that the actions in question are those "which may either redound to the damage or benefit of [one's] neighbours," presumably because these actions are the most important for one's conservation. They are also actions concerning which there has been much "false reasoning" and "folly." (*DC* 2.1n)

67 See Gauthier, "Thomas Hobbes," pp. 548–9; Kavka, *Theory*, p. 291; Hampton, *Tradition*, pp. 35–42, and "Ethical Naturalism"; Darwall, *Internal*, pp. 58–60, "Internalism," pp. 162–4, and "Motive and Obligation," pp. 140–1.

not specify what counts as an end (and so, for example, cannot identify an agent's ends with the objects of his desires). Call this the "thin" view. The thin view might appeal because claims concerning the best means to reach an end can be reduced to testable, non-normative claims about cause and effect. There is not much evidence to show that Hobbes sees this appeal.[68] But the point to be made here is that Hobbes could not use the thin view to support his instrumentalism. Hobbes is not agnostic about ends: "[W]hatsoever is the object of any mans Appetite or Desire; that is it, which he for his part calleth *Good*." (*L* 6/120; also 15/216, *EL* I.7.3, I.17.14, *DC* 3.31) He holds the "thick" view standardly called "instrumental": practical reasoning specifies means to reach a *particular* end, namely the satisfaction of one's desires. Since the thin view says nothing about ends, it does not support Hobbes against those who take (for example) one's pleasure, or perfection, or the satisfaction of *every-one's* desires, as the reason-giving end. Nor does naturalism help. For taking (say) the satisfaction of everyone's desires as the end has the same attraction, for the naturalist, as taking one's own desires as the end. Claims about both sorts of end are equally reducible to non-normative claims (about desires).

Hobbes might hold the thin view. It would, however, preclude him from arguing for his choice of ends on the basis of practical reason. Since, on the thin view, practical reason cannot support any end, it cannot support taking the agent's desires as providing ends.[69] It is possible that Hobbes could give some other sort of reason for privileg-ing the agent's desires. But the threat is that these reasons, whatever they are, could favour an alternative end, such as the satisfaction of

---

68 Darwall agrees. He appeals to Hobbes's "general epistemology and metaphysics." See Darwall, "Motive and Obligation," pp. 140–1, "Internalism," pp. 162–3, and *Internal,* pp. 60–1. Hampton enlists Hobbes by claiming that in "[a]ttacking what he called the 'filth and fraud' in Greek philosophy (D[e] C[orpore], *EW* i, Ep. Ded., ix), Hobbes dismissed the existence of any *Summum Bonum,* the prescriptive entity that his academic contemporaries were most likely to embrace." This is poor evidence. The passage criticising Greek philosophy in *De Corpore* does not mention the *sum-mum bonum,* or indeed any particular Greek moral belief. Where Hobbes does attack the *summum bonum,* his attack is not directed to any queerness it has as a prescriptive entity. His complaint is that "the Felicity of this life, consisteth not in the repose of a mind satisfied. . . . Felicity is a continuall progresse of the desire, from one object to another." (*L* 11/160) See Hampton, "Naturalism," p. 333.

69 For this point, and the distinction between thin and thick views (put slightly differently), see Stephen Darwall, *Impartial Reason* (Ithaca, NY: Cornell University Press, 1983), pp. 15–16, 45–8.

everyone's desires. And again, the naturalism Hampton and Darwall ascribe to Hobbes cannot help him. Instead, it makes any argument for the instrumental theory more difficult, by ruling out the possibility of justifying one's desires as ends by appeal to practical reason. Naturalism of the brand Hampton and Darwall propose leads most naturally to the elimination of the normative altogether, since the thin theory, taken by itself, offers no guidance.[70] Given this, it is no surprise that Hobbes is not keen on the naturalism he has been offered.

There is a further objection. Hobbes supposes that practical reason can only serve desires. But there is another sense of practical reason, found in both moral and non-moral cases (and quite compatible with Hobbes's general view of reason as calculation.) We often think that it is rational to avoid arbitrariness. Thus one who ignores relevant evidence or decides on the basis of irrelevant evidence is irrational. One whose desires make arbitrary distinctions is also irrational.[71] When Sidgwick argues against rational egoism, it is just this sense of irrationality that he relies on: The rational egoist makes a limitation to himself that "we see . . . is arbitrary and without foundation in reason; we deny its validity and substitute . . . the wider statement of which that affirmed a part."[72] I shall consider this argument in 3.3. The point here is that, given this quite ordinary sense of rationality, further argument is needed to show that means–ends reasoning stands alone.

Since Hobbes does not offer this further argument, I continue treatment of the instrumental theory in Chapter 2.

1.4

It may seem odd that I have not considered any straightforward argument *in Hobbes* for rational egoism. (For the remainder of the Chapter, I use "rational egoism" to involve either self-defence or self-interest.) Instead, I have canvassed his commentators. The reason is that no clear-

70 This is Hampton's conclusion. See Jean Hampton, "Ethical Naturalism," pp. 348–9, and "Rethinking Reason," *American Philosophical Quarterly* 29, 1992, pp. 232–3, to which I am indebted. Darwall himself rejects the naturalistic internalism he ascribes to Hobbes. See Stephen Darwall, *Impartial Reason*, p. 199, "Internalism," pp. 166–9, *Internal*, pp. 16–20, 324–32, and "Autonomist Internalism and the Justification of Morals," *Nous* 24, 1990, pp. 261–6.
71 For examples, see Parfit, *Reasons and Persons*, pp. 122–6.
72 Sidgwick, "The Establishment of Ethical First Principles," *Mind* 4, 1879, p. 107.

cut argument is to be found.[73] The best candidate appears in the *Elements* and *De Cive* but not *Leviathan*.

> [F]orasmuch as necessity of nature maketh men to will and desire *bonum sibi*, that which is good for themselves, and to avoid that which is hurtful . . . it is not against reason that a man doth all he can to preserve his own body and limbs, both from death and pain. And that which is not against reason, men call RIGHT, or *jus*, or blameless liberty of using our own natural power and ability. It is therefore a *right of nature*: that every man may preserve his own life and limbs, with all the power he hath. (*EL* I.14.6)

> [E]very man is desirous of what is good for him, and shuns what is evil, and this he doth by a certain impulsion of nature, no less than that whereby a stone moves downward. It is therefore neither absurd nor reprehensible, neither against the dictates of true reason, for a man to use all his endeavours to preserve and defend his body and the members thereof from death and sorrows. But that which is not contrary to right reason, that all men account to be done justly, and with right. . . . Therefore the first foundation of natural right is this, that *every man as much as in him lies endeavour to protect his life and members*. (*DC* 1.7; also ded. 90, pref. 99, *EL* I.14.10)

This may be a version of Kavka's argument, considered in 1.1. It may also be a version of the argument from instrumental rationality considered in 1.3. Or it may reflect, less reputably, what Sidgwick described as "the quasi-theistic assumption that what is natural must be reasonable."[74]

Of course Hobbes may be claiming only that self-defence is excusable – since we have no choice but to defend ourselves, self-defence is a "blameless liberty" and "neither absurd nor reprehensible."[75] As Hobbes puts the point while arguing for inalienability, "[w]hen a man has arrived to this degree of fear" – of death or bodily injury – "we cannot expect but he will provide for himself either by flight or fight." Flight or fight occurs "by natural necessity. . . . [H]e can do no otherwise." (*DC* 2.18) Similarly, "[i]f a man by the terrour of present death, be compelled to doe a fact against the Law, he is totally Excused. . . . Nature . . . compells him to the fact." (*L* 27/345–6) But this does not

---

73 For a much clearer presentation of the argument from practicality, see the discussion of John Clarke in 4.3.

74 Sidgwick, *Outlines*, p. 192. Sidgwick also suggests the argument from practicality at *Methods*, p. 89, and the argument from instrumental rationality at *Outlines*, p. 165.

75 Ewin, *Virtues*, p. 83.

agree with (sensible) admissions elsewhere that people will give up their lives to save their reputations, or to avoid great pain, or out of religious conviction or political loyalty. (*EL* I.9.6, I.16.11, *DC* 3.12, 6.13, 18.1, *L* 15/210–11, *DH* 11.6, *B* 71, 94) Some are "stout enough to bear" wounds or death. (*DC* 2.18)[76] Nor does it support the conclusion that self-defence is "done justly, and with right." We typically excuse what we do not find right; excuses usually bear on responsibility, not justification. Nor would it support preemptive strikes – these are not part of a "flight or fight" response. However these arguments are taken, then, they fail to establish the right of nature.

Hobbes does not give a good argument for rational egoism. This is not surprising. I suggest that Hobbes is an *unreflective* rational egoist. He is a rational egoist without careful arguments in favour of rational egoism.

This explains some puzzling features. A reflective rational egoist would say more than Hobbes does at *DC* 1.7 and *EL* I.14.6. He would not omit these passages – the best candidates for a defence of rational egoism to be found – from his masterwork, *Leviathan*.[77] And when he comes to defend the crucial connection between self-preservation and following his laws of nature, he would say (as his commentators have) a great deal about the Foole's worry. The Foole argues that it is rational to be unjust where injustice pays. Hobbes replies that the reputation of being just is needed for admission into a confederacy, and so injustice never pays. (*L* 15/203–6) Here one expects a detailed discussion of the worry that, by deception, the Foole can get the reputation without being just; Machiavelli had famously praised this very deception. Hobbes himself is sceptical about knowledge of other people, making the Foole's job easier.[78] But Hobbes says only that the Foole "cannot reasonably reckon upon" mistakes by the confederacy, without further explanation. (*L* 15/205; also *L* 27/342) A reflective rational egoist would say more. He would certainly not omit the worry entirely, as in the *Elements* and *De Cive*.

My interpretation might seem to make Hobbes look bad. But given the context, Hobbes did not need careful arguments for rational egoism. Consider some of the various contexts in which Hobbes can be placed.

Suppose that Hobbes is placed in the context of contemporary En-

---

76 Kavka, *Theory*, p. 331.
77 There is a shadow of them in the arguments for inalienability and at *L* 15/209–10.
78 See Marshall Missner, "Skepticism and Hobbes's Political Philosophy," *Journal of the History of Ideas* 44, 1983, pp. 407–28.

glish political issues.[79] In particular, he wants to argue that the sovereign can tax without consent, that defeated Royalists should take the Engagement, that "mixed monarchies" are a mistake, that Charles II can abandon the Anglicans, and that Church must be subordinate to the State. On each issue, the upshot of Hobbes's argument is that his policies are needed for peace.[80] Hobbes sometimes adds that peace is good because it is in the self-interest of each, but his argument would stand or fall without this. It requires only that one sees peace as good.

Or suppose, as Quentin Skinner argues, that Hobbes is worried by the rhetorical tradition of *paradiastole,* in which one action can be described as both virtuous and vicious. Hobbes's solution is to argue that virtues or vices are constituted by their connection to peace: A disposition is virtuous provided it conduces to peace. Again, the question of why peace is good need not be answered, provided one finds peace good.[81]

Or suppose that Hobbes is placed in the Grotian natural law tradition. Grotius justifies his laws of nature in various ways: by appeal to our sociableness, by appeal to "more advanced" authorities, and by appeal to self-interest. Hobbes attacks the first two justifications. (*EL* I.15.1, *DC* 1.2, 2.1) With an agenda set by Grotius, justification by appeal

---

79 See Sommerville, *Context,* chs. 1–2; Quentin Skinner, "Conquest and Consent: Thomas Hobbes and the Engagement Controversy," in *The Interregnum,* ed. G. E. Aylmer (London: Archon, 1972); Goldie, "Reception," pp. 595, 614; and Tuck, *Government,* pp. 320–5.

80 Of course Hobbes also relies on particular claims about, say, covenanting. But as Sommerville admits, these claims usually have little connection to self-preservation. (Sommerville, *Context,* pp. 51, 55) For example, many note that Hobbes fails to give a rational egoist justification for why it is rational to keep covenants extorted by fear. He argues simply that "what I lawfully Covenant, I cannot lawfully break." (*L* 14/198) One can invent a rational egoist justification. Perhaps breaking such a covenant would ruin one's reputation as a cooperator or perhaps one needs to discourage the policy of killing captives, given that one may become a captive again. But even those who offer these justifications worry that they fail: The members of one's community can distinguish covenants among themselves and covenants with others; the likelihood of becoming a captive again may be outweighed by the loss of paying the ransom; kidnapping is best dealt with, not by committing oneself to paying, but by always refusing payment. See Daniel M. Farrell, "Reason and Right in Hobbes' *Leviathan,*" *History of Philosophy Quarterly* 1, 1984, pp. 307–8; Richard Nunan, "Hobbes on Morality, Rationality, and Foolishness," *Hobbes Studies* 2, 1989, pp. 47–8; and Curley, "Reflections," pp. 193–4, 202–3 (which includes some of these attacks on the rational egoist justification).

81 See Quentin Skinner, "Thomas Hobbes: Rhetoric and the Construction of Morality," *Proceedings of the British Academy* 76, 1990, pp. 1–61.

Hobbes

to self-interest is the obvious choice. It is not until later that one finds a developed, secular, more-or-less utilitarian alternative that new rational egoists would need to defeat.

One might object that Hobbes's own theoretical ambitions must be frustrated by the lack of a good argument for rational egoism. But even here the lack is unimportant. Hobbes describes "moral philosophy" as knowledge of "those duties which unite and keep men in peace." (*EW* i 8) The laws of nature, "the sum of *moral* philosophy," give "the meanes of peaceable, sociable, and comfortable living." (*DC* 3.32; *L* 15/216; also *EL* I.15.1–2, I.17.2, *DC* 1.15, 2.1–2, 3.27n, 3.31, *L* 13/188, 15/214–15, 18/233, 26/314) "[T]he goodness of actio[n] consists in this, that it was in order to peace"; "moral virtues . . . are those whereby what was entered upon [society] can be best preserved." (*DC* 3.32, *DH* 13.9) Thus Hobbes sometimes downplays traits, such as drunkenness, which harm the individual without jeopardising peace. Where he does not downplay them, he connects them with disobedience to the other laws of nature, and so to peace. (*DC* 3.32, *L* 15/214, *DH* 13.9; *DC* 3.25, 3.27n, 4.19) And he often treats "peace" as interchangeable with "preservation" or "advantages"; for example, "I cannot understand what . . . cruelty . . . can advance toward peace, or the preservation of any man." (*DC* 3.27n; also [e.g.] *DC* 2.2, 10.1)

On this view of the Hobbesian enterprise, two sorts of argument are needed: An argument to show that following the laws of nature is indeed necessary for peace and an argument to show that peace is good. Rational egoism is irrelevant to the former. As Hampton notes, this is simply a piece of causal knowledge, defended like any other.[82] Rational egoism does help to show the latter, that peace is good. But again, Hobbes does not need rational egoism here: *Any* sensible normative position will find peace to be good, and so Hobbes, after arguing that a state of war is nasty, just notes that "all men agree on this, that Peace is Good." (*L* 15/216; also *DC* 3.31)[83]

The recent interest in Hobbes is welcome. But some of the reasons for this interest make arguments for rational egoism unimportant. Thus

82 Jean Hampton, *Tradition,* pp. 47–8, "Ethical Naturalism," pp. 337–8, "Hobbes's Science of Moral Philosophy," in *Knowledge and Politics,* ed. Marcelo Dascal and Ora Gruengard (Boulder, CO: Westview Press, 1989), pp. 52–6.

83 For a similar emphasis on peace, see Bernard Gert's introduction to *Man and Citizen* and Howard Warrender, "Hobbes and Macroethics: The Theory of Peace and Natural Justice," in *Hobbes's "Science of Natural Justice",* ed. C. Walton and P. J. Johnson (The Hague: Nijhoff, 1987). I disagree with Gert and Warrender, however, in claiming that Hobbes remains a rational egoist, albeit an unreflective one.

37

one might value Hobbes because of his emphasis on peace. Yet it is because of this emphasis that Hobbes does not need an argument for rational egoism. Since peace is usually necessary both for each and for all, any tension between rational egoism and, say, utilitarianism is submerged. Indeed, Hobbes even gives utilitarian rather than rational egoist arguments for particular laws of nature.[84]

Alternatively, one might value Hobbes because of his scepticism: he accepts a world in which there is "want of a right Reason constituted by Nature" and in which competing views of right reason bring conflict. (*L* 5/111) But Hobbes's helpful response is not to offer an argument for, say, rational egoism as *really* bearing the mark of right reason. His response is to note that, whatever one's view of right reason, peace is good – and he could say this even were he sceptical about rational egoism itself. This is an advantage of Hobbes's theory: It suits a pluralistic, sceptical age. But it is an advantage that makes him a poor place to look for arguments for rational egoism. I have argued that his contemporary admirers, though more reflective, do no better.

---

84 See Kavka, *Theory,* pp. 371–3. The same holds for advice to the sovereign. Hobbes advises that the sovereign should care for those who cannot work and that colonists "are not to exterminate those they find there." One can invent rational egoist arguments for these positions. But the arguments are not found in Hobbes. He writes only that "it is Uncharitablenesse in any man, to neglect the impotent." (*L* 30/387) Thus nineteenth-century utilitarians who admired Hobbes were not totally misguided; George Grote, for example, praises Hobbes because "he judged of right and wrong by the test of utility." See George Grote, "Notice of Sir William Molesworth's Edition of the Works of Hobbes," in *The Minor Works of George Grote* (London: J. Murray, 1873), p. 67.

Chapter 2

The instrumental theory

I<small>T</small> might seem misguided to consider the instrumental theory in a work on rational egoism – apart, at least, from any role the theory plays in the exegesis of Hobbes.[1] For combining an instrumental account of rationality with the denial of psychological egoism allows the possibility that one might act rationally against one's self-interest, and so makes room for morality in a way that rational egoism does not.[2] The instrumental theory, however, is not really a friend of morality. For it makes rational sacrifice, though not impossible, often unlikely. Sacrifice will fail to be rational whenever my interests – both self- and other-regarding – happen not to be best served by it. In this the instrumental theory resembles rational egoism: Both make the rationality of obeying moral demands contingent on features of the agent that are often absent. It is worth, then, asking whether Hobbes missed good arguments for the instrumental theory.

There is a further reason for considering the instrumental theory: given the falsity of psychological egoism, it is, as noted, inconsistent with rational egoism. One might, then, attack rational egoism by supporting the instrumental theory. I shall focus on the instrumental theory as an egoist-like threat to morality, but it is worth keeping in mind that rational egoism is also threatened.

---

1 I shall henceforth refer to what I called the "thick view" as "the instrumental theory." According to the instrumental theory, it is necessary and sufficient, for an action to be rational, that it best contribute to the satisfaction of the agent's desires.
2 This point is made by W. K. Frankena, *Thinking About Morality* (Ann Arbor: University of Michigan, 1980), pp. 84–90, and "Sidgwick and the Dualism of Practical Reason," in Goodpaster, *Perspectives on Morality*, pp. 203–4; Parfit, *Reasons and Persons*, pp. 127–33, 450, 462; and Richard B. Brandt, "Rationality, Egoism, and Morality," in Brandt, *Morality, Utilitarianism, and Rights* (New York: Cambridge University Press, 1992), pp. 97–8. For the rise of "process" rather than "content" conceptions of rational action, see Frankena, "Rational Action," pp. 180, 188–9.

In 2.1 I argue against attempts to justify the instrumental theory. In 2.2 I argue that Hume, often read as the classic instrumentalist, suggests an argument *against* the instrumental theory.

2.1

Often, defenders of instrumental reason do no more than assert their belief. Gilbert Harman, for example, says of the purely instrumental theory only that "[i]t seems to me that some such theory must be correct."[3] John Harsanyi finds it "quite unsatisfactory" to think that the pain of another person can directly provide me with reason to act. The pain "cannot be the whole reason. Besides some condition in him (namely, his need for my help) there must be also some condition in me that will give me a reason to help him." But Harsanyi does not defend this question-begging stipulation.[4] Richard Fumerton rejects the same possibility in the same fashion: "[t]he oddness of supposing that I could have reason to pursue as an end something to which I am completely and utterly indifferent seems to me so great that it is difficult for me to take the view seriously."[5] Others offer various slightly more complex arguments. (I shall sometimes write of arguments for hypothetical imperatives and against categorical imperatives, since that is the language in which much of the debate over instrumental reason is put.)

The appeal to naturalism

Naturalists such as Larry Laudan suppose that "one ought to do x" is puzzling, since we do not know what could justify it. He has no patience with traditional appeals to intuition or reflective equilibrium. But "if one's goal is y, then one ought to do x" removes the puzzle, since it can be justified by ordinary empirical means and so should be adopted as the proper gloss on "one ought to do x." Naturalists, then, can adopt

---

3 Gilbert Harman, "Human Flourishing, Ethics, and Liberty," *Philosophy and Public Affairs* 12, 1983, p. 320. See also Gilbert Harman, *The Nature of Morality* (New York: Oxford University Press, 1977), p. 133, and "Moral Relativism Defended," *Philosophical Review* 84, 1975, p. 9. Insofar as Harman offers any reason for dismissing rivals to the instrumental theory, his argument seems to be that rivals must see a "possible source of motivation in reason itself." (Harman, "Relativism," p. 9) For a reply, see the discussion of Mackie below.

4 John Harsanyi, "Does Reason Tell Us What Moral Code to Follow and, Indeed, to Follow Any Moral Code at All?" *Ethics* 96, 1985, p. 50.

5 Richard A. Fumerton, *Reason and Morality: A Defense of the Egocentric Perspective*, (Ithaca, NY: Cornell University Press, 1990), p. 155.

instrumental rationality, and hence naturalists can have a normative rather than purely descriptive theory.[6]

The problem is the same as suggested above. No empirical means are offered to specify reason-giving goals. Laudan simply assumes that the desires of individual scientists supply goals. Some will disagree – preferring, say, the desires of "science" or the scientific community.[7] Thus the same reason for finding "one ought to do x" puzzling afflicts the identification of goals with the desires of individual scientists. The objection is not merely the familiar complaint that the instrumental theory cannot judge (non-instrumental) desires and so cannot do all the normative work we want done.[8] Rather, it is that the naturalistic rationale for adopting the instrumental theory precludes having any theory of ends, and so the theory can do *no* normative work.

Laudan admits that "[m]ethodology gets nowhere without axiology."[9] But he does not admit that the rationale for his methodology – empirical testability – rules out axiology. In reply to a similar criticism, Laudan stresses that his axiology asks that goals be realisable and that realisability is an empirical matter.[10] But this does not give an empirical rationale for identifying the desires of individual scientists with goals. And when Laudan does argue in favour of identifying the desires of individual scientists with goals, his argument consists in a straightforward appeal to intuition. Concerning the "aims of science" suggestion, he writes that "I cannot accept the violence it does to our usual notion of rationality, entailing among other things that agents who acted effectively so as to promote their ends may turn out to be irrational (*viz.*, if their actions failed to promote 'the' ends of science)."[11] If appeal to "our usual notion of rationality" is permitted here, it is unclear why it is not also permitted at the level of methodology, rather than banned by the demand for empirical testability. It is also unclear that our intuitions

6 See Larry Laudan, "Progress or Rationality? The Prospects for Normative Naturalism," *American Philosophical Quarterly* 24, 1987, pp. 23–5. For a similar view, see Ronald N. Giere, "Scientific Rationality as Instrumental Rationality," *Studies in the History and Philosophy of Science* 20, 1989, pp. 377–84.

7 This, for example, is the view of Alexander Rosenberg, who shares Laudan's enthusiasm for instrumentalism. See Alexander Rosenberg, "Normative Naturalism and the Role of Philosophy," *Philosophy of Science* 57, 1990, pp. 34–43.

8 For this worry, see Harvey Siegel, "What Is the Question Concerning the Rationality of Science?" *Philosophy of Science* 52, 1985, pp. 520–2.

9 Laudan, "Progress," p. 29.

10 Larry Laudan; "Normative Naturalism," *Philosophy of Science* 57, 1990, p. 51; and "Relativism, Naturalism and Reticulation," *Synthese* 71, 1987, p. 232.

11 Laudan, "Progress," pp. 22–3.

support the claim that "good reasons are instrumental reasons; there is no other sort."[12]

A similar objection can be made against naturalistic attempts to support the instrumental theory by appeal to "internalism."[13] Internalism requires that reasons motivate; motivation proceeds through desires; desires, then, provide reason-giving ends.

This argument is controversial.[14] Suppose, however, that it succeeds. One can still ask whether naturalism supports internalism. Darwall argues that it does.

> The considerations said to be reasons are themselves simply matters of fact of which we can take notice and consider. But in what does their property of being reasons itself consist? The internalist answer is that their status as reasons consists in their capacity to move agents when contemplated under certain conditions. . . . [T]he internalist move seems the only alternative to treating the property of being a reason as a further, non-natural property that is itself the object of a special sort of cognitive act.[15]

But this is inconclusive. The internalist offers one possible naturalistic analysis of being a reason: to be a reason for action is to motivate under certain conditions. There are other naturalistic analyses available. One might, for example, say that to be a reason for action is to be conducive to pleasure or to satisfy the desires of all parties concerned. Darwall

---

12 Larry Laudan, "Aim-less Epistemology?" *Studies in the History and Philosophy of Science* 21, 1990, p. 320.

13 By "internalism," I mean what Darwall calls "constitutive existence internalism": Motivation is at least a necessary condition for the truth of a moral claim. This is to be distinguished from "judgement" internalism, which claims that motivation is the necessary result of sincere assent to a moral claim, and from "non-constitutive existence internalism," which claims that motivation is a necessary effect of knowledge of a moral claim, but denies that motivation is relevant to the truth or understanding of the claim itself. See Darwall, "Internalism," pp. 155–8.

14 It is controversial in at least three ways. Some deny internalism. Some wield internalism as a way of discovering motivations, rather than as a way of constraining reasons. And some doubt that desires are needed for motivation. See, for example, David O. Brink, *Moral Realism and the Foundations of Ethics* (New York: Cambridge University Press, 1989), pp. 37–50; Christine Korsgaard, "Skepticism About Practical Reason," *Journal of Philosophy* 83, 1986, pp. 23–4; David McNaughton, *Moral Vision* (Oxford: Blackwell Publisher, 1988), pp. 106–13. (There are also worries concerning exactly how desires "provide" reasons, which I put aside here. See Darwall, *Impartial Reason*, pp. 33–4, 37–8, 58.)

15 Darwall, *Impartial Reason*, p. 56.

could reply that the identification of being a reason with these properties is not open to observation. A "special sort of cognitive act" is needed. But the same holds for the internalist analysis. In each case, an identification of two properties is offered – conduciveness to pleasure, or motivation, is identified with being a reason – for which simple observation seems indecisive. Without some naturalistic way of choosing between these alternatives, naturalism fails to provide guidance and hence normativity.[16]

The appeal to ordinary language

Philippa Foot's famous attack on categorical imperatives notes that it would follow, from an acceptable moral categorical imperative, that anyone has a reason to do what the imperative enjoins. But Foot finds the latter impossible, since "[i]rrational actions are those in which a man in some way defeats his own purposes, doing what is calculated to be disadvantageous or to frustrate his ends. Immorality does not *necessarily* involve any such thing."[17] An agent's reasons depend only on his "interests and desires": "I believe that a reason for acting must relate the action directly or indirectly to something the agent wants or which it is in his interest to have."[18]

Foot's position is unusual. She allows reasons of prudence, not based on the desires of the agent. She also allows reasons that do not motivate.[19] One wonders why she does not also allow reasons based on the desires or interests of others. Her reply is that "there is no such thing as an objectively good *state of affairs*. Such constructions as 'a good state of affairs,' 'a good thing that p,' are used subjectively, to mark what fits in with the aims and interests of a particular individual or group. Divorced from such a background these expressions lose their sense."[20] This argument can take modest or ambitious interpretations. On the modest interpretation, the point is that no one has shown how the interests and desires of one person give reasons, by themselves, to other

---

16 For a further worry about internalism, see 4.8.

17 Philippa Foot, "Morality as a System of Hypothetical Imperatives," in *Virtues and Vices* (Berkeley and Los Angeles: University of California, 1978), p. 162.

18 Foot, "Reasons for Action and Desires," p. 151, and "A Reply to Professor Frankena," p. 179 (both in *Virtues*); see also Foot, "Moral Beliefs" (in *Virtues*), p. 130n6, "Reasons for Action and Desires," p. 156, and " 'Is Morality a System of Hypothetical Imperatives?' A Reply to Mr. Holmes," *Analysis* 35, 1974–5, pp. 53, 56.

19 Foot, "Reasons for Action and Desires," pp. 148–50, 156n2, "Reply to Professor Frankena," p. 179.

20 Foot, "Reasons for Action and Desires," p. 154.

people. This was, at one time, Foot's gloss on her argument.[21] One appropriate reply is to argue, as I shall in 2.2, that the same consider-ations that show that the interests and desires of the agent provide reasons also show that the interests and desires of others provide rea-sons. On the ambitious (and more natural) interpretation, Foot's point is that it is senseless to speak of reasons that do not depend on the inter-ests and desires of the agent. In a later paper, she may seem to endorse this claim, by arguing, through appeal to ordinary language, that the truth of expressions such as "a good state of affairs" is "speaker-relative."[22] But she admits that one can give the expression a non-speaker-relative meaning, as she thinks utilitarians do, and that it has an ordinary, non-speaker-relative meaning, deriving from the virtue of benevolence. She is concerned to show that neither move aids the utili-tarian.[23] The point here, however, is that admitting a non-speaker-relative meaning prevents her from arguing that, because "good state of affairs" is speaker-relative, it is senseless to speak of reasons that do not depend on the interests and desires of the agent. She is left with the modest claim that she has not seen an argument for such reasons.

The appeal to motivation

J. L. Mackie's attack on "objective values" is an attack on categorical imperatives.[24] Mackie's main argument is from "queerness." Categori-cal imperatives are queer because knowledge of them

> provides the knower with both a direction and an overriding motive; something's being good both tells the person who knows this to pursue it and makes him pursue it. An objective good would be sought by anyone who was acquainted with it, not because of any contingent fact that this person, or every person, is so constituted that he desires this end, but just because the end has to-be-pursuedness somehow built into it.[25]

Mackie thinks there are no such objects of knowledge.

One problem is that the defender of categorical imperatives need not claim, with Kant, that knowledge of them motivates regardless of one's

---

21 See Foot, "Reasons for Action and Desires," p. 156, and "Morality as a System of Hypothetical Imperatives," pp. 168n8, 172–3.
22 Philippa Foot, "Utilitarianism and the Virtues," *Mind* 94, 1985, pp. 199–202.
23 Ibid., pp. 203–9.
24 J. L. Mackie, *Ethics: Inventing Right and Wrong* (Harmondsworth: Penguin Books, 1977), p. 29.
25 Ibid., p. 40. I discuss Mackie further in 2.2.

desires.[26] He need claim only that, when true, a categorical imperative *justifies* regardless of one's desires. The "authority" of moral demands can be understood in terms of a justification, rather than a motivation, that is independent of one's desires.[27]

Another problem is that hypothetical imperatives fail just as categorical ones do. Consider a piece of instrumental reasoning:

(1) I desire to leave the room. (Suppose I have no conflicting desires.)
(2) I know that walking through the door is the best way of leaving the room.
(C) Therefore it is reasonable – I ought – to walk through the door.

I might know (1), (2), and (C) but fail to be motivated to walk through the door. I might suffer from weakness of will. Hypothetical imperatives, like categorical ones, can fail to motivate.[28] Of course, in this case, one wants to say that I have a reason – a justification – for walking through the door. But if this justification is not defeated by noting that it is possible to fail to be motivated, then the justification offered by a categorical imperative also cannot be defeated by noting that it is possible to fail to be motivated.[29]

---

26 See, for example, Immanuel Kant, *Foundations of the Metaphysics of Morals*, trans. Lewis White Beck, (Indianapolis: Bobbs-Merrill, 1969), Ak. 417–9, 454–5.

27 Foot, Brink, and Peter Railton suggest that categoricity might be understood in terms of the "scope" or "application" of an imperative. This resembles my view in that reference to motivation is dropped. But they also drop reference to justification, since they hold the instrumental theory (or, in Foot's case, the instrumental theory along with a theory of prudence). For all three, obeying categorical moral demands is irrational where one's desires are not served by following them. This hardly preserves the authority of morality. (Foot does not mind this, but Railton may. He ends by writing that "the basis of morality is not to be found in the agent's reasons alone, but in the reasons or well-being of others he might affect." The reference to "reasons" suggests that, contrary to his official view, he abandons the purely instrumental theory.) See Foot, "Morality as a System of Hypothetical Imperatives;" David Brink, "A Puzzle About the Rational Authority of Morality," *Philosophical Perspectives* 6, 1992, pp. 7–10; and Peter Railton; "Some Questions About the Justification of Morality," *Philosophical Perspectives* 6, 1992, pp. 27–54; and "Moral Realism," *Philosophical Review* 95, 1986, pp. 201–3. The quotation is from Railton, "Questions," p. 49.

28 Brink worries that it "seems possible to be unmoved by agent-neutral considerations." (Brink, "Puzzle," p. 11) Since it is also possible to be unmoved by agent-relative considerations, this argument does not hurt agent-neutrality.

29 For a similar point, see Korsgaard, "Skepticism," pp. 12-15; and Hampton, "Ethical Naturalism," p. 349.

The appeal to the social sciences

David Gauthier defends instrumental reason by remarking that it "is almost universally accepted and employed in the social sciences. . . . Social scientists may no doubt be mistaken, but we take the onus of proof to fall on those who would defend universalistic rationality."[30] Similarly, David Brink writes that "[a]gent-relative assumptions seem to underlie many formal and informal discussions of individual rationality in philosophy, economics, and politics."[31]

The problem is that it is unclear why the social sciences should be thought of as providing the correct account of practical reason. The worry is not only that the social sciences are notoriously bad at both explanation and prediction. It is that success at explanation and prediction seems irrelevant to establishing a theory of practical reason. Suppose there is a suffering person in the room. I could easily alleviate his pain, but I have no desire to do so; I want to leave the room. Gauthier's economist tells me that I have reason to go to the door but not to help the suffering person. When I ask why, the economist replies that my reasons depend on my desires because citing my desires (along with my beliefs) suffices to explain and predict my behaviour. As Brink puts it, "if an agent has not already formed desires for the welfare of other people, it's hard to see how the welfare of others could explain his behaviour in any way."[32] But this is surely irrelevant. I could agree with the economist that my beliefs and desires will explain my action, but still wonder what I have reason to do or – what comes to the same thing – wonder what desires I have reason to have. If so, the appeal to the social sciences neither establishes the instrumental theory nor puts the onus of proof on the defender of non-instrumental reason.

The appeal to weakness

Gauthier writes that the instrumental theory

> possesses the virtue . . . of weakness. Any consideration affording one a reason for acting on the maximising [instrumental] conception, also affords one such a reason on the universalistic conception. But the converse does not hold. On the universalistic conception all persons have in effect the same basis for rational choice – the interests of all – and this assumption, of the impersonality or impartiality of reason, demands defence.[33]

30 Gauthier, *Morals by Agreement*, p. 8.
31 Brink, "Puzzle," p. 2.
32 Ibid., p. 11.
33 Gauthier, *Morals by Agreement*, p. 8.

There are two replies. First, this argument does not show that the instrumental theory is weaker than theories other than the universalistic theory. A deontologist might claim that reason prohibits promise breaking. If so, it is not true that any reason for acting on the instrumental theory is also a reason for acting on the deontological theory. For the instrumental theory might well find reason for promise breaking – something the deontologist finds no reason for. The same is true for hedonists: my desire for x gives me a reason on the instrumental theory, but will not for the hedonist, where x is unconnected to pleasure.

Second, one need not hold that any reason on the instrumental theory is also a reason on the universalistic theory. Suppose one has reason to do what one is justified in doing. Say that on the instrumental theory, I am justified, given my desires, in going to a movie tonight. It does not follow that, on the universalistic theory, I am justified in going to a movie tonight. The desires of others might make it such that I am justified in doing volunteer work instead.

Gauthier might object that, on the universalistic theory, my desire to go to the movie still provides *some* reason or justification; it is simply outweighed by the desires of others. It is important to mark the contribution of losing desires. To the latter claim, the universalist might agree. But he need not agree that the contribution of losing desires must be marked by saying that they provide some reason or justification. Their contribution can be marked by saying that they have some impact on the winning, reason-giving set of desires or by saying that, absent the other desires, they would have provided reasons.

Admittedly, there is a sense in which Gauthier is right. One might argue for the universalistic conception by arguing for the instrumental conception and then invoking extra considerations, such as arbitrariness. In this case, the instrumental conception is weaker, in that one requires whatever justifies the instrumental conception along with further premises to arrive at the universalistic conception. But this argument for weakness depends on arriving at the universalistic conception by a specific argument. One might use another argument, such as the argument I shall ascribe to Hume in the next section, which makes the case for the instrumental conception and the universalistic conception depend on the same considerations.

The appeal to analyticity

Kant is no defender of the instrumental theory. But he sets up the issue of hypothetical and categorical imperatives in a way that comforts the instrumentalist. Hypothetical imperatives are easily explicable; categorical imperatives require "difficult and special labours."[34] If these labours fail, as most suppose, Kant is left with only hypothetical imperatives. It is worth seeing whether the explanation of hypothetical imperatives is indeed so easy.

Kant asks how hypothetical, prudential, and categorical imperatives are "possible."[35] To show how they are possible is to show "how the constraint of the will, which the imperative expresses . . . can be conceived."[36] It is to explain the normative "must." In the case of hypothetical imperatives, the explanation "requires no particular discussion."[37]

> Whoever wills the end, so far as reason has decisive influence on his action, wills also the indispensably necessary means to it that lie in his power. This proposition, in what concerns the will, is analytical; for, in willing an object as my effect, my causality as an acting cause, i.e., the use of the means, is already thought, and the imperative derives the concept of necessary actions to this end from the concept of willing this end.

> [I]f I know the proposed result can be obtained only by [a certain] action, then it is an analytical proposition that, if I fully will the effect, I must also will the action necessary to produce it. For it is one and the same thing to conceive of something as an effect which is in a certain way possible through me and to conceive of myself as acting in this way.[38]

Suppose that I will to leave the room and know that walking through the door is the only way of doing so. Then I must walk through the door – I am constrained to walk through the door – because willing to leave the room is the same as conceiving of myself as walking through the door.[39]

---

34 Kant, *Foundations,* Ak. 420.
35 Ibid., Ak. 417.
36 Ibid.
37 Ibid.
38 Ibid.
39 I put aside one difference between Kant and the instrumentalist: Kant's "willing" is more weighty than the instrumentalist's "desiring." It might perhaps be replaced by "desiring, all things considered." The second difference requires more comment. Kant's argument applies only to the necessary means, not to the most efficient, or even the minimally efficient, means. Since there is rarely only one means, this limits the applicability of the hypothetical imperative. Kant might reply that the imperative directs one to will at least one of the sufficient means. But this is consistent with choosing a highly inefficient means, such that a person obeying the hypothetical imperative would be condemned as irrational by the instrumental theory and, indeed, by any conception of rationality. Kant might, instead, try building the notion of efficiency into the end. For example, I do not will merely to leave the room. I will to

Now, many hold that rational people must will the means to their ends, because this is (perhaps part of) what it means to be rational. Kant seems important because he appears to provide an argument for this claim: it is rational to take the necessary means to one's ends *because* willing an end and conceiving of oneself as taking the necessary means to it are the same. On this reading, what is distinctive about Kant is not the claim that it is analytic that rational people take the necessary means to their ends, but rather Kant's attempt *to show* that this is analytic.

This attempt fails. To see why, consider two possible candidates for the claim Kant takes to be analytic:

(1) If I will an end, then I will the necessary means to that end.
(2) If I am rational, then, if I will an end, I will the necessary means to that end.

The first passage quoted supports treating (2) as analytic. And Kant soon rephrases the hypothetical imperative as "whoever wills the end wills also (necessarily according to reason) the only means to it which are in his power."[40] More decisively, Kant has reason to reject taking (1) as analytic. For Kant holds that it must be possible to fail to obey imperatives. If (1) is analytic, then it is impossible to will an end without willing the necessary means to it. It is impossible, then, to violate the imperative that "commands the willing of the means to him who wills the end."[41]

Suppose, then, that Kant takes (2) as the analytic claim. His explanation of analyticity then plays no role. The explanation notes that willing an end is "one and the same thing" as willing the necessary means to that end. This would support taking (1) as analytic. But since no mention is made of rationality, this is irrelevant to (2). To show that (2) is analytic requires showing that it is part of the concept of rationality that anyone who wills an end must also will the necessary means. What Kant needs, but does not supply, is an argument to show that thinking

leave the room in an efficient manner. For these two differences between Kant and the instrumentalist, see Kurt Baier, "Comments," in *Reason, Ethics, and Society*, ed. J. B. Schneewind (La Salle: Open Court, 1996), pp. 252, 258–9, 282n57; and Thomas E. Hill, Jr., "The Hypothetical Imperative," *Philosophical Review* 82, 1973, pp. 432–8.
40 Kant, *Foundations*, Ak. 417–18.
41 Ibid., Ak. 419. This point is made by Hill, "Hypothetical," p. 431; Jean Hampton, "On Instrumental Rationality," in Schneewind, *Reason, Ethics, and Society*, pp. 96, 115n21; Baier, "Comments," pp. 255–9, 261.

of a rational person and thinking of a person who wills the necessary means to his ends are "one and the same thing."[42]

This suggests a different, less ambitious reading of Kant. Perhaps he is not trying to argue that (2) is analytic. It is, after all, difficult to convince someone that a claim is analytic, should that person not already agree. On this reading, Kant is noting that we suppose a rational person is one who, when he wills an end, also wills the necessary means. These two willings are "one and the same thing" in the mind of a rational person. In making this claim, Kant is not trying to convince someone that (2) is analytic. He is merely rephrasing (2). This interpretation excuses Kant from confusing (1) and (2). But it does not give him an argument for the analyticity of (2). Like many defenders of the instrumental theory, he has merely asserted it.

2.2

It may seem odd that I have not discussed Hume – the most famous instrumentalist. This is because Hume is best seen as suggesting an argument against rather than for instrumentalism.

Hume is not an instrumentalist: "[a]ctions may be laudable or blameable; but they cannot be reasonable or unreasonable."[43] But Hume's official reason for rejecting instrumentalism is unimpressive. He allows that a passion can be unreasonable in two ways: "When a passion . . . is founded on the supposition of the existence of objects, which really do not exist [or] [w]hen in exerting any passion in action, we chuse means insufficient for the design'd end, and deceive ourselves in our judgement of causes and effects." However, he adds that " 'tis not the passion, properly speaking, which is unreasonable, but the judgement."[44] Later

---

42 For the same point, see Baier, "Comments," pp. 259–61, 285n70, 285n71. There is a trivial sense in which (2) could be supported by showing that willing an end is the same as willing the necessary means to that end. If willing an end is the same as willing the necessary means to that end, then the consequent of (2) is always true, and so (2) is always true. The problem is that "If I am irrational, then, if I will an end, I will the necessary means to that end" is supported equally well.

43 Hume, *Treatise*, p. 458. See Jean Hampton, "Does Hume Have an Instrumental Conception of Practical Reason?" and Elijah Millgram, "Is Hume a Humean?" both in *Hume Studies* 21, 1995, pp. 57–74, 75–94. Hampton thinks Hume, as a "naturalist," is right to reject the instrumental theory, but she does not provide textual evidence to show that naturalism drives Hume's rejection. Millgram thinks Hume's rejection of instrumentalism relies on a "thoroughly discredited" semantic theory. (p. 87) Both depend on *Treatise*, pp. 415 and 458, addressed below.

44 Hume, *Treatise*, p. 416.

he admits that, "in a figurative and improper way of speaking," one might call actions "unreasonable" when they suffer from either of these liabilities.[45] His reason for not endorsing the instrumental theory is that passions and actions are "original facts and realities, compleat in themselves," and so are insusceptible to "agreement or disagreement either to the *real* relations of ideas, or to *real* existence and matter of fact."[46] A passion "contains not any representative quality, which renders it a copy of any other existence or modification," and so cannot "be oppos'd by, or be contradictory to truth and reason; since this contradiction consists in the disagreement of ideas, consider'd as copies, with those objects, which they represent."[47] The judgements accompanying passions and actions represent, and so can be reasonable; the passions and actions themselves do not represent.

This is not a good reason for resisting the instrumental theory. First, the view that passions do not represent may be inconsistent with Hume's (plausible) claims elsewhere. For he may hold that passions are partially constituted by representations of their intentional objects.[48] Second, even were this not so, Hume should have no objection to calling the *judgement* "action x is unreasonable" a reasonable or unreasonable judgement; it cannot be excluded on the grounds that it fails to represent.[49] Third, one might grant Hume the connection between reasonableness and correct representation, yet still hold that actions are subject to a special sort of criticism when they are insufficient for their ends or founded on non-existent objects. The criticism is special in that it depends on finding a mistaken representation. One who believes that practical reason is purely instrumental would, on this proposal, now

45 Ibid., p. 459.
46 Ibid., p. 458.
47 Ibid., p. 415.
48 For discussion, see Annette Baier, *A Progress of Sentiments* (Cambridge, MA: Harvard University Press, 1991), pp. 160–4; Rachel Cohon, "On an Unorthodox Account of Hume's Moral Psychology"; Annette Baier, "Response to My Critics," *Hume Studies* 20, 1994, pp. 179–94, 211–4; Millgram, "Humean," pp. 83–4, 91–2nn28–9; Daniel Shaw, "Reason and Feeling in Hume's Action Theory," *Hume Studies* 18, 1992, pp. 355–60; and Páll Árdal, "Some Implications of the Virtue of Reasonableness in Hume's *Treatise*," in *Hume: A Re-evaluation*, ed. Donald W. Livingston and James T. King (New York: Fordham University Press, 1976), p. 101.
49 See Robert J. Fogelin, *Hume's Skepticism in the Treatise of Human Nature* (London: Routledge & Kegan Paul, 1985), pp. 131–2; Francis Snare, *Morals, Motivation, and Convention* (New York: Cambridge University Press, 1991), pp. 72, 77; Jonathan Harrison, *Hume's Moral Epistemology* (Oxford: Oxford University Press [Clarendon], 1976), p. 25.

claim that criticism that depends on finding a mistaken representation is the only cogent sort of criticism. Hume has not, so far, shown any problem for *this* position.[50]

(Hume may agree. Despite his strictures, he describes acts as reasonable or unreasonable.[51] He also speaks of characters as reasonable or unreasonable.[52] In "Of the Standard of Taste," Hume notes that some think "sentiment has a reference to nothing beyond itself" and that "no sentiment represents what is really in the object." But he rejects the conclusion that "[a]ll sentiment is right."[53] For he supposes, like the instrumentalist, that a sentiment is "erroneous" when it is not the product of "good sense." He differs from the instrumentalist only in requiring that "true" sentiments must pass not just the test of good sense, but other tests as well.[54] Finally, one of Hume's anti-rationalist arguments in the second *Enquiry* depends on instrumentalism.[55] Hume imagines a chain of questions and answers that ends by explaining the desire for money by the desire for pleasure. He then comments that "beyond this it is an absurdity to ask for a reason. It is impossible . . . that one thing can always be a reason why another is desired."[56] This implies, as the instrumentalist would expect, that the desire for pleasure is a reason for the desire for money, since money is a means to pleasure.)

---

50 I leave aside the question of whether an instrumental theory should endorse Hume's claim that a passion or action "must be accompany'd with some false judgement, in order to its being unreasonable." (Hume, *Treatise*, p. 416) Some claim that the reasonableness of an action or passion depends not on whether the underlying judgements are false, but rather on whether they are supported by the agent's evidence. Hume himself sometimes links "reasonable" and "unreasonable" to evidence in this way. (e.g., Hume, *Treatise* pp. 138, 167, 222, 369, 550, *An Enquiry Concerning Understanding*, in *Enquiries*, ed. L. A. Selby-Bigge and P. H. Nidditch (Oxford: Oxford University Press [Clarendon], 1975), pp. 42, 158, *Essays*, ed. Eugene F. Miller (Indianapolis: Liberty, 1985), pp. 365n, 433n179, *Dialogues Concerning Natural Religion*, ed. Norman Kemp Smith [London: Thomas Nelson & Sons, 1947], pp. 148, 156, 166, 187, 190) For the objection, see Barry Stroud, *Hume* (London: Routledge & Kegan Paul, 1977), p. 162; Harrison, *Epistemology*, p. 20; Árdal, "Reasonableness," pp. 94–5. For another worry about *Treatise*, p. 416, see the discussion of weakness of will below.
51 Hume, *Treatise*, pp. 156, 232, *Essays*, pp. 494, 610, 646, *Dialogues*, p. 131.
52 Hume, *Treatise*, pp. 111, 350, *Enquiry Concerning Understanding*, pp. 125, 131, *An Enquiry Concerning Morals*, p. 191, *Essays*, pp. 65, 81, 313, 540, 636, *Dialogues*, pp. 128, 154.
53 Hume, *Essays*, p. 230.
54 Ibid., pp. 240–1, 232–41.
55 This is also noted by Millgram, "Humean," pp. 85–6, 93n34.
56 Hume, *Enquiry Concerning Morals*, p. 293; also p. 277.

But Hume has a better, unofficial argument against instrumentalism. Reconsider the claim to instrumental rationality described in 2.1:

(1) I desire to leave the room. (Suppose I have no conflicting desires.)
(2) I know that walking through the door is the best way of leaving the room.
(C) Therefore it is reasonable – I ought – to walk through the door.

One can ask how (C) follows from (1) and (2). One is tempted to reply by simply repeating the premises: I ought to walk through the door because I desire to leave the room and I know that walking through the door is the best way of leaving the room. Of course one might add a premise:

(3) I ought to do what best satisfies my desires.

Neither of these replies, however, adds anything to the initial argument, in the sense that no one with doubts about the argument would be persuaded by these manoeuvres. Some way of justifying the inference is needed.

Hume suggests one route. His strategy for justifying claims about what one ought to believe or do resorts, in the end, to our taking certain cases as credible. For example, the justification of the rules to judge of causes and effects starts by taking certain cases as credible instances of cause and effect. Hume then asks what properties the objects have, such that we do think they are cause and effect.

> Here is a billiard ball lying on the table, and another ball moving towards it with rapidity. They strike; and the ball, which was formerly at rest, now acquires a motion. This is as perfect an instance of the relation of cause and effect as any which we know, either by sensation or reflection. Let us therefore examine it.[57]

The first three rules to judge of causes and effects are justified by what this examination reveals: cause and effect must be contiguous and constantly conjoined, and the cause must precede the effect. The other rules "we derive from experience": they give proven strategies for finding what the first three rules identify as causes.[58]

Hume follows the same procedure for moral principles.

---

57 Hume, "Abstract of the *Treatise*," p. 649.
58 Hume, *Treatise*, p. 173.

[W]e shall consider every attribute of the mind, which renders a man an object either of esteem and affection, or of hatred and contempt. . . . The only object of reasoning is to discover the circumstances on both sides, which are common to these qualities; to observe that particular in which the estimable qualities agree on the one hand, and the blameable on the other; and thence to reach the foundation of ethics, and find those universal principles, from which all censure or approbation is ultimately derived.[59]

Hume justifies what one could call "rules to judge of virtue and vice" by supposing that we can identify some instances of virtue and vice. We then ask what properties these instances have, such that we think they are virtues or vices. The answer is that virtues are qualities useful or agreeable to their possessor or those he affects. Rules for recognising virtues and vices are justified by reference to this definition.

Aesthetic norms are found in the same way. To discover the "true standard," Hume appeals to great works of art that have stood the test of time. The "foundation" of "the rules of composition" is "experience; nor are they any thing but general observations, concerning what has been universally found to please in all countries and in all ages."[60] The "general rules of beauty" are "drawn from established models" such as Homer, Terence, and Virgil.[61] If "no excellent models had ever been acknowledged . . . it would not have been so easy to silence the bad critic."[62] The "best way of ascertaining" delicacy of taste is "to appeal to those models and principles, which have been established by the uniform consent and experience of nations and ages."[63] The difficulty of finding the standard is "not so great as it is represented" because "[j]ust expressions of passion and nature are sure, after a little time, to gain public applause, which they maintain for ever."[64] Again, norms are derived from initially credible examples.[65]

Hume uses, then, the same strategy made famous by Nelson Goodman and John Rawls. As Goodman puts it for deduction, "[p]rinciples of deductive inference are justified by their conformity with accepted deductive practice. Their validity depends upon accordance with the

---

59 Hume, *Enquiry Concerning Morals,* pp. 173–4; also pp. 289, 312, *Enquiry Concerning Understanding,* pp. 6, 15.
60 Hume, *Essays,* p. 231.
61 Ibid., p. 235.
62 Ibid., p. 236.
63 Ibid., p. 237.
64 Ibid., p. 242.
65 For defence of this interpretation, see my "Hume's Moral Theory?" *History of Philosophy Quarterly* 12, 1995, pp. 317–31.

particular deductive inferences we actually make and sanction. . . . Justification of general rules thus derives from judgements rejecting or accepting particular deductive inferences."[66] On this view, one expects that Hume would justify (3), or the inference from (1) and (2) to (C), by our taking the derivation of (C) from (1) and (2) (or a similar case) as an instance of good practical reasoning that justifies inferring (C). Alternatively, it is our approval of the trait of inferring (C) from (1) and (2) that justifies inferring (C).

This is a point about Hume's method of justifying normative claims. One could use this method given a variety of ways of understanding what it is to accept such a claim. But here Hume has a particular account, one that gives him a further argument for the role of approvals in justification. For Hume, to accept a normative claim is in part to have a particular feeling of approval or disapproval. This is why the transition from "is" to "ought" must be explained by "our own sentiments," by our approvals and disapprovals.

> Take any action allow'd to be vicious. . . . Examine it in all lights, and see if you can find that matter of fact, or real existence, which you call *vice*. In which-ever way you take it, you find only certain passions, motives, volitions and thoughts. There is no other matter of fact in the case. The vice entirely escapes you, as long as you consider the object. You can never find it, till you turn your reflexion into your own breast, and find a sentiment of disapprobation, which arises in you, towards this action.[67]

Hume does not think facts about "the object" – presumably facts other than its effects on spectators – entail approval. The approval depends on the sentiments of the spectators. And so any justification of a claim such as "justice is a virtue" or "one ought to be just" requires more than facts about justice. Our approval is needed. Similarly, the "ought" introduced in (C) escapes us, until we reflect not only on (1) and (2), but also on our approval. And the justification of (C) requires, in addition to (1) and (2), this approval.

One might object that the "ought" of (C) need not receive the analysis of a moral "ought." One might distinguish ought-judgements of the understanding, such as the rules to judge of causes and effects, from moral ought-judgements and identify (C) with the former. It is unclear,

---

66 Nelson Goodman, *Fact, Fiction, and Forecast* (Cambridge, MA: Harvard University Press, 1983), pp. 63–4. For Rawls, see especially John Rawls, "Outline of a Decision Procedure for Ethics," *Philosophical Review* 60, 1951, pp. 177–97, where justifying moral principles is compared with justifying rules of inductive logic.

67 Hume, *Treatise*, pp. 468–9.

however, how Hume could make the distinction. Worse, there is no textual evidence that he makes it. And in his moral writings, he suggests various virtues to cover the trait of inferring (C) from (1) and (2): strength of mind, prudence, forethought, good sense, resolution, discernment, sagacity, presence of mind.[68] This suggests that, if a distinction were made, Hume would see the "ought" of (C) as falling in the moral rather than "theoretical" camp.

So far, no argument against the purely instrumental theory has emerged. But the Humean strategy for justifying normative claims has two consequences, both bad for the instrumentalist.

First, attempts to draw a significant distinction between hypothetical and categorical imperatives fail. Consider Mackie again. Mackie argues that, in any argument that concludes with a categorical imperative, "there will be something which cannot be objectively validated – some premise which is not capable of being simply true, or some form of argument which is not valid as a matter of general logic, whose authority or cogency is not objective, but is constituted by our choosing or deciding to think in a certain way."[69] Hypothetical imperatives, on the other hand, "follow from causal statements."[70] Mackie admits that we often speak of reasons that do not depend on present desires. We speak of prudential reasons or say: " 'Surely if someone is writhing in agony before your eyes, or starving on your doorstep, this is in itself, quite apart from your feelings, a reason for you to do something about it if you can; if you don't admit that, you just don't know what a reason is.' " But Mackie objects that such reasons depend upon an "institution" or choice, and "nothing compels us to reinterpret the requirements of an institution, however well established, however thoroughly enshrined in our ordinary ways of thinking and speaking, as objective, intrinsic, requirements of the nature of things."[71]

On Hume's view, hypothetical imperatives depend on choice or institution just as categorical imperatives do. To a sceptic about the argument for (C), we cannot reply that the argument from (1) and (2) to (C) is "valid as a matter of general logic" or that (3) is "simply true" given

68 Hume, *Treatise*, pp. 610–11, *Enquiry Concerning Morals*, pp. 239–43.
69 Mackie, *Ethics*, p. 30. See also Mackie, *Hume's Moral Theory* (London: Routledge & Kegan Paul, 1980), p. 62.
70 Mackie, *Theory*, p. 62. See also Mackie, *Ethics*, pp. 27–8.
71 Mackie, *Ethics*, pp. 79–80. For consideration of a similar example, with a different conclusion, see Thomas Nagel, *The View from Nowhere* (New York: Oxford University Press, 1986), pp. 160–1 or John Skorupski, *John Stuart Mill* (London: Routledge & Kegan Paul, 1989), p. 311.

"the nature of things."[72] We can, and probably would, reply that the sceptic does not "know what a reason is." We might, that is, defend the connection as a matter of choice or institution. If so, hypothetical and categorical imperatives simply belong to different institutions or result from different choices. From the point of view of the (non-institutional, non-optional) "nature of things," they are on a par.

Mackie might reply by claiming, as above, that criticism that depends on finding a mistaken representation is the only cogent sort. But this both requires argument and faces an objection. One cannot support (C) simply by noting (1), (2), and that I hold no (relevant) mistaken representations and so cannot be criticised. One must still show how (1) and (2) support (C) rather than some other ought-claim or none at all. If the support comes from our approvals, then it is unclear why cogent criticism is restricted to finding mistaken representations. After all, our approvals sometimes call for criticisms that are not restricted in this way, as in the case of the person writhing in agony. Surely the kind of consideration needed to support (C) can sometimes furnish criticism of claims like (C).

To avoid this problem, Mackie might say that (1) and (2) cause me to go to the door, and that, since I have no mistaken representations, my going to the door cannot be criticised and so is reasonable. On this view, however, *any* action I perform without mistaken representations is reasonable. For example, (1) and (2) might be true yet fail, through weakness of will, to cause me to go to the door. Here, contrary to the instrumental theory, not going to the door turns out to be reasonable.[73]

---

72 See Hampton, "Hobbes and Ethical Naturalism," pp. 347–9, and "Instrumental Conception?" pp. 59, 70. Sidgwick may make this point in writing that "[w]hen (e.g.) a physician says, 'If you wish to be healthy you ought to rise early,' this is not the same thing as saying 'early rising is an indispensable condition of the attainment of health.' This latter proposition expresses the relation of physiological facts on which the former is founded; but it is not merely this relation of facts that the word 'ought' imports: it also implies the unreasonableness of adopting an end and refusing to adopt the means indispensable to its attainment." (*Methods* p. 37) R. M. Hare also makes the point, in response to Max Black's claim that the inference from (1) and (2) to (C) is valid – though Hare supposes that only a non-cognitive act of endorsement can justify the inference from (1) and (2) to (C). See R. M. Hare, "Wanting: Some Pitfalls," in Hare, *Practical Inferences* (Berkeley and Los Angeles: University of California Press, 1971), pp. 44–51; and Max Black, "The Gap Between 'Is' and 'Should,'" *Philosophical Review* 73, 1964, pp. 165–81.

73 See Don Hubin, "Irrational Desires," *Philosophical Studies* 62, 1991, pp. 28, 42n10; or Michael Smith, "Reason and Desire," *Proceedings of the Aristotelian Society* 88, 1987–8, pp. 245–7.

Second, there is no reason for thinking that our approvals are limited to the inferences sanctioned by the instrumentalist. Suppose that I have no desire to help the person writhing in agony before my eyes; my desire is to leave the room. Many will deny that I ought to walk through the door rather than help. Many will no longer approve of concluding (C) from (1) and (2) or endorse (3).[74] This suggests that claims of instrumental reasonableness will not always win approval when they conflict with moral (or prudential) instances or approvals. Indeed, one might even try to argue that they win approval *only* when they do not conflict with moral (or prudential) approvals.

I do not deny that we often approve of concluding (C) from (1) and (2). Nor do I deny that it is part of our concept of a rational person that she (sometimes) wills the necessary means to her ends. But there is no reason for thinking that instrumental rationality exhausts practical rationality. For we sometimes suppose that the desires of others can provide me with reasons directly. This latter thought does not need a special and dubious defence, to be conducted while the instrumentalist, secure with a firmly founded theory, looks on with a critical eye.[75] Both accounts of rationality rest on the same footing – both are backed by appeal to the sort of inferences we are willing to admit.

One might still admit only those inferences licenced by the instrumental theory. But the rationale for doing so is not given by appeal to some extra-normative commitment, such as naturalism or the other appeals canvassed in 2.1. Like the rationale for licensing rational egoist or utilitarian inferences, the rationale for the instrumental theory must come from examining the normative judgements we are willing to accept.

Sidgwick shares the approach just sketched. He does not, however, say much about instrumentalism. He thinks that, on normative grounds, more can be said for rational egoism and utilitarianism. I return to this, briefly, in the next chapter. The point here is that, since instrumentalism lacks a special foundation, moral theories with which it conflicts – and, for that matter, rational egoism – need not have special fear of it.

---

74 Black concedes this, after noting a similar counter-example, but supposes the argument remains valid because the "ought" in (C) is not an all-things-considered ought. If the instrumentalist makes Black's reply, however, he admits that his theory does not exhaust practical reasoning. (Black would not mind, since he thinks facts about the pain of others can justify ought claims.) See Black, "'Is' and 'Should,'" pp. 175–6, 180–1.

75 For a particularly clear instance of thinking the contrary, see Gauthier, "Why Contractarianism?" pp. 18–20.

Chapter 3

Sidgwick

SIDGWICK is the most astute defender and the most astute critic of rational egoism. His astuteness is evidenced in numerous ways.

First, Sidgwick takes rational egoism seriously. He is not much concerned with whether it qualifies as a moral theory. Perhaps it does not – but since there is "wide acceptance" of it, it deserves consideration as a theory of reasons for action. (ME 119) Sidgwick asks the general question "What do I have most reason to do?"

Second, in answering this question, Sidgwick holds that virtue does not always pay. He refuses to settle for the comfortable and popular reconciliation of morality and rational egoism. (ME 162–75, 502–9)

Third, Sidgwick is aware, as no one before or since, of the history of rational egoism. His *Outlines of the History of Ethics* contains the best, and indeed almost the only, history of the position.

Fourth, he rejects the arguments uncovered in this history that purport to establish rational egoism on the basis of psychological egoism. Here I shall, briefly, give his reasons.

Say psychological egoism is true. This does not exclude the possibility that I take my pleasure from doing what I take to be right, while holding that, say, utilitarian considerations make right acts right. (ME 40–1) Belief in psychological egoism, then, does not compel belief in rational egoism. One might reply that, at least, if maximising psychological egoism is true, then no end conflicting with my pleasure can be dictated by reason. Sidgwick agrees, but adds that it does not follow that my *pursuing* my pleasure is dictated by reason. For a course of action to be dictated by reason, it must be possible to deviate from it. Reason cannot be said to guide me to maximise my happiness where I cannot but maximise my happiness. (ME 34–5, 41) Now, non-maximising psychological egoism allows the possibility of guidance. Sidgwick thinks that, were it true, it might provide an argument for rational egoism:

If it can be shown that the ultimate aim of each of us in acting is always solely *some* pleasure (or absence of pain) to himself, the demonstration certainly suggests that each *ought* to seek his own *greatest* pleasure. As has been said, no cogent inference is possible from the psychological generalisation to the ethical principle: but the mind has a natural tendency to pass from the one position to the other: if the actual ultimate springs of our volition are always our own pleasures and pains, it seems *prima facie* reasonable to be moved by them in proportion to their pleasantness and painfulness, and therefore to choose the greatest pleasure or least pain on the whole. (*ME* 42; also 412)

Sidgwick does not defend this claim to prima facie reasonableness. One suspects he would not defend it, for elsewhere he argues that appeals to nature, or natural tendencies, are thought to support normative conclusions only given theological assumptions about design or bad arguments that assign normative weight to the common, the original, or the inevitable. (*ME* 80–3) He also finds both maximising and non-maximising psychological egoism false. (*ME* 42–54) If so, rational egoism must stand on grounds unconnected to motivation.[1] I shall argue that Sidgwick suggests three such grounds.

Fifth, Sidgwick shows astuteness in a further, more controversial way: He does not hold a purely instrumental theory of rationality. He rejects it by noting that

[w]e do not all look with simple indifference on a man who declines to take the right means to his own happiness, on no other ground than that he does not care about happiness. Most men would regard such a refusal as irrational, with a certain disapprobation; they would thus implicitly assent to Butler's statement that 'interest, one's own happiness, is a manifest obligation.' In other words, they would think that a man *ought* to care for his own happiness. The word "ought" thus used is no longer relative: happiness now appears as an ultimate end, the pursuit of which . . . appears to be prescribed by reason 'categorically.' (*ME* 7)

Sidgwick adds that many think moral duties are sometimes "binding . . . without regard to ulterior consequences," and that utilitarians think the general happiness is an end "categorically prescribed." (*ME* 8; also

---

1 Sidgwick grants that, were psychological egoism true, it would be "useless to point out to a man the conduct that would conduce to the general happiness, unless you convince him at the same time that it would conduce to his own." (*ME* 84–5) This does not help rational egoism, however, both because psychological egoism is false and because the arguments against drawing a normative conclusion – whether rational egoist or utilitarian – remain.

26, 35–6, FC 482–3) We think some ultimate ends, such as fame, are irrational. (*ME* 9, 155–6) Were there compelling arguments for the instrumental theory, this appeal to what we think would be unsatisfactory. But since there are no such arguments, the onus is on the instrumental theorist to show that what we think is mistaken.

In 3.1, I explain Sidgwick's methodology. I argue in favour of seeing common sense as epistemically significant. Since I shall argue that common-sense views concerning morality and prudence do not support rational egoism, it is important to explain and defend this claim. In 3.2, I clarify Sidgwick's view of the status of rational egoism. I argue that his considered view is that rational egoism is neither self-evident nor of the highest certainty. In 3.3 and 3.4, I consider his arguments for rational egoism based on the distinctness of persons and the systematisation of common sense. In Chapter 4, I consider his argument for rational egoism from historical consensus. I argue that these arguments in favour of rational egoism fail and that Sidgwick suggests two good arguments against rational egoism, from systematisation and arbitrariness.

Before proceeding, two preliminaries are needed.

First, Sidgwick takes rational egoism to be the view that "the rational agent regards quantity of consequent pleasure and pain to himself as alone important in choosing alternatives of action; and seeks always the greatest attainable surplus of pleasure over pain." (*ME* 95; also 119–20) Pleasure is "feeling which the sentient individual at the time of feeling it implicitly or explicitly apprehends to be desirable; desirable, that is, when considered merely as feeling." (*ME* 131; also 42–3, 127) Sidgwick's discussion supposes that rational (and psychological) egoism takes hedonistic forms, and so he often writes of "egoistic hedonism" and "psychological hedonism" rather than "rational egoism" and "psychological egoism." Since I think Sidgwick's arguments are relevant to any non-vacuous variety of rational or psychological egoism, I use the wider labels.

The second preliminary concerns Sidgwick's self-evident axioms. He gives various statements of the axioms; he sometimes gives the same axiom different names; and he often distinguishes between the axioms and the "principles" of which they reveal the self-evident element. For ease of reference, I shall assign names to the canonical statements of the axioms as follows:

> The axiom of consistency: "'[I]t cannot be right for A to treat B in a manner in which it would be wrong for B to treat A, merely on the ground that they are two different individuals, and without there being any

difference between the natures or circumstances of the two which can be stated as a reasonable ground for difference of treatment.'" (*ME* 380) (Sidgwick often calls this the axiom of justice.)

The axiom of temporal irrelevance: "[T]he mere difference of priority and posteriority in time is not a reasonable ground for having more regard to the consciousness of one moment than to that of another." (*ME* 381) (Sidgwick often calls this the axiom of prudence.)

The axiom of personal irrelevance: "[T]he good of any one individual is of no more importance, from the point of view (if I may say so) of the Universe, than the good of any other." (*ME* 382)

The axiom of the whole: "[A]s a rational being I am bound to aim at good generally, – so far as it is attainable by my efforts, – not merely at a particular part of it." (*ME* 382)

From the axioms of personal irrelevance and of the whole, Sidgwick derives

The axiom of rational benevolence: "[E]ach one is morally bound to regard the good of any other individual as much as his own, except in so far as he judges it to be less, when impartially viewed, or less certainly knowable or attainable by him." (*ME* 382)[2]

In setting out the axioms in this way, I do not mean to prejudge controversial issues. I intend only to make reference to the axioms easier.

3.1

Sidgwick's methodology is controversial. Some think he relies almost entirely on an appeal to self-evidence.[3] Others think he appeals first and foremost to coherence with common-sense morality.[4] Still others think he does both, and is inconsistent.[5] I shall argue that he does both, but

2 I leave aside the question of whether the axiom of rational benevolence is self-evident. J. B. Schneewind argues that, since it is a deduction, it is not. Sidgwick, however, repeatedly treats it as self-evident. (*ME* xxxv, 388, 400, 421, 462n, 498, 505, 507) See J. B. Schneewind, *Sidgwick's Ethics and Victorian Moral Philosophy* (Oxford: Oxford University Press [Clarendon], 1977), pp. 294–5.

3 See Peter Singer, "Sidgwick and Reflective Equilibrium," *The Monist* 57, 1974, pp. 490–517.

4 John Rawls, *A Theory of Justice* (Cambridge, MA: Harvard University Press, 1971), p. 51n.

5 David Brink, "Common Sense and First Principles in Sidgwick's *Methods*," *Social Philosophy and Policy* 11, 1994, pp. 179–201; Steven Sverdlik, "Sidgwick's Methodology," *Journal of the History of Philosophy* 23, 1985, pp. 537–53.

that there is no inconsistency. I shall also defend Sidgwick's account of
the role of common-sense morality in justification.

In the *Methods*, Sidgwick gives four epistemic tests for any proposition: The proposition must be clear and precise; it must be seen as self-
evident by careful reflection; it must be consistent with other propositions accepted as self-evident; and there must be little disagreement
about its truth. (*ME* 338–42) He introduces these tests by writing that

> I now wish to . . . decide whether [some] formulae possess the charac-
> teristics by which self-evident truths are distinguished from mere opin-
> ions. . . . There seem to be four conditions, the complete fulfilment of
> which would establish a significant proposition, apparently self-evident,
> in the highest degree of certainty attainable: and which must be approxi-
> mately realised by the premises of our reasoning in any inquiry, if that
> reasoning is to lead us cogently to trustworthy conclusions. (*ME* 338)

Sidgwick goes on to apply the tests to common-sense morality, concluding that the "self-evidence [of its principles] becomes dubious or vanishes altogether." (*ME* 343) This suggests that the epistemic tests are
tests for self-evidence.

In his epistemological writings, Sidgwick holds the appealing position that we should proceed by making explicit the methods we use to
discover error, rather than by offering a priori methods derived from a
philosophical view of knowledge. (*LK* 466) He gives tests for freedom
from error. The first test, "intuitive verification," asks for "clearness,
distinctness, precision in our concepts, and definite subjective self-
evidence in our judgement." (*LK* 466) Sidgwick often refers to propositions passing these tests as self-evident.[6] This test is "useful." (*LK* 461;
also VB 584, *LK* 451) But self-evidence is insufficient, for we have all too
often discovered that what passes this test proves unacceptable. (VB
585, 587, *LK* 450–1, 460–2, EP 108) This is the fate, for example, of "a

6 For example, such propositions have "self-evidence in the belief itself." (*LK* 464)
   "[O]ur certainty of . . . truth is . . . obtained by contemplating them alone, and not in
   connection with any other propositions." (VB 586; also EP 106, 108–9, *ME* 98, 211–12,
   379, 383) In his attack on common-sense morality, he treats showing that a claim is not
   known a priori, that it is derivative, or that it requires a further reason for assent as
   showing that it is not self-evident. (e.g., *ME* 346, 348, 359; 354–6) (Here, a priori cannot
   mean "without experience," since Sidgwick allows observation sentences to be self-
   evident. Observation sentences can be self-evident because they are not inferred from
   any other propositions. For a similar construal of self-evidence, see Thomas Reid,
   Essays on the Intellectual Powers of Man, in Reid, *Philosophical Works* [Hildesheim: Georg
   Olms Verlag, 1967], vol. 1, p. 434.)

thing cannot act where it is not" or "it [is] just to give every man his own." (VB 585, *LK* 462) When we do discover error, it is by seeing the inconsistency of the proposition with other propositions we hold. (*LK* 461–2, 466) New theories are usually accepted, not by virtue of new data, but by seeing that they better harmonise the existing data. (*M* 606–7) This is illustrated "by the method by which in my work on Ethics Common Sense is led to Utilitarianism." (*LK* 462) The intuitive verification "requires to be supplemented by a discursive verification." (VB 590; also *LK* 462, *M* 347, 605–8, *PSR* 219) This justifies an intrapersonal consistency test. It has "special and pre-eminent importance." (*LK* 466–7) Consistency between my beliefs is not enough, however; we sometimes detect error by finding that our beliefs are inconsistent with the beliefs of unconstrained experts. (*LK* 466, *M* 609–11, EP 109, *PSR* 217, 219) A "Social or Oecumenical Verification" is needed. (*LK* 464) This test explains why Sidgwick provisionally takes "Common Sense as the point of departure." (*LK* 464) In sum, "if we find that an intuitive belief appears clear and certain to ourselves contemplating it, that it is in harmony with our other beliefs relating to the same subject, and does not conflict with the beliefs of other persons competent to judge, we have reduced the risk of error with regard to it as low as it is possible to reduce it." (*LK* 465; also EP 109, *LK* 419)

Sidgwick's epistemological views force reinterpretation of the tests of the *Methods*. The tests "establish a significant proposition, apparently self-evident, in the highest degree of certainty attainable." (*ME* 338) The highest degree of certainty comes not with self-evidence, but with, in addition, discursive and social verification. Thus Sidgwick applies the tests *to* putative self-evident propositions, but the tests are not themselves all tests for self-evidence. He is not *just* separating self-evident propositions from "mere opinions." He is testing for freedom from error. This explains why they so closely resemble the tests suggested in the epistemological writings.[7]

---

7   The first edition makes the point more clearly. The tests are introduced as follows: "The truths of science are known to us in two ways, by direct intuition, or by processes of inference. . . . For our present purposes, we need only examine the characteristics of the former, intuitively known, truths. . . . There would seem to be four conditions, the complete fulfilment of which would establish a proposition in the highest degree of certainty attainable." (*ME* (1) 317) Reflecting back, Sidgwick writes that he inquired whether common-sense morality provided axioms that "were really clear, self-evident, coherent, and universally admitted." (*ME* (1) 388; also EP 109)

I think this interpretation is correct. There is one glitch. The intrapersonal consistency tests in and outside of the *Methods* seem to differ. In the *Methods*, a self-evident proposition reaches the highest degree of certainty through consistency with other self-evident propositions. Outside the *Methods*, Sidgwick is not entirely clear. Sometimes the proposition must be consistent with propositions that might conflict with it (*LK* 462, 465, 466, EP 109, VB 590); "what we commonly agree to take for knowledge" (*M* 607); beliefs "we find ourselves naturally impelled to hold" (*M* 347); or propositions "equally strongly affirmed by us." (*LK* 461) The last agrees with the *Methods;* the other suggestions do not. The worry is that, if the tests differ, the *Methods* tests may after all be tests for self-evidence, as they initially appeared to be.[8]

Again, however, this conclusion is inconsistent with Sidgwick's explicit claim that self-evidence alone does not yield the highest degree of certainty. One must, then, read the *Methods* tests as tests for freedom from error rather than simply self-evidence. This is not so odd. Sidgwick straightforwardly treats the fourth test as a test for truth and certainty (*ME* 341–2); he describes the second test as asking by itself whether an axiom is "really self-evident" (*ME* xxxiv); he notes, in discussing the second test, that asking for self-evidence is "valuable" but not "complete" protection against error (*ME* 339); and, after having pronounced the axioms to be self-evident, he adds that his confidence in them would be increased should they agree with the conclusions of Samuel Clarke and Kant. (*ME* 384)

It is also not odd to read the intrapersonal consistency test as demanding consistency with propositions of equal certainty. Sidgwick might plausibly think that the certainty of a self-evident proposition, consistent with all other self-evident propositions and held by all, is unimpaired by conflict with a proposition that is not self-evident. Indeed, this is one way in which he supposes common sense can be criticised: "[W]e should expect that the history of Moral Philosophy . . . would be a history of attempts to enunciate, in full breadth and clearness, those primary intuitions of Reason, by the scientific application of which the common moral thought of mankind may be at once systematised and corrected." (*ME* 373–4; also *LK* 465)

It is true that Sidgwick can be misleading. As noted, he sometimes suggests that the *Methods* tests are tests for self-evidence. He is often hunting self-evident propositions, without always noting that, in addi-

8 For this inference, see Schneewind, *Victorian*, p. 268.

tion to self-evidence, they must have the highest certainty. (e.g., *ME* 211–12, 373–86)[9] And when he applies these tests to common-sense morality, he is willing to use *any* of the tests to discredit a claim to self-evidence. I think the laxness is understandable and should not be taken to show, again, that the tests are really all for self-evidence. For Sidgwick is also lax in stating whether he is denying self-evidence or "ultimate certainty" or "rational conviction." (*ME* 343–50, 353, 356, 358–60; 214; 357) He does not care; he need only show that common-sense morality does not provide propositions of the highest certainty.

Moreover, Sidgwick holds that the consistency tests, while not direct tests for self-evidence, still have an effect on our reflection on any proposition. Reflection is "aided . . . by communication with other minds." (*ME* 212; also 2, 28, 101, 373) A qualification demanded by consistency "suggests a doubt whether the correctly qualified proposition will present itself with the same self-evidence as the simpler but inadequate one." (*ME* 341) The self-evidence of a proposition "becomes dubious or vanishes altogether" with these qualifications. (*ME* 343) The point is not limited to qualifications: I might, for example, come to see how a proposition could be false by seeing its negation become plausible through being embedded in a system of propositions I had not considered. Sidgwick thinks this is true of "a thing cannot act where it is not." The hypothesis of universal gravitation "destroyed any intuitive certainty in it for most of us." (*LK* 462) Reflection on other propositions can also make one see self-evidence where it was not obvious: "[A] proposition may be self-evident . . . though in order that its truth may be apparent to some particular mind, there is still required some rational process connecting it with propositions previously accepted by that mind." (*EP* 106) The difference between a test and a causal influence shows how Sidgwick can admit the possibility of an "ultimate difference of intuitive judgement"; in such a case, the demands of consistency do not cause one to retract the claim to self-evidence. (*LK* 466)

Sidgwick, then, combines the appeal to self-evidence with the appeal to common-sense morality. One might ask why, if he distrusts judgements of self-evidence, he includes them at all. One reason is that Sidgwick's predecessors and opponents looked for self-evidence. Another, better reason is that Sidgwick is looking for propositions of the "highest certainty." It is these, he hopes, that will allow "escape from the doubt-

9 The hunt in Sidgwick, *Methods*, III.XIII, does, however, begin by asking whether we can attain "intuitive propositions of real clearness *and certainty.*" (*ME* 373, italics added)

fulness, disputableness, and apparent arbitrariness of current moral opinions." (*ME* 378–9; also 102–3, 497) He thinks, plausibly, that self-evidence adds certainty to that brought by discursive and social verification. In the case of "fundamental assumptions which lack self-evidence, but are confirmed or not contradicted by other beliefs relating to the same matter and accepted by Common Sense," there is "imperfect certitude." (*LK* 465) A self-evident proposition has a further source of certainty – itself.[10]

The value of self-evidence can be seen in another way. Consider a coherent system of beliefs. Whether or not I should believe the system does not depend solely on its internal consistency, nor on its consistency with other possible systems. I want to know which of the many possible consistent systems to hold. One of Sidgwick's examples of the intuitive test is the empiricist requirement that beliefs concern particulars and be as close to non-inferential as possible. Sidgwick spends most of his time arguing that meeting this criterion does not guarantee certainty. But his insistence on the value of intuitive criteria can be seen as (in part) an insistence that the information supplied by the senses plays a crucial role in the choice of beliefs.

On this picture, common-sense morality enters most obviously in social verifications. It also enters in discursive verifications. For even if common-sense morality contains no self-evident propositions, I shall argue that the self-evident propositions Sidgwick finds leave room for much consistency-testing on the (lower) level of certainty at which much ethical debate must exist. Sidgwick stresses this role for common-sense morality in his ethical society addresses. (*PE* 6–8, 15) Finally, the *Methods* suggests another general strategy for supporting a moral theory. In addition to applying the epistemic tests, one can argue that those who hold one theory should, on grounds they already accept, switch to another theory. These grounds may be some axioms taken as self-evident by the target theory, or they may be other claims accepted by the target theory. (*ME* 419–22, 497 EP 106–7) Sidgwick calls this "proof" –

---

10 This is why Sidgwick is unsure, at the close of the *Methods,* about justifying belief in an afterlife on the ground that the belief brings consistency. He notes that proponents of self-evidence reject this justification; proponents of coherence should accept it; Sidgwick himself, demanding both self-evidence and coherence, assigns "imperfect certitude" to an afterlife. (*ME* 509) Elsewhere he argues that self-evidence is not needed for a " 'working philosophy of religious belief.' " (*M* 605–8) He also notes that some propositions passing the consistency tests but lacking self-evidence feel as certain as self-evident propositions, but he insists that they remain "provisional." (*PSR* 243)

"a line of argument which on the one hand allows the validity, to a certain extent, of the maxims already accepted, and on the other hand shows them to be not absolutely valid, but needing to be controlled and completed by some more comprehensive principle." (*ME* 420) Since common-sense morality is itself a theory, any "proof" of rational egoism or utilitarianism must address it.

In numerous places, Sidgwick notes that he combines the epistemic tests, including the appeal to self-evidence, and the various appeals to common-sense morality. (*PE* 52–3, *ME* 400, *UG* 35, *EP* 106–7) The same combination is found in his political writings.[11] Sidgwick thinks "[t]he two methods are in no way antagonistic." (*PE* 53) Some disagree. Steven Sverdlik objects that self-evident propositions "are known to be true as soon as their meaning is understood" and so appealing to self-evidence leaves no room for appealing to common-sense morality. "The contradiction . . . consists in asserting that the principles of Benevolence, Prudence, and Justice are so certain that they do not admit of further substantiation and that they do admit of such substantiation."[12] There are two replies.

First, I shall argue below that Sidgwick's self-evident propositions do not establish substantive positions such as utilitarianism. Thus even if Sidgwick justified these propositions by self-evidence alone, he would need to do more to establish a substantive position. Common-sense morality could then have a role. (Other arguments, which are neither considerations of self-evidence nor appeals to common-sense morality, also have a role: for example, common-sense prudential beliefs and beliefs about personal identity, an afterlife, and the ultimately good.)

Second, Sidgwick does not agree that self-evident propositions "do not admit of further substantiation." He sees the worry: "It may be thought . . . that so long as any proposition presents itself as self-evident, we can feel no need of anything more . . . since self-evidence, *ex vi termini*, leaves no room for any doubt that a supplementary criterion could remove." But he makes the expected reply:

> [T]his view does not sufficiently allow for the complexity of our intellectual processes. If we have once learnt . . . that we are liable to be mistaken in the affirmation of apparently self-evident propositions, we may surely retain this general conviction of our fallibility along with the special im-

---

11   See Stefan Collini, "The Ordinary Experience of Civilized Life: Sidgwick's Politics and the Method of Reflective Analysis," in Schultz, *Essays*, pp. 333–68.

12   Sverdlik, "Methodology," pp. 548–9. For the same objection, see Brink, "Common Sense," p. 191.

pression of the self-evidence of any proposition we may be contemplating; and thus however strong this latter impression may be, we shall still admit our need of some further protection against the possible failure of our faculty of intuition. (EP 108–9)

Sidgwick can say this because, unlike Sverdlik, he characterises self-evidence in terms of (degrees of) certainty rather than knowledge.[13]

Brink has a further objection to combining the epistemic tests, including tests for self-evidence, with the appeal to common-sense morality. Sidgwick motivates the search for self-evident propositions, in part, by a regress argument; the regress argument rules out circular reasoning; but the appeal to common-sense morality is circular: "[P]articular common moral beliefs are justified by appeal to moral principles that subsume and explain them, and these principles are justified by their ability to subsume and explain common moral beliefs."[14]

This oversimplifies in two ways.

First, common moral beliefs provide a check on judgements of self-evidence, but they do not provide the initial justification.[15] Sidgwick emphasises that "it makes a fundamental difference whether [consistency tests] are used as supplementary to the characteristic of apparent self-evidence, or as substitutes for it." (EP 108; also *ME* 101, 341) The philosopher, "though . . . expected to establish and concatenate at least the main part of the commonly accepted moral rules, . . . is not necessarily bound to take them as the basis on which his own system is constructed." (*ME* 373)

13 (i) Apart from this, I follow Sverdlik's strategy here – though he treats the "further protection" as confirming a putative self-evident proposition as really self-evident, rather than as providing a separate test for freedom from error. See Sverdlik, "Methodology," pp. 549–50. (ii) To this, Brink objects that "Sidgwick appears to claim that the discursive justification of first principles exhausts their justification." In support, he quotes Sidgwick's conclusion that "[i]f systematic reflection upon the Morality of Common Sense thus exhibits the Utilitarian principle as that to which Common Sense naturally appeals for the further development of its system which this same reflection shows to be necessary, the proof of Utilitarianism seems as complete as it can be made." (*ME* 422; Brink, "Common Sense," p. 192) But Brink misreads the passage. Sidgwick writes of "proof," not complete justification. (Brink sees this rejoinder, but gives a puzzling reply; see 192n13) And even if one equates "proof" with justification, the claim that the proof is "as complete as it can be made" is most naturally taken to encompass not only the argument based on common sense, but also the appeals to the axioms made earlier in the chapter that the passage concludes.
14 Brink, "Common Sense," p. 192. I think it is unclear whether Sidgwick does rule out circular reasoning by appeal to a regress argument, but I shall let this pass here.
15 For the point, see Schneewind, *Victorian*, p. 350.

Second, before arriving at any self-evident principles, Sidgwick supposes that common-sense morality has *"prima facie* claim to proceed on reasonable principles." (*ME* xxvii; also 9) This is why he considers it, and not various other possibilities, as a serious rival to rational egoism and utilitarianism. Elsewhere he writes that general consent "may afford a sufficient ground for a practical decision: certainly if I found myself alone *contra mundum,* I should think it more probable that I was wrong than that the world was, and such a balance of probability is enough to act on." (EP 109) The "extent to which [a moral belief] has found favour with thoughtful persons affords a *prima facie* presumption that there are elements of sound reason in it." (*PE* 70) Given specialisation, the social verification is "practically most prominent"; one must *"provisionally* accept the judgement of Common Sense." (*LK* 464–5) Consistency considerations, without self-evidence, are sufficient for "the kind and degree of certitude which we require for a "'working philosophy.'" (*M* 606; also *PE* 5, 8, 15) Indeed, one must study common-sense morality "with reverent care and patience" since it incorporates the otherwise uncodifiable "continuous experience of social generations." (*PE* 35) There is even an evolutionary argument for the *approximate* reliability of common-sense morality: "[S]o far as any moral habit or sentiment was unfavourable to the preservation of the social organism, it would be a disadvantage in the struggle for existence, and would therefore tend to perish with the community that adhered to it." (*ME* 465; also xxiii, *PE* 47–8)[16] For Sidgwick, then, there is some reason to believe common-sense morality, even without showing that it derives from any propositions of greater certainty.[17] It has "imperfect certitude."

Putting these two points together, one can see that Sidgwick's procedure is not circular. I believe some self-evident proposition p on the basis of seeing its self-evidence and seeing that it agrees with common-sense morality. If I have no reason to trust common-sense morality other than noting p, seeing the agreement with common-sense morality

16 Sidgwick goes on to argue that the evolutionary argument does not show that common-sense morality conforms perfectly to utilitarianism. (*ME* 465–7) But this does not impugn the evolutionary argument as an argument for the credibility of common-sense morality, both because utilitarianism may not be the best moral theory and because imperfections in common-sense morality are compatible with its credibility.

17 I write "greater certainty" rather than "self-evidence" because, again, I shall argue that, for Sidgwick, although much of common-sense morality can be derived from utilitarianism, utilitarianism is not self-evident.

should not increase my confidence in p. But where there is independent reason for believing in common-sense morality, agreement with it increases my confidence in p.[18]

I close this section by considering worries about common-sense morality. Sidgwick thinks agreement with common-sense morality should increase one's certainty. Peter Singer and R. M. Hare disagree. Singer asks

> [w]hy should we not . . . make the . . . assumption, that all the particular moral judgements we intuitively make are likely to derive from discarded religious systems, from warped views of sex and bodily functions, or from customs necessary for the survival of the group in social and economic circumstances that now lie in the distant past? In which case, it would be best to forget all about our particular moral judgements, and start again from as near as we can get to self-evident moral axioms.[19]

The point is not simply that our judgements may be wrong. The worry is that their credibility does not survive reflection on their origins.

Now, Singer directs his objection to one who treats common-sense morality as providing all the evidence there is for a moral theory. As noted, this is not Sidgwick's position:

> For myself, I feel bound to say that though I have always been anxious to ascertain and disposed to respect the verdict of Common Sense in any ethical dispute, I cannot profess to regard it as final and indisputable: I cannot profess to hold that it is impossible for me ever to be right on an ethical point on which the overwhelming majority is clearly opposed to me. (FC 474)[20]

18 Brink considers something like this reply. He rejects it because he takes the claim that common-sense moral beliefs lack self-evidence to entail that they lack initial credibility. I do not see the inference. See Brink, "Common Sense," p. 192n12.

19 Singer, "Reflective Equilibrium," p. 516. See also Daniel Little, "Reflective Equilibrium and Justification," *Southern Journal of Philosophy* 22, 1984, pp. 378–9; and Richard Brandt, *A Theory of the Good and the Right* (Oxford: Oxford University Press [Clarendon], 1979), p. 21. As F. H. Hayward notes, many of Sidgwick's contemporaries objected to Sidgwick's disinterest in the origins of our moral views. See F. H. Hayward, *The Ethical Philosophy of Sidgwick* (London: Swan Sonnenschein, 1901), pp. 258, 264, 267.

20 Singer agrees. He directs the objection at Rawls. At times, Singer roughly agrees with my account of the role of common-sense morality in Sidgwick. ("Reflective Equilibrium," pp. 507–9) At other times, he suggests that the appeal to common-sense morality is entirely part of a "proof" of utilitarianism directed at one who believes common-sense morality, and so is not a "test of the validity of moral theories." (pp.

Nonetheless, Sidgwick does not think that one should "forget all about" common-sense morality.

The reason is that, for Sidgwick, learning that thoughtful people agree with my position should increase my certainty – even without any investigation into the status of common-sense morality. Of course, if an investigation shows some error the thoughtful people make, then their agreement no longer increases certainty. But where there is agreement, the burden lies on Singer to find the error. Hypothetical suggestions concerning the causes of agreement are not enough. Thus Sidgwick is quite willing to admit that limited information, limited sympathy, the "perverting influence" of authority, and "false religions" all cause common-sense morality to go wrong. (*ME* 464; also 455) Like Singer, he notes that portions of common-sense morality may be "the survival of a sentiment which once was useful but has now ceased to be so." (*ME* 456) But he asks that these bad influences be demonstrated, not assumed. And, even where they are demonstrated, Sidgwick does not think a belief is so easily made less credible by noting its origin. Singer needs to show that the causes "are more likely to produce a false belief than a true one." (EP 111; also *ME* 212–13, 383, *PSR* 164) Thus it may be, for example, that discarded religions, particularly those discarded on abstruse theological grounds, produce more truths than falsehoods in morality, and so showing their influence would not suffice.[21]

Like Singer, Hare argues that common-sense morality has no "proba-

498–501, 514, 516–17) Sometimes he runs these two readings together: For example, he writes that Sidgwick employs common-sense morality "as some kind of confirmation of a result independently arrived at, and in particular as an *ad hominem* argument addressed to the supporter of common-sense morality," or that Sidgwick rightly employed common-sense judgements "as supporting evidence, or as a basis for *ad hominem* arguments, but never so as to suggest that the validity of the theory is determined by the extent to which it matches them." (pp. 498, 517) The pure ad hominem interpretation is ruled out, not only by the methodological writings, but also by Sidgwick's claim that "the Utilitarian argument cannot be fairly judged unless we take into account the cumulative force which it derives from the complex character of the coincidence between Utilitarianism and Common Sense." (*ME* 425) Perhaps Singer is best read as holding that, for Sidgwick, fit with common-sense morality is neither the sole nor the most important test. For the same worry about Singer, see Sverdlik, "Methodology," pp. 543–4.

21 Where the issue is not initial credibility but rather the final verdict, Sidgwick adds that discredited causal antecedents do not discredit a belief – they discredit only where the discredited claims are given as *reasons* for the belief. For example, the retributivist theory of punishment may descend from a culture of revenge and blood feuds, but that does not discredit it. (*PSR* 167–71, 174)

tive force." He is anxious to prevent claims about the meaning of moral terms from entailing claims about substantive moral issues.[22] For example, suppose that, in ancient Greece, I hold that slavery is wrong. Hare wants my position to be possible without my being guilty of misusing the word "wrong." I agree with others about the meaning of "wrong"; I disagree with others about what things are wrong. If so, the test for understanding "wrong" must not be agreement with common judgements of wrongness. All this, however, does not show that common-sense morality has no probative force. It shows only that common-sense morality has no probative force when it is employed along with a theory of meaning that takes agreement with common-sense judgements about what is wrong as a conclusive test for understanding the meaning of "wrong." Since common-sense morality can be employed in other ways, Hare has not established that it lacks probative force. And Sidgwick, of course, does not suppose common-sense morality has probative force through employment with any theory of meaning – he does not think "right" and "wrong" are definable, other than by equally normative phrases such as "reasonable." (*ME* 32, FC 480–3; *ME* vii, 5–6, 23, 27, 36–37, 77, 112n, 173, 344, 507, FC 475–80, SE 411)[23] He also, again, does not think an appeal to common-sense morality exhausts a full justification.

Hare has another objection to common-sense morality. Common-sense morality sometimes makes mistakes: For example, it disapproved of mixed bathing. Hare concludes that we must have some criteria for knowing when to trust common-sense morality.[24] Sidgwick can agree; he draws the same conclusion when discussing errors in general. (VB 583, *LK* 433–4) But he need not agree that common-sense morality has no probative force. Suppose I believe p on the basis of arguments that are independent of common-sense morality. I then notice that p is part of common-sense morality – that is, others, after reflection, hold p (and not simply because they know I hold p). Sidgwick thinks this should increase my confidence in p. Agreement makes it less likely that I have made an error.[25] Noting that others sometimes hold false beliefs does

---

22 R. M. Hare, "The Argument from Received Opinion," in Hare, *Essays on Philosophical Method* (London: Macmillan Press, 1971), pp. 122, 119.

23 See Schneewind, *Victorian*, pp. 221, 303–4, 417–18; and Hayward, *Ethical System*, pp. 24, 38, 50. For the general point that differences in moral beliefs do not entail differences in meaning, see FC 480.

24 Hare, "Received Opinion," p. 118.

25 Hare might seem to agree when he notes that "many heads are better than one, and many ordinary men in the course of generations may have seen aspects of the

not undercut this, unless there is reason to think that they hold false beliefs as often as they hold true ones – something one example, such as mixed bathing, does not show.

I turn to the evaluation of rational egoism, considering how it fares under Sidgwick's intuitive, discursive, and social tests.

3.2

In this section, I shall clarify Sidgwick's view of the status of rational egoism: Sidgwick's considered judgement is that rational egoism is neither self-evident nor of the highest certainty.

As some critics have noted, there is a gap between the axioms, as first and most carefully presented, and both rational egoism and utilitarianism. In his initial presentation, Sidgwick supposes the axioms reveal "a self-evident element" in "the principles of Justice, Prudence, and Rational Benevolence." (*ME* 382; also xxxv) The axioms are the "basis" for thinking morality is reasonable. (*ME* 383) The "axiom of Prudence, as I have given it, is a self-evident principle, *implied in* Rational Egoism." (*ME* 386, italics added) The axiom of Rational Benevolence is "required as a rational *basis* for the Utilitarian system." (*ME* 387, italics added; also xxii, xxxv, 496)[26] This suggests that neither rational egoism nor utilitarianism possess self-evidence or the highest certainty.

Sidgwick gives one reason for the gap: In the arguments for the axioms, there is no argument for identifying the good with happiness, as both rational egoist and utilitarian wish. (*ME* 381, 388, 421n1) This argument comes in the next chapter. There, Sidgwick recognises that many disagree about hedonism; nowhere does he claim that hedonism possesses self-evidence or the highest certainty. (*ME* 399–401, UG 35)

There is a further reason for a gap between the axioms and rational egoism or utilitarianism. Consider rational egoism.[27] The discussion of the axiom of temporal irrelevance runs as follows:

> The proposition 'that one ought to aim at one's own good' is sometimes given as the maxim of Rational Self-love or Prudence: but as so stated it

question which in our relatively brief experience we have ignored." (Hare, "Received Opinion," p. 128) He does not, however, take agreement to affect the certainty of some moral principle. Agreement is relevant only in that disagreement should prompt reconsideration of the form or application – but not the substance – of moral principles. (pp. 128, 134–5)

26 See Schneewind, *Victorian*, pp. 304–6.
27 I consider utilitarianism at the end of the section.

does not clearly avoid tautology; since we may define 'good' as 'what one ought to aim at.' If, however, we say 'one's good on the whole,' the addition suggests a principle which, when explicitly stated, is, at any rate, not tautological. I have already referred to this principle as that 'of impartial concern for all parts of our conscious life': – we might express it concisely by saying 'that Hereafter *as such* is to be regarded neither less or more than Now.' . . . All that the principle affirms is that the mere difference of priority and posteriority in time is not a reasonable ground for having more regard to the consciousness of one moment than to that of another. (*ME* 381)

The second half of this passage, starting with "we might express it concisely," states the irrelevance of time. This is necessary for both rational egoism and utilitarianism; it does not favour either.[28] The first half of the passage may claim only that rational egoists must accept temporal irrelevance. Yet the first half might also be read as claiming that "one ought to aim at one's own good on the whole" is self-evident. This fits some of the other statements of the axiom elsewhere in the *Methods:* One should have "equal and impartial concern for all parts of one's conscious life," or "seek . . . one's own good on the whole, repressing all seductive impulses prompting to undue preference of particular goods." (*ME* 124n1, 391–2)[29] But these claims, like those in the first half of the passage, suggest two points: (a) time is irrelevant; (b) I should have concern for my life (rather than no concern, or concern for the lives of others). The question is whether Sidgwick intends (b). There are various reasons for thinking he does not.

First, (a) is presented as a clarification of the first half. (a) states "[a]ll that the principle affirms." Second, Sidgwick intends the axioms to be clear, precise and distinct. (*ME* 338–9, *LK* 461, 463, 465–6) A "distinct notion of any object [is] one that is not liable to be confounded with that

---

28 This is noted by Georg von Gizycki, in the course of asking Sidgwick for a defence of rational egoism. He grants the irrelevance of time, but notes "I cannot recognize it as a basis for 'Rational Egoism,' since it is equally involved in 'Rational Benevolence.' In what way does it hold less good for conduct towards others than for that towards one's self? Ought not the father or mother to take into account also their child's future as well as its present? And ought not all men to consider the future generations, and not say, '*Après nous le déluge*'?" Von Gizycki adds that, when the axiom is thus understood, it cannot conflict with the axiom of rational benevolence. See his review of the fourth edition of *Methods, International Journal of Ethics* 1, 1891, pp. 120–1; Schneewind, *Victorian*, p. 361; and Hayward, *Ethical System*, pp. 122, 131, 133–7, 144.

29 It is not true of *ME* 383, where the self-evident proposition is "'I ought to prefer a present lesser good to a future greater good.'"

of any different object." (*LK* 449) Presumably, then, the axiom should not run together two separate points. Since Sidgwick explicitly favours (a), this counts against (b). Third, Sidgwick claims that the axiom is "implied in" rational egoism. (*ME* 386) This is true of (a). (b) gives a much stronger connection: The axiom virtually implies rational egoism.[30] And fourth, after stating the axioms, Sidgwick concludes that he has revealed "the permanent basis of the common conviction that the fundamental precepts of morality are essentially reasonable." (*ME* 383) He has arrived "at the fundamental principle of Utilitarianism." (*ME* 387) The "clear and self-evident principles" are "perfectly consistent with Utilitarianism." (*ME* xxiii) They are "not only not incompatible with a Utilitarian system, but even seem required to furnish a rational basis for such a system." (*ME* 496) "[C]onsideration of Intuitionism in its most philosophical form" leads "at once to Utilitarianism." (PC 564; also *ME* 388, 406–7, UG 31, M 90) These are puzzling claims to make, if he has just asserted (b) among the axioms.

Admittedly, Sidgwick is sometimes misleading. He writes that "even if a man admits the self-evidence of the principle of Rational Benevolence, he may still hold that his own happiness is an end which it is irrational for him to sacrifice to any other; and that therefore a harmony between the maxim of Prudence and the maxim of Rational Benevolence must be somehow demonstrated, if morality is to be made completely rational." (*ME* 498) If the "maxim of prudence" says only that time is irrelevant, no harmony with the maxim of rational benevolence need be demonstrated. Sidgwick seems to understand the "maxim of prudence" as claiming (b) as well as (a).[31]

But there is an alternative. After introducing the axioms, Sidgwick notes that he has "tried to show how in the principles of Justice, Prudence, and Rational Benevolence as commonly recognised there is at least a self-evident element." (*ME* 382; also xxxv) There is a distinction between the principles "so far as they are self-evident" and their wider, more popular understanding. (*ME* 391) On the wider reading, the "prin-

---

30 Schneewind notes that in the third and fourth editions, Sidgwick writes that the axiom is "the self-evident principle on which Rational Egoism is based." The "implied in" phrasing first appears in the fifth edition. Schneewind comments that "[i]t is doubtful whether much is to be made of the difference between 'implied in' and 'required as a basis for.'" On my reading, Sidgwick has good reason to make the change, perhaps in reply to von Gizycki's review of the fourth edition. See Schneewind, *Victorian*, p. 306. For the same point against him, see John Skorupski, "Sidgwick's Ethics," *Philosophical Quarterly* 29, 1979, p. 167.

31 For a similar understanding of the axiom, see *ME* 383–4, 418.

ciple of prudence" states (a) and (b); insofar as it is self-evident, it states (a). When Sidgwick claims that the principles must be harmonised, he may have in mind their wider readings, and so he need not be claiming that (b) is self-evident. This fits the problematic passage: It refers to the self-evidence of rational benevolence, but not of the "maxim of prudence" when the latter is given the wider reading. (*ME* 498)

Of course, after the first edition, Sidgwick does link the axiom of temporal irrelevance and rational egoism. The axiom is "implied in" rational egoism. (*ME* 386) This needs to be explained. I suggest that Sidgwick links the irrelevance of time with rational egoism for two reasons. First, when he tries to show our agreement that time is irrelevant, he gives an egoistic example as "[t]he form in which it practically presents itself to most men," viz. "Prudence is generally exercised in restraining a present desire . . . on account of the remoter consequences of gratifying it." (*ME* 381)[32] Second, Sidgwick starts consideration of the axiom, not with a discussion of time, but with the traditional injunction to "aim at one's own good." (*ME* 381) The irrelevance of time emerges as the "self-evident element" in this injunction. (*ME* 382) Rational egoism, then, has "priority in the knowledge of . . . mind" in arriving at the irrelevance of time.[33]

There is an additional advantage to an interpretation denying that rational egoism has the highest certainty. Propositions of the highest certainty must be mutually consistent. But Sidgwick holds that rational egoism and utilitarianism are inconsistent. By this he means that, in some cases, they issue conflicting prescriptions.[34] If he adds that rational egoism and utilitarianism have the highest certainty, there is a puzzle.[35]

32 Similarly, when Sidgwick tries to show our agreement with the maxim of benevolence, he gives a utilitarian example; see *ME* 382, quoted in 3.4.
33 For priority in mind as opposed to logical priority, see EP 106, *LK* 41–2.
34 Critics have noted a further sense: They make different properties right-making, and so are inconsistent even were they to agree in their prescriptions. See G. E. Moore, *Principia Ethica* (New York: Cambridge University Press, 1903), pp. 102–3; C. D. Broad, *Five Types of Ethical Theory* (London: Routledge & Kegan Paul, 1930), p. 253; David Brink, "Sidgwick's Dualism of Practical Reason," *Australasian Journal of Philosophy* 66, 1988, pp. 304–5, and "Sidgwick and the Rationale for Rational Egoism," in Schultz, *Essays*, p. 205.
35 See Brink, "Dualism," pp. 304–5, "Rationale" p. 205; Marcus Singer, "The Many Methods of Sidgwick's Ethics," *The Monist* 58, 1974, p. 446; James Seth, "The Ethical System of Henry Sidgwick," *Mind* 10, 1901, pp. 180–1; Sverdlik, "Methodology," p. 553.

Critics have devised two replies to avoid concluding that rational egoism and utilitarianism lack self-evidence and the highest certainty. Both replies put the problem in terms of inconsistent self-evident propositions rather than inconsistent propositions of the highest certainty. Both solve the problem by claiming that rational egoism and utilitarianism are consistent. Both have well-documented textual difficulties.

First, J. B. Schneewind and Mackie argue that Sidgwick could say that rational egoism and utilitarianism specify different right-making properties, while neither claims that its right-making property is the only such property. There is then no inconsistency in the statements of the two theories. Rational egoism and utilitarianism continue to offer inconsistent prescriptions, but this is a contingent matter. It could be resolved by the "moral government of the world," whereby acting as a utilitarian always maximises one's own happiness. (*ME* xx, etc.)[36] The problem, as Schneewind admits, is that when Sidgwick states rational egoism and utilitarianism, he usually presents each as claiming the sole right-making property. For example, the rational egoist "regards quantity of consequent pleasure and pain to himself *as alone* important in choosing between alternatives of action." (*ME* 95, italics added; also *ME* 6, 174, 403)[37] And, as noted, Sidgwick takes the axioms to be consistent with, and required to prove, utilitarianism; these are puzzling claims to make, if he has just asserted, among the axioms, that my own interest is one right-making property.

Second, Brink takes utilitarianism to be a self-evident moral theory and rational egoism to be a self-evident theory of rationality. They do not conflict, because they have different subject matters. Rational egoism specifies what we have reason to do; utilitarianism specifies what it is moral to do.[38] The problem here is that Sidgwick does not separate "rational egoism" and "rational benevolence" from "ethical egoism" and "utilitarianism."[39] He is looking for "a theory of rational action as a

---

36 Schneewind, *Victorian*, p. 373; Mackie, "Sidgwick's Pessimism," in Schultz, *Essays*, p. 170.

37 For further evidence and discussion, see Schneewind, *Victorian*, p. 373; Skorupski, "Sidgwick's Ethics," pp. 167–8; and Brink, "Rationale," p. 235n8. Brink notes that Sidgwick usually formulates rational egoism and utilitarianism in terms of "ultimate" ends or standards, which again suggests, though does not entail, that each is intended to offer the sole right-making property.

38 Brink, "Dualism" and "Rationale," pp. 202–6.

39 See Brink, "Dualism," pp. 296–9; Frankena, "Sidgwick's Dualism of Practical Reason"; Henry S. Richardson, "Commensurability as a Prerequisite of Rational Choice:

whole." (*PSR* 29; also *ME* 9, 12, 14, 78) As noted above, right actions are reasonable ones. For Sidgwick, "the 'authority of Conscience' is the authority of Reason in its application to practice." (*LE* 326) "[T]he choice between the alternatives of 'rational' and 'irrational' conduct . . . is [what] alone . . . concerns us, from an ethical point of view." (FC 479) These are not merely "linguistic" points.[40] For one should see Sidgwick as attractive *because* he asks the most general question "What do I have most reason to do?" On Brink's interpretation, Sidgwick is left with a theory of what reason says on the one hand and a moral theory on the other. It is unclear what status the moral theory should have in the face of what reason says. The Sidgwick who has "taken service with Reason" with "no intention of deserting" and who has "an extraordinary belief in *following reason*" would dispense with the moral theory. (*M* 508, 557) There would be no dualism of practical *reason*, no "fundamental contradiction in our apparent intuitions of what is Reasonable in conduct," no doubts because practical reason is "divided against itself," no need for "non-rational impulses" to decide, no requirement of "Moral order" for "rational conduct," no fear of a "lapse" into Hume's view that "ultimate ends are determined by feeling, not reason." (*ME* 508, *PSR* 243, *PE* 10-11, FC 485) This is not simply a textual observation about Sidgwick: If our moral theory and our theory of rationality conflict, the latter should win. Otherwise, there is no check on whether our moral theory is justified.[41]

Critics are driven to these positions because they both take the consistency test as a test for self-evidence and suppose rational egoism and utilitarianism are self-evident. My interpretation avoids the resulting difficulties. The consistency test is a test for the highest certainty, not for self-evidence. Thus Sidgwick *could* say that rational egoism and utilitarianism are self-evident and inconsistent. Both lack the highest certainty. This may be his position. For he claims, at times, that both are self-evident. In the case of rational egoism, he finds "with as much clearness and certainty as the process of introspective reflection can give" that "it would be irrational to sacrifice any portion of my own happiness unless

An Examination of Sidgwick's Position," *History of Philosophy Quarterly* 8, 1991, pp. 183, 196n26.
40 Brink, "Dualism," p. 305.
41 Brink should agree. He writes that "norms of rationality . . . have a kind of primacy. . . . [T]hey are the norms . . . with which other norms (e.g., moral norms) must agree. . . ." (Brink, "Rationale," p. 203)

the sacrifice is to be somehow at some time compensated by an equiv-alent addition to my own happiness." (FC 483) The claim that the dis-tinction between persons is fundamental and so determines "the ulti-mate end of rational action for an individual" seems self-evident. (FC 484) The precept to "seek . . . one's own good on the whole, repressing all seductive impulses prompting to undue preference of particular goods" is also self-evident. (*ME* 391–2; also *ME* (1) 388) At one point, he is explicit about the opposition between the two self-evident claims. He notes that rational egoism "seems self-evident, although it *prima facie* contradicts the equally self-evident proposition that my own good is no more to be regarded than the good of another." (FC 484; also *ME* xx, 498, *ME* (1) 460–1)

Yet this is not, I think, Sidgwick's considered view. He agrees that rational egoism and utilitarianism do not possess the highest certainty. But when he distinguishes between rational egoism and utilitarianism, on the one hand, and the "self-evident element" expressed by the ax-ioms on the other, he suggests that neither rational egoism nor utilitar-ianism is self-evident. This is also the result one would expect from the "careful reflection" that yields self-evidence: Reflection on the inconsis-tency of rational egoism with other beliefs of the same certainty should (though need not) lead one to doubt its self-evidence. Sidgwick sug-gests exactly this when he writes that from the inconsistency "it would seem to follow that the apparently intuitive operation of the Practical Reason, manifested in these contradictory judgements, is after all il-lusory." (*ME* 508) In this way the puzzle raised by the critics is doubly dissolved. Sidgwick is left saying, plausibly, that rational egoism and utilitarianism really are inconsistent.

I have not considered whether the axioms support utilitarianism any better than they support rational egoism. One might suppose they do, in two ways. First, the axiom of consistency might seem to rule out rational egoism. The axiom states that "it cannot be right for A to treat B in a manner in which it would be wrong for B to treat A, merely on the ground that they are two different individuals, and without there being any difference between the natures or circumstances of the two which can be stated as a reasonable ground for difference of treatment." (*ME* 380) One might object that the rational egoist does justify different treatment of himself without giving any reason beyond noting that he is one of the individuals.

This is too quick: Rational egoism does not violate the axiom. Sup-pose I say it is right for me to break my promise to you, because breaking maximises my happiness. The axiom precludes my adding that it is wrong for you to break your promise to me, when breaking maximises your happiness. But rational egoism does not add this, for it claims that what is right for each person is that he maximise his own happiness. It is right for me to break, and for you to break. This explains why Sidgwick does not deploy the axiom of consistency against rational egoism.

Second, the axiom of personal irrelevance is the only self-evident axiom that concerns the distribution of good between persons. (*ME* 382) As Schneewind notes, there is still a gap between this and utilitarianism: Sidgwick must identify the good with happiness, link the good with the right and the reasonable, and argue that the good should be maximised.[42] These arguments might fail. But Sidgwick can at least point out that the rational egoist has these tasks as well – and without any supporting axiom regarding the distribution of good between persons.

Yet again this is too quick. If the axiom of personal irrelevance is taken to have these consequences for distribution, then it is inconsistent with Sidgwick's various declarations of the reasonableness of rational egoism. According to the epistemic test requiring agreement, this counts against it. Sidgwick can reply that his most careful statement of the axiom is that "the good of any one individual is of no more importance, *from the point of view (if I may say so) of the Universe*, than the good of any other." (*ME* 382, italics added) This is consistent with asserting rational egoism: As Broad puts it, the rational egoist can "remark that, after all, he is not the Universe, and therefore it is not obvious that he ought to take the Universe's point of view."[43] But this defence concedes that another argument must be made to move from the axioms to utilitarianism: One must argue for taking up the point of view of the universe.[44] Thus, although there is no axiom supporting the rational egoist's distribution, Sidgwick supposes there are other considerations favouring it, and the axiom intended to support utilitarianism does so

42 Schneewind, *Victorian*, pp. 307–9.
43 Broad, *Five Types*, pp. 244–5. Broad thinks, however, that the rational egoist must deny the axiom of the whole, viz. "as a rational being I am bound to aim at good generally . . . not merely at a particular part of it." (*ME* 382) If so, Sidgwick's claim to highest certainty must again be given up. But the rational egoist could also agree here: He agrees that he is bound to aim at his good generally, and not merely a particular part of it. I follow Schneewind, *Victorian*, p. 363; cf. Broad, *Five Types*, p. 245.
44 Presumably the axiom of rational benevolence, deduced in part from the axiom of personal irrelevance, should incorporate reference to the point of view of the universe.

only given their defeat. Given this, Sidgwick is right when he claims, as he usually does, only that the axioms are consistent with and needed to prove utilitarianism, and that the issue between rational egoist and utilitarian turns on the rationality of taking up the universe's point of view. (*ME* xxi–xxiii, 387, 496, *M* 90; *ME* 420–1, 497–8)[45]

It might seem unsatisfying that the axioms do so little. Sidgwick admits that they "are of too abstract a nature, and too universal in their scope, to enable us to ascertain by immediate application of them what we ought to do in any particular case." (*ME* 379; also 462) On my reading, things seem worse: The axioms seem not even to resolve theoretical issues. But they still have a point. They suggest where the debate between rational egoist and utilitarian must be located: The issue turns on the rationality of taking up the point of view of the universe. Further, Sidgwick takes one of his great achievements to be showing that "the opposition between Utilitarianism and Intuitionism was due to a misunderstanding." (*ME* xxii) "[T]he common antithesis between Intuitionists and Utilitarians must be entirely discarded." (*ME* 496; also xiii, PC 564, UG 31, *M* 75) As Schneewind notes, this is historically important, given the long-standing opposition between intuitionists and utilitarians.[46] That the axioms do not settle the issue between utilitarians and rational egoists does not prove their futility.

3.3

Although Sidgwick's considered view is that rational egoism is neither self-evident nor of the highest certainty, he still finds it as credible as

45 The claim that Intuitionism leads "at once to Utilitarianism" is misleading, but Sidgwick's gloss shows that he again makes a cautious claim: "I hold that the only moral intuitions which sound philosophy can accept as ultimately valid are those which at the same time provide the only possible philosophical basis of the Utilitarian creed." (PC 564) Similarly, writing that "I arrive, in my search for really clear and certain ethical intuitions, at the fundamental principle of Utilitarianism" is misleading, but one can think of the axiom as stating the principle; it merely leaves out that an argument for the point of view of the universe is needed. (*ME* 387) These two strategies can also be used on *ME* 388 and UG 31. In *ME* (1), the axiom supporting utilitarianism makes no mention of the point of view of the universe, and Sidgwick concludes discussion of the axioms by claiming the "suppression" of rational egoism. (*ME* [1] 366; 360, 363, 364, 365) He concludes the book, however, with the dualism. In later editions, Sidgwick cleared the tension by specifying that the axioms suppress rational egoism only once the universal point of view is taken, or once reference to the universal point of view is built into the axioms. (SE 411)

46 Schneewind, *Victorian*, pt. 1, *passim*.

utilitarianism. In the next two sections and in Chapter 4, I consider his arguments for rational egoism.

In a series of reviews of the *Methods,* Georg von Gizycki asked Sidgwick for a defence of rational egoism.[47] In reply, Sidgwick admits that "the assumption upon which the rationality of Egoism is based has been denied by philosophers." The assumption, whose denial Sidgwick finds "absurd," is that "the distinction between any one individual and any other is real and fundamental, and that consequently 'I' am concerned with the quality of my existence as an individual in a sense, fundamentally important, in which I am not concerned with the quality of the existence of other individuals." (FC 484) Call this the "distinction passage."

The distinction passage was added to the fourth edition of the *Methods* and retained through the seventh and last. (*ME* 498) Before its insertion, Sidgwick admits that "I had made no attempt to show the irrationality of the sacrifice of self-interest to duty." (FC 484) This confirms the argument, above, that Sidgwick did not take the axiom of temporal irrelevance to establish rational egoism. It also indicates that Sidgwick did not take the appeal to agreement to establish rational egoism, though presumably agreement helped the case; from the first edition, rational egoism was seen as a serious and undefeated contender. The distinction passage, then, bears a great deal of the weight of the argument for rational egoism.[48]

The distinction passage might seem obviously true: *Of course* I am distinct from other people. I have a separate history and spatiotemporal position. I have separate interests and memories, and (apparently) special access to my mental contents. But Sidgwick cannot intend these mundane facts. He needs the distinction passage to be true in a specific sense, a sense such that he can infer that "I do not see how it is to be proved that this distinction is not to be taken as fundamental in determining the ultimate end of rational action for an individual." (*ME* 498; FC 484) He takes this result to be inconsistent with the "proposition that

47 See, for example, von Gizycki, "Review," pp. 120–1.
48 Hayward emphasises it, but laments "[a] whole book we find devoted to an examination of egoism as a *method;* but only a few words, and those originally inserted in a journal, to an examination of its fundamental postulate, though the latter was accepted by himself!" See Hayward, *Ethical System,* p. 131; also pp. 104–5, 117, 130. Recently, the passage has been cited against Nagel, but without accompanying gloss. See Eric Mack, "Moral Individualism: Agency-Relativity and Deontic Restraints," *Social Philosophy and Policy* 7, 1989, p. 87; and Peter Singer, *Practical Ethics* (New York: Cambridge University Press, 1979), p. 208.

my own good is no more to be regarded than the good of another." (FC 484) This suggests a constraint on the interpretation of the distinction passage. Sidgwick holds that a non-normative claim cannot, by itself, entail a normative conclusion. (*ME* 1–2, 23–38, 79, 81, 98, 213, SE 412, *O* 182, EP 107–8, *PE* 68, FC 480, *PSR* 22–4, 235–41) Since he draws normative conclusions from the distinction passage, he must intend either a normative reading of the passage or a non-normative reading conjoined with relevant normative claims. The mundane facts noted above are not themselves normative, nor do they look like promising candidates to be joined with some normative principle.

I shall offer three interpretations of the distinction passage. The first is non-normative; the second and third are normative. In each case, I am interested both in whether the interpretation fits the text and in whether it gives a rationale for rational egoism. I think that the first and second interpretations are textually plausible, but that none of the interpretations give Sidgwick a convincing argument.

The personal identity interpretation

Sidgwick supposes that "[i]t undoubtedly seems to Common Sense paradoxical to ask for a reason why one should seek one's own happiness on the whole." (*ME* 418) However, one might sensibly ask this question if one holds "as Hume and his followers maintain" that "the permanent identical 'I' is not a fact but a fiction." (*ME* 419) Elsewhere Sidgwick characterises Hume as holding that we "are each and all 'nothing but bundles of different perceptions, succeeding one another with inconceivable rapidity.'" (*LK* 410) Hume argues for "the impossibility of finding a self in the stream of psychical experience." (*LK* 453; also 454, GG 610) If Hume is right, it makes sense "to ask for a reason why one should seek one's own happiness on the whole." (*ME* 419) Since I do not persist through time, it is unclear why the bundle that I now am should sacrifice for some future bundle. In this way, Sidgwick notes, utilitarianism and rational egoism could be equally challenged: The utilitarian is asked why one person should sacrifice for another person, and the rational egoist is asked why a present bundle of experience should sacrifice for a future bundle. Sidgwick concludes, however, that utilitarianism and rational egoism are *not* equally challenged, for common sense "does not think it worth while to supply the individual with reasons for seeking his own interest." (*ME* 419)[49]

49 As Brink notes, there is another interpretation of Sidgwick's view of Hume. Sidgwick puts his question by asking "why . . . should one part of the series of feelings into

Sidgwick does not say, here, whether or why common sense is right. He does, however, refer the reader to the chapter in which the distinction passage occurs. (*ME* 419n1) There, the distinction passage is not explicitly connected to the discussion of personal identity. But the reference suggests that the distinction passage constitutes Sidgwick's agreement with common sense.[50] And in the paper in which the distinction passage first appears, Sidgwick introduces it by writing that "the denial [of the assumption on which the rationality of egoism is based] seems to Common Sense so absurd that a serious demand for its explicit statement is rather paradoxical." (*FC* 484) This suggests that the distinction passage is asserting, against Hume, that personal identity is a fact.[51]

which the Ego is resolved be concerned with another part of the same series?" (*ME* 419) Sidgwick may think that for Hume, I persist over time, but that my continuity is merely that of a "series of feelings." This suggests a challenge to rational egoism based, not on denying continuity, but on giving a particular account of the continuity. I think the passages about Hume from outside the *Methods* make this reading unlikely. An interpretation that denies continuity also has the advantage that it becomes much harder to defend rational egoism. For while it is not obvious that accepting a particular account of my continuity should alter my concern, I cannot maintain concern where I do not persist. Here Brink replies that this "simply dissolves the question of how to distribute goods and harms among persons as misconceived. . . . [C]omplete skepticism about personal identity dissolves the debates between egoism and its rivals and does not so much defeat egoism or its rationale." This is not so: The issue of distribution remains, though it is distribution to fleeting bundles rather than persons. And if the rationale for rational egoism rests on persistence, as Brink holds, the rationale is surely gone. See Brink, "Rationale," pp. 221–3, and for discussion of the argument against rational egoism from a particular account of continuity, pp. 224–33; and Parfit, *Reasons and Persons,* pp. 307–12.

50 Further evidence is provided by the first through third editions. There, neither the distinction passage nor the reference to the final chapter in the discussion of personal identity appears.

51 (i) I say "asserting" because Sidgwick never explains why Hume is wrong. This is a drawback to this defence of rational egoism. For the assertion, see *PSR* 86 and *ME* (1) 102–3. (ii) This interpretation may be suggested by Parfit, *Reasons and Persons,* pp. 138–9, 312, 521. But Parfit supposes that "if what is fundamental is that we are different persons, each with his own life to lead, this supports the claim that the supremely rational aim, for each person, is that his own life go as well as possible." (329; 138) My interpretation does not move as quickly from the distinction passage to normative claims. (iii) This interpretation is also suggested by Brink, "Rationale," pp. 208–9, 224, and "Common Sense," p. 185. Like Parfit, however, Brink is tempted by a normative gloss: the "passage . . . suggest[s] a *normative* claim that goes beyond the metaphysical separateness of persons. . . . Sidgwick's appeal to the separateness of persons implicitly invokes th[e] principle that the *rationality* of sacrifice requires compensation." This is unlikely, given that Sidgwick offers the distinction passage as support for this principle. (*FC* 483–4) I discuss Brink's principle below. See David

On this interpretation, the distinction passage replies to one attack on rational egoism – the attack based on claiming that personal identity is a fiction. Sidgwick can conclude, as he wishes, that rational egoism is not open to an attack parallel to the one utilitarianism faces. (*ME* 418–19) The distinction passage makes a non-normative point with normative implications, since it denies the claim on which an attack is based.[52]

Now suppose that the argument from personal identity is the only plausible attack on rational egoism. Then Sidgwick is right to claim: "I do not see how it is to be proved that this distinction is not to be taken as fundamental in determining the ultimate end of rational action for an individual." (*ME* 498; FC 484) The only way of proving this has been discredited. If one also supposes that rational egoism is established by discrediting all plausible attacks on it, then Sidgwick is also right to claim that the rationality of rational egoism has been established and utilitarianism contradicted. (FC 484) However, if either of these suppositions is false, then the distinction passage establishes less than Sidgwick thinks – it establishes only that *one* attack on rational egoism fails.

The first supposition, claiming that the argument from personal identity is the only plausible attack on rational egoism, makes a very bold claim. Consider three other attacks on rational egoism, all suggested by Sidgwick. (I examine the first two attacks in more detail below.)

First, one might attack rational egoism as arbitrary. (EP 106–7) It need not help rational egoism to reply that personal identity is a fact, since the charge of arbitrariness need not hang on any claims about personal identity. One might grant that I am separate and continuous over time, but ask why this is relevant to distribution. Sidgwick seems to admit this, noting that "even if the reality and essentiality of the distinction between one individual and another be granted, I do not see how to prove its fundamental practical importance to anyone who refuses to admit it." (FC 485)[53]

Brink, "Rationale," p. 209, and "The Separateness of Persons, Distributive Norms, and Moral Theory," in *Value, Welfare, and Morality*, ed. Ray Frey and Christopher Morris (New York: Cambridge University Press, 1993), p. 255.
52 This interpretation solves a puzzle Parfit raises. He wonders why Sidgwick did not take the distinction passage to have anti-utilitarian consequences for distributive justice. (Parfit, *Reasons and Persons*, p. 521n109) If Sidgwick is merely denying a particular objection, this is understandable.
53 Parfit suggests three possible explanations for why utilitarians do not take the separateness of persons to have anti-utilitarian distributive consequences: (a) utilitarians overlook separateness; (b) utilitarians deny separateness, by supposing the collec-

Second, Sidgwick argues in favour of utilitarianism by claiming it best systematises common-sense morality. Since utilitarianism conflicts with rational egoism, this is a problem for the latter. Perhaps this argument fails. But even if it does, it is unlikely that it fails because personal identity is a fact. If so, noting that personal identity is a fact is an insufficient defence of rational egoism.

Third, Derek Parfit notes that Sidgwick runs together two challenges to rational egoism. Sidgwick supposes the rational egoist might be asked "[a] 'Why should I sacrifice a present pleasure for a greater one in the future?' [b] 'Why should I concern myself about my own future feelings any more than about the feelings of other persons?'" (*ME* 418) Sidgwick dismisses both challenges by claiming that personal identity is a fact. At best, however, this replies to (b); the rational egoist can answer (b) by saying "because my future feelings are mine, and not someone else's."[54] Sidgwick seems to assume that only the view that personal identity is a fiction could underwrite (a) and thus that he has answered (a) as well. But Parfit's work shows that this is not so: Rational egoism can be challenged by the Present-Aim theorist – one who asks with Sidgwick "I do not see why the axiom of Prudence should not be questioned, when it conflicts with present inclination." (*ME* 418) The Present-Aim theorist provides a rationale for asking (a) that does not depend on any appeal to personal identity: Why should I sacrifice a currently desired lesser pleasure for a greater future pleasure that I do not now desire?[55]

One reply to this last worry should be noted. Brink argues that the

tion of individuals is itself an individual; (c) utilitarians deny separateness by holding reductionist views of personal identity. Only (c) supports rather than undermines utilitarianism. (Parfit, *Reasons and Persons*, p. 331) Sidgwick suggests another explanation, which also supports: (d) utilitarians admit separateness, but do not see any argument showing that it is relevant to distribution. Surely (d) is more common than (a)–(c).

54 "At best" because one might argue that the "depth" of the sense in which they are mine, and the degree to which my future self is connected to me, both affect the rationality of my concern. See Parfit, *Reasons and Persons*, pp. 307–18.

55 See ibid., pp. 138–42, and, in general, pt. 2. Hayward makes the same point: "Why not add, 'We are concerned with the quality of our *present* existence in a sense, fundamentally important, in which we are not concerned with the quality of future existence'; in other words, why not express in philosophic language the exhortation 'Let us eat, drink and be merry, and seize the passing hour?' This concrete principle would stand opposed to the 'prudential' maxim in the same manner as the declaration quoted above [the distinction passage] stands opposed to the maxim of benevolence." See Hayward, *Ethical System*, p. 146.

distinction passage, conjoined with the principle that sacrifice is rational only when compensated, gives Sidgwick a reply to (a) as well as (b). Brink plausibly reads the distinction passage as claiming not only that persons are enduring, but also that they are separate, perhaps in that they are not parts of one consciousness. This might be directed against T. H. Green and F. H. Bradley.[56] By itself, noting that persons are separate in this sense does not have relevant normative implications. Almost all utilitarians agree that persons are separate in this sense, without being committed to rational egoism. But conjoined with the principle that sacrifice is rational only when compensated, the distinction passage lets one conclude, since I am separate and enduring, both that compensating you does not compensate me and that I will be around for compensation. This gives the rational egoist a rationale for being indifferent to the time at which compensation comes, but rightly concerned with who gets the compensation. The rational egoist need not be neutral about time and person, as the utilitarian is, nor give relative treatments of time and person, as the Present-Aim theorist does.

Now as with Sidgwick, this at best defeats one sort of objection to rational egoism – the objection from (a) that Parfit has developed. Without an argument to show that this objection is the only serious one, rational egoism is not established.[57] But more importantly, Brink relies on the principle that sacrifice is rational only where it is compensated. Without this principle, the distinction passage does no work. Sidgwick may indeed hold the principle. (FC 483, *ME* 498, quoted above)[58] But the justification of rational egoism requires defence of it.[59] Sidgwick initially presents the distinction passage *as* the defence of the principle, along with noting that the principle is widely held and self-evident. (FC 483–4) While the latter two considerations may be seen as a defence of the principle, it is hard to see how the distinction passage is such a defence – unless it is understood as undercutting the personal identity objection to rational egoism, as suggested above. If so, debate over the

56 Brink, "Rationale," pp. 208–9, 224, and for those who deny separateness, "Puzzle," pp. 14–15.
57 Brink realises this; see "Rationale," pp. 214–15.
58 See Hayward, *Ethical Philosophy*, pp. 107–8; Brink, "Rationale," p. 209.
59 Brink admits that cases in which the uncompensated sacrifice is small and the gain to others is large are problems for the principle. We are not keen to say that uncompensated sacrifice is irrational here. He defends the principle by moving to an objective – non-desire-based – account of welfare. This defence is not open to Sidgwick, given his preference-hedonism. See Brink, *Moral Realism*, pp. 72–4.

principle must centre on the claims that it is widely held and self-evident and that the argument from personal identity is the only serious challenge. Simply stating the principle and the distinction passage is insufficient, even as a reply to Parfit.

In sum: On this interpretation, the distinction passage holds that I am separate and enduring. This undercuts an objection to rational egoism based on a Humean view of personal identity, but does no more.

The point of view interpretation

In various places, Sidgwick indicates that there are two normative points of view: the "point of view of the universe" and the point of view of the individual.

> No doubt it was, from the point of view of the universe, reasonable to prefer the greater good to the lesser, even though the lesser was the private happiness of the agent. Still, it seemed to me also undeniably reasonable for the individual to prefer his own. (*ME* xx)

> [I]t is . . . reasonable for an individual to make an ultimate sacrifice of his happiness for the sake of the greater happiness of others, as well as reasonable for him to take his own happiness as ultimate end; owing . . . to the double view which he necessarily takes of himself as at once an individual essentially separate from other individuals, and at the same time essentially a part among similar parts of a larger whole. (*FC* 486)

> [There is an] inevitable twofold conception of a human individual as a whole in himself, and a part of a larger whole. There is something that it is reasonable for him to desire, when he considers himself as an independent unit, and something again which he must recognize as reasonable to be desired, when he takes the point of view of a larger whole. (*ME* [3] 402; see also *ME* 404–5, 420–1, SE 411)

The distinction passage may simply assert that the individual's point of view is important and non-arbitrary.[60]

Yet more is needed. Sidgwick cannot defend the claim that these two points of view are reasonable by arguing that they are the only possible points of view. I might take the point of view of my family, country, race, or species. Sidgwick does not think these points of view are reasonable: "It is, of course, possible to adopt an end intermediate between [individual and general happiness], and to aim at the happiness of some limited portion of mankind, such as one's family or nation or race: but

---

60 This is Schneewind's interpretation. I take *ME* (3) 402 from him, *Victorian*, p. 369. See pp. 365–6, 369–70, 418, 420; and Hayward, *Ethical Philosophy*, pp. 104–6, 117.

any such limitation seems arbitrary, and probably few would maintain it to be reasonable *per se.*" (*ME* 10)[61] He comments that

> [f]or egoism pure and simple . . . there is . . . much to be said; but I have never seen, nor can I conceive, any ethical reasoning that will provide even a plausible basis for the compound proposition that a man is bound to sacrifice his private interest to that of the group of human beings constituting his state, but that neither he nor they are under any similar obligation to the rest of mankind. (*PE* 68)

Similarly, to aim at the happiness of humans, rather than sentient beings, is "arbitrary and unreasonable." (*ME* 414; also EP 106–7) But then Sidgwick must explain why the individual and universal points of view are not also arbitrary and unreasonable. In particular, he must explain why a limitation, say, to one's family is arbitrary and unreasonable, while a limitation to oneself is not.

It will be hard to find an explanation that privileges the individual's point of view and the point of view of the universe, but nothing in between. For suppose I favour the point of view of the individual because, with Broad, I note that I *am* an individual, not a hive member. One problem is that this argument cuts against the universal point of view just as it cuts against the point of view of the family or nation. If I try to save the universal point of view by adding that it, unlike the point of view of any smaller group, avoids making arbitrary distinctions, then I must explain why my individual point of view is not also arbitrary. I cannot reply by repeating that I am an individual; I might just as well say that I am a member of a group and so should take its point of view. Perhaps I could say that *if* I go beyond my own point of view, I cannot stop short of the universal point of view. But this does not show how Sidgwick could hold both individual and universal points of view as reasonable. It also remains open to the worry that I am a group member as well as an individual.

One might try a metaphysical argument. There is, I might say, nothing more to a human group than the individuals composing it. The point of view of the individual is basic. This argument faces several objections. One problem is that, again, this cuts against the point of view of the universe. Another problem is that, on a plausible interpretation, the sense in which the point of view of the individual is basic does not show that it is privileged. There may be – as Sidgwick thought –

---

61 For Sidgwick, a distinction is arbitrary when there is no good reason for drawing it. (e.g., *ME* 267–8, 268n, 298, 378, 447) For a different use, see *ME* 293n.

"social facts," facts not reducible to facts about individuals. (*PSR* 152–5, 159) If so, one could grant that, without individuals, there is no group. For once there are individuals, there is more to a group than the individuals composing it. And this "more" may make it reasonable to adopt the point of view of the group. Learning that the group would not survive the death of its members would not alter this.

Sidgwick does not try these arguments. The reason, perhaps, is that he thinks that "few would maintain" the ultimate reasonableness of taking a point of view between one's own and the universe. (*ME* 10) He does not suppose that "national egoism" asks for or receives the support of either philosophers or "the common moral consciousness of mankind." (*PE* 68) Positions between rational egoism and utilitarianism are ruled out because few hold them. But this does not establish that rational egoism and utilitarianism escape arbitrariness while intermediate positions do not. It gives merely "provisional" support. Further, Sidgwick does allow one position other than rational egoism and utilitarianism – common-sense morality. And one might think that common-sense morality endorses intermediate goals as ultimate. It is unlikely that tariffs, or "Buy Canadian" campaigns, or sentiments in wartime or at international sporting matches are endorsed entirely on rational egoist or utilitarian grounds. One might reply that these must be irrational phenomena – but that is what requires proof.

Since some viewpoints are arbitrary, it is tempting to ask whether the viewpoint of the individual is arbitrary. At one point, this is just what Sidgwick asks. Suppose I hold that "'all pain of human or rational beings is to be avoided.'" I need to show why rationality is a reason for caring about some pains and not others. Sidgwick thinks it is not: "[T]he difference of rationality between two species of sentient beings is no ground for establishing a fundamental ethical distinction between their respective pains." I should come to hold that "'all pain is to be avoided.'" (EP 106–7) Sidgwick does not explain why differences in rationality are no ground. But the obvious thought is this: Pain should be avoided because it is unpleasant, and so it is unpleasant whether felt by a rational or non-rational being.

Sidgwick then applies the same strategy to rational egoism. Suppose I hold that "'it is reasonable for me to take my own greatest happiness as the ultimate end of my conduct.'" I need to show why the fact that some happiness is mine is a reason for caring about that happiness and not that of others. Sidgwick suggests it is not: "[T]he happiness of any other individual, equally capable and deserving of happiness, must be no less worth aiming at than my own." I should come to hold that "'happiness generally is to be sought.'" (EP 107) Again, Sidgwick does not explain why differences in who feels the happiness are no ground. But again, there is an obvious thought: Happiness should be promoted because it is pleasant, and so it is pleasant whether felt by me or someone else.[62]

Sidgwick thinks the first argument succeeds. Indeed, animals provide one of the very few places where he explicitly corrects, on utilitarian grounds, what some take to be common sense. (*ME* 431) He is tempted by the second argument, and sometimes gives it without noting any problems. (e.g., *ME* [3] 360, 363–6, *ME* 500, *LE* 346–7) At one point, he assigns the argument a role in the case for hedonism. (*ME* 403) But in the end, he thinks it fails. When asked why, he argues that the rational egoist can simply "confin[e] himself" to his own point of view. (*ME* 420) The distinction passage is intended to show that doing so is reasonable and hence to show that the second argument fails. This is why it directly follows the claim that the rational egoist can "declin[e] to affirm" the universal point of view. (*ME* 498)

There are two ways in which the distinction passage could undermine the second argument. First, the passage might claim that I do not need to show why the fact that some happiness is mine is a reason for caring about that happiness and not that of others. This is "fundamental."[63] Second, the passage might deny that happiness should be promoted because it is pleasant. Happiness, it says, should be promoted because it is pleasant *and mine.*

Neither of these alternatives is attractive. Against the first, Sidgwick admits that it is fair to ask for a justification of rational egoism. (FC 484, *ME* xv) More generally, "when we are dealing with any subject where there is a conflict of opinion as to first principles, we can hardly refuse to give reasons for taking our side in the conflict: as rational beings conversing with other rationals it seems absurd that we should not be able to explain to each other why we accept one first principle rather than another." (EP 106) As Sidgwick notes, this raises a problem for first

---

62 Mackie holds that the disagreement between the rational egoist and utilitarian turns on whether "good" is a one- or two-place predicate. He is pessimistic about resolving the disagreement because he sees no way to force the rational egoist to the one-place reading. The strategy above shows that this need not justify pessimism. The utilitarian can agree that "good" is two-place, but ask the rational egoist why the second place should be occupied by "for me" rather than "for all." See Mackie, "Pessimism."

63 For emphasis on not trying to prove first principles, see Reid, *Intellectual Powers*, pp. 230–4, *Essays on the Active Powers of the Human Mind*, in Reid, *Works*, vol. 2, p. 637.

principles. He suggests it be solved by "establish[ing] some general criteria for distinguishing true first principles . . . from false ones." (EP 107) These criteria are those discussed in 3.1; I am arguing that rational egoism does not fare well on them.

There is a further worry. Even were it true that I do not need to show the relevance of my connection to the happiness, I would still need to show that the relevance of my connection to it is one of those claims that do not need further proof. Sidgwick could not say merely that he has no further reasons, since this might well be a sign that his position should be rejected. He would not, for example, allow a defence of the relevance of rationality, in the argument excluding animals, that simply claimed that rationality is relevant. Sidgwick does not give criteria for selecting principles that do not require further defence. Reid does; I argue in 4.6 that rational egoism does not meet these.

The second suggestion is that happiness should be promoted not because it is pleasant, but because it is both pleasant and mine. In the context of these arbitrariness arguments, this is unhelpful. Again, Sidgwick would not allow, as an objection to the first argument, that pain should be avoided because it is unpleasant *and* felt by rational beings. The relevance of the addition, in each case, is what is disputed. Worse, Sidgwick's grounds for finding rationality irrelevant seem to commit him to finding my connection to the happiness also irrelevant. If it is the unpleasantness of pain that makes it wrong to limit concern to rational beings, it is the pleasantness of happiness that makes it wrong to limit concern to oneself. One might change the second argument to reflect this more closely: Pain should be avoided because it is unpleasant, and so it is unpleasant whether felt by myself or someone else.

In sum: On this interpretation, the distinction passage holds that the individual's point of view is important and non-arbitrary. But the distinction passage merely asserts this, without explaining why this is so.

I have not considered whether the point of view of the universe fares any better. The arbitrariness argument suggests that it does: The point of view of the universe, unlike the other points of view, draws no distinctions with respect to the distribution of happiness and, hence, cannot be accused of arbitrariness. The point of view of the universe aims at the greatest total amount of happiness; any distribution that calls for a lesser amount faces the charge of arbitrariness. The argument for utilitarianism thus parallels a popular argument for egalitarianism: We should distribute equally, unless there is special reason for not doing so; there are no special reasons for not doing so (because, for example, our qualities are a matter of luck, and luck does not ground desert); hence we should distribute equally.

Sidgwick does not think this argument for utilitarianism works. He holds that the distinction between oneself and all other sentient creatures is not an arbitrary basis for normative distinctions, while any distinction between sentient creatures, oneself excluded, is an arbitrary basis for normative distinctions. I have argued that Sidgwick does not successfully defend this position, and that the most plausible explanation for refusing to discriminate between animals and humans – the unpleasantness of pain, whether felt by an animal or a human – is a reason for refusing to discriminate between oneself and others. Here it is worth noting, briefly, a different reply to the arbitrariness argument in favour of the point of view of the universe.

The reply (offered by Singer) is that my desire for my own happiness *makes* the distinction between myself and others non-arbitrary. Similarly, if I care about humans but not animals or Canadians but not Americans, my caring makes these distinctions non-arbitrary.[64] To avoid obvious problems – racists with false beliefs, and the like – one could add that it is my fully informed desires that are relevant. But the information must be non-normative: It cannot contain, for example, the knowledge that the distinction between myself and others is non-arbitrary. That conclusion must arise from the process.

One problem with this reply is that it is unlikely to privilege myself in the way required by Sidgwick's rational egoism. There is no reason to think that my desires, given full information, would single out my own happiness as their object. Since the issue here, however, is not whether rational egoism can be established but rather whether the arbitrariness argument for the point of view of the universe can be blocked, I put this aside.

Sidgwick would not be sympathetic to the reply. For the reply simply restates a contention of the instrumental theory: It holds that the desires of the agent always provide decisive reasons. Since there are no good arguments for the purely instrumental theory, the theory of arbitrariness it supports is undefended and fares no better than Sidgwick's own claim that the distinction between oneself and others is "fundamental."

---

64 Singer accepts this objection against his own statement of the arbitrariness argument. See Peter Singer, "Reasoning Towards Utilitarianism," in *Hare and Critics*, ed. Douglas Seanor and N. Fotion (Oxford: Oxford University Press [Clarendon], 1988), p. 158.

One might object that we often do take the agent's desires as making non-arbitrary distinctions.[65] My preference for kippers over sardines makes my choice of kippers over sardines, while in the grocery, non-arbitrary. Sidgwick agrees: "[I]t is *pro tanto* expedient that the mere preferences of an individual should be treated by others as legitimate grounds for inequality in the distribution of his property and services." But this is derived from the (utilitarian) value of freedom of action, and constrained by "what the interests of others clearly require." (*ME* 442; also 268, 447n) As the example of Sidgwick's shows, one can accept that there are cases in which the agent's desires create non-arbitrary distinctions, without accepting that they always do. Where my preference for, say, hiring whites over blacks conflicts with "what the interests of others clearly require," we do not think my desire creates a non-arbitrary distinction. (One might reply that my desire gives me *a* reason to hire whites over blacks, although it is outweighed by other reasons, and so my choice of a white would not be arbitrary. But if so, the charge of arbitrariness could be replaced by a charge of irrationality – I do not do what I have most reason to do.)

Suppose, however, that the argument to privilege the point of view of the universe fails. Many points of view would be left in the running. The rational egoist could then claim at least a draw. But Sidgwick should not agree. Considering various distributions of the same total of happiness, he claims the happiness should be distributed equally, since "this principle seems the only one which does not need a special justification; for . . . it must be reasonable to treat any one man in the same way as any other, if there be no reason apparent for treating him differently." (*ME* 417) Elsewhere, he notes that, in the absence of desert claims, equality is "the only mode of distribution that is not arbitrary." (*ME* 447) Different points of view can be thought of as different plans for distribution, and so, where there is no "special justification" for any one point of view, Sidgwick should find only an equal distribution non-arbitrary. This is a defeat for both the utilitarian and rational egoist.

The separateness of persons interpretation

The distinction passage may suggest, to contemporary readers, the familiar claim that persons are separate.[66] This point is now deployed

65 See Daniel Shaw, "Reason and Feeling in Hume's Action Theory," *Hume Studies* 18, 1992, p. 366.
66 Parfit, *Reasons and Persons*, p. 329; Brink, "Rationale," pp. 208–9, 224.

against the utilitarian, just as Sidgwick deploys the distinction passage.[67] Perhaps, then, the distinction passage simply makes the separateness point. I think it does not, and that if it did, this would not help
rational egoism. To show this requires specifying what is intended by
the charge that utilitarianism ignores the separateness of persons.

The separateness of persons is sometimes noted to derail an argument for utilitarianism. Suppose that utilitarians, including Sidgwick,
argue for utilitarianism by treating interpersonal cases as intrapersonal.[68] They claim (i) it is rational for an individual to sacrifice at one
point in his life to get a greater benefit at a later point, and then suppose
(ii) it is rational to sacrifice the interests of one individual, to get greater
benefit for the collection of individuals. Noting the separateness of
persons points out a disanalogy: In (i), the same entity sacrifices and
gains; in (ii), different entities sacrifice and gain. If so, (i) does not
support (ii).

This might be a good objection, and a good interpretation of the
distinction passage, if Sidgwick argues from (i) to (ii). The distinction
passage would find Sidgwick raising a popular objection to his own
argument for utilitarianism. However, Sidgwick does not argue from (i)
to (ii), and so it is unlikely that the distinction passage is an objection to
such an argument. The axiom of temporal irrelevance makes point (i).
(*ME* 381) Sidgwick then makes point (ii). (*ME* 382) He does note that the
reasoning is the same in both cases: We compare the part (one person at
one time, or one person) and the whole (one person over time, or all
people).

67 See, for example, Rawls, *Theory*, pp. 27, 187; Nozick, *Anarchy*, pp. 32–3; Samuel
 Scheffler, *The Rejection of Consequentialism* (Oxford: Oxford University Press [Claren-
 don], 1982), pp. 11–12.
68 Rawls, *Theory*, pp. 23–30, 187–8. A. R. Lacey and Brink agree. Lacey supposes that
 "Sidgwick tries to derive the maxim of Universal Good [personal irrelevance] from
 that of Temporal Indifference by analogy." He then objects that "the wholes in
 question are not of the same type, being in the one case goods 'that succeed one
 another in the series of our conscious states,' and in the other the goods 'of all
 individual . . . sentient existences.' [T]here is a link uniting the parts into a whole in
 the former case that does not operate in the latter, namely a unifying consciousness."
 (see A. R. Lacey, "Sidgwick's Ethical Maxims," *Philosophy* 34, 1959, p. 219) Brink
 writes that Sidgwick "finds temporal-neutrality self-evident, and the analogy leads
 him to accept person-neutrality. We may wonder whether this argument shows that
 utilitarianism is the object of a fundamental intuition, because its constituent axiom –
 person-neutrality – seems really to be a theorem derived from the axiom . . . of
 temporal-neutrality together with an analogy between intertemporal and interpersonal distribution." (Brink, "Common Sense," p. 195; see also "Separateness," p. 254)

[J]ust as [the notion of the good on the whole of an individual] is constructed by comparison and integration of the different 'goods' that succeed one another in the series of our conscious states, so we have formed
the notion of Universal Good by comparison and integration of the goods
of all individual human – or sentient – existences. And here again, just as
in the former case, by considering the relation of the integrant parts to the
whole and to each other, I obtain the self-evident principle that the good
of any one individual is of no more importance, from the point of view . . .
of the Universe, than the good of any other. (*ME* 382)

But Sidgwick is simply noting a similarity. He is not claiming that the
argument for (ii) stands on the truth of (i) and the similarity of the cases.
(Indeed, in the first edition, he argues for (ii) without mentioning (i).)
The argument for (ii), as for (i), is that it passes the various epistemic
tests. If so, noting the separateness of persons, in the sense of noting a
disanalogy between intrapersonal and interpersonal cases, does not
hurt the argument for the axiom of personal irrelevance.

But the critics of utilitarianism have more in mind. In noting the
separateness of persons, they are not only attacking an argument for
utilitarianism. They are also making the normative claim that the sacrifices utilitarians impose are unjust. To say that persons are separate is
not to give an argument for claiming that utilitarianism is unjust; it *is*
the claim that what utilitarianism demands is unjust. The critics can
defend the charge by developing a theory of justice and then showing
that utilitarianism diverges from it.

On this reading, the separateness of persons is an old objection to
utilitarianism. My concern here is not the objection, but rather whether
this reading of the separateness of persons makes sense of the distinction passage. It does not. For Sidgwick endorses no alternative moral
theory, other than rational egoism, by which utilitarianism stands condemned. He has argued that common-sense morality, which might condemn utilitarianism, collapses *into* utilitarianism. In rational egoism,
Sidgwick does have a rival normative theory that condemns utilitarianism. And the distinction passage could be taken to express condemnation from the point of view of this theory. But then the distinction
passage has not yielded any defence of rational egoism. It simply tells
us what rational egoism says about utilitarianism. Just as the separateness of persons charge depends on, rather than establishes, the superiority of a non-utilitarian theory of justice, so the distinction passage
would depend on, rather than establish, rational egoism.

There is a further drawback. Perhaps the idea behind separateness is
that, if persons are separate, we must justify our moral theory to each of

them, and each gets a veto over any decision. From this one might infer something like rational egoism. But if one makes further assumptions, one infers something quite different. Thus if one assumes that it would be unfair for the persons with veto power to know about their identities, one might get Rawls or average utilitarianism. If one assumes that no decisions could be made where all can veto, one might offer suggestions for what, in the absence of unanimity, is needed for justification – perhaps, as Thomas Nagel suggests, minimising the biggest complaint and so privileging the worst-off.[69] Again, this does not support rational egoism. If one assumes that one can justify a moral theory to someone by arguing for its theory of the good, without giving any special role to the interests of one's interlocutor, one might, again, get utilitarianism. The separateness of persons can support rational egoism only should all these assumptions be discarded.[70]

I conclude that, however it is read, the distinction passage does not give Sidgwick a convincing argument for rational egoism. At best, on the personal identity interpretation, it defeats one argument against rational egoism.

3.4

Sidgwick emphasises systematisation among his epistemic tests. He spends a great deal of time arguing that utilitarianism explains and makes precise common-sense morality and some time arguing that rational egoism is inconsistent with common-sense morality. From this, critics have drawn various conclusions. Singer argues that, since Sidgwick remains divided between utilitarianism and rational egoism, systematisation must mean little. Schneewind suggests that utilitarianism's superiority here explains why Sidgwick is a utilitarian. And Sverdlik thinks Sidgwick "stumbled at this point, and ignored the resources his own methodology provided." All agree that rational egoism fails to systematise, at least when compared to utilitarianism.[71] Schnee-

69 Thomas Nagel, "Equality," in *Mortal Questions* (New York: Cambridge University Press, 1979), p. 123.
70 For excellent criticism of the connections drawn between separateness and various moral theories, see Dennis McKerlie, "Egalitarianism and the Separateness of Persons," *Canadian Journal of Philosophy* 18, 1988, pp. 205–26; and Brink, "Separateness."
71 Peter Singer, "Reflective Equilibrium," p. 506; Schneewind, *Victorian*, p. 361; Sverdlik, "Methodology," p. 552. Schneewind does note that rational egoism can systematise some of common-sense morality. See Schneewind, *Victorian*, p. 359, and

wind and Sverdlik conclude that this provides an argument against rational egoism.

Systematisation does provide an argument against rational egoism. But the issue is not so simple. Sidgwick is interested in what it is most rational to do, not simply in what it is moral to do. One expects him to consider more than common-sense morality. And this is what one finds: Sidgwick supposes that rational egoism systematises some common-sense moral beliefs *and* common-sense prudential beliefs. At first glance, this suggests an argument for, rather than against, rational egoism.

Sidgwick consistently ties rational egoism to common sense. (*ME* 7, 120, 419) He considers rational egoism as "a *prima facie* tenable principle for the systematisation of conduct." (*ME* 199) Hobbes can be seen as giving such an account. (*ME* 103n) In *Methods*, II.IV, Sidgwick treats common-sense prudential beliefs much as he later treats common-sense moral beliefs. The former beliefs are "very deficient in clearness and consistency." (*ME* 153) There is "great instability and uncertainty in the most decisive judgements of common sense." (*ME* 157; also 460–1) For example, common sense recommends wealth. But it does not say what to do when wealth conflicts with fame or leisure or friendship. It is not even certain about recommending wealth: Many think that habit accustoms one to luxury so that the wealthy get no more pleasure than the poor and, indeed, are perhaps worse off, given their addiction to luxury and the labour and anxiety (some) undergo to keep it. Furthermore, wealth is often condemned by those who reflect most carefully on the sources of happiness. (*ME* 154–5, 157–8) At best, a "tolerably coherent body of probable doctrine, not useless for practical guidance" can be derived from common-sense judgements of prudence. (*ME* 158) For precision and consistency, as well as practical guidance, one must replace common-sense judgements of the sources of happiness with the maximising principle rational egoism provides, along with empirical studies of the sources of happiness. This lets us say when to choose wealth over other goods and explains the vacillations of common sense. (In the case of wealth, Sidgwick supposes that wealth on average brings more happiness than its lack, but that common-sense reservations are correct when understood as noting that wealth will not bring as much happiness as many think, and none at all to some. (*ME* 159–60) Rational

"First Principles and Common-sense Morality in Sidgwick's Ethics," *Archiv für Geschichte der Philosophie* 45, 1963, p. 155.

egoism bears the same relation to common-sense prudential beliefs that utilitarianism bears to common-sense moral beliefs.

So it might seem that the appeal to system does not help utilitarianism. But common-sense beliefs are not neatly divided into prudential and moral beliefs. We have common-sense beliefs about what it is reasonable to do when prudence and morality conflict. Sidgwick considers these cases. He supposes, for example, that "all admit that we have a general duty of rendering services to our fellow-men and especially to those who are in special need, and that we are bound to make sacrifices for them, when the benefit that we thereby confer very decidedly outweighs the loss to ourselves." (*ME* 348–9)[72] Sidgwick thinks that utilitarianism is needed here, to answer "how far we are bound to give up our own happiness in order to promote that of our fellows." (*ME* 349) Rational egoism can neither explain our common-sense belief nor make it precise. Utilitarianism is superior to rational egoism in systematising our common-sense beliefs about cases where prudence and morality conflict.

There is an obvious objection. Utilitarianism does not seem to endorse the general duty noted. Utilitarians should claim that we have a more radical duty of rendering services, to those in special need or not, whenever the benefit we confer outweighs by *any* amount the loss to ourselves. Utilitarianism captures the common-sense duty no more than rational egoism does.

Sidgwick has a reply. In the face of the objection that "in laying down that each agent is to consider all other happiness as equally important with his own, Utilitarianism seems to go beyond the standard of duty commonly prescribed," he gives a series of indirect considerations to show that, in practice, utilitarian demands do not exceed those of common sense. We can best increase the happiness of those around us; most can do little to help more than a few people; excessive assistance encourages improvidence; helping those we know gives us the added pleasure of seeing their pleasure; beneficence from personal affection is reciprocated, and so encourages rather than depresses the incentive of those benefited; we are incapable of an active general benevolence, and so, if we are to be benevolent (and resist self-interest) at all, it must be to friends and family; expectations would be disappointed were those close to us not favoured; the family is needed for the care of children, and partial affections are needed for the family; close personal ties

---

72 This passage is noted by Seth, "System," p. 185, in his argument to show that rational egoism is not endorsed by common sense.

make possible help of the sort that cannot be purchased (such as various sorts of advice). (*ME* 431–9) The utilitarian, then, endorses the more radical duty as a practical rule only where these indirect considerations are silent or outweighed. The help must greatly outweigh the cost for it to be clear that the indirect considerations are overcome.

The rational egoist might object that he, too, can offer indirect considerations to capture the common-sense view. We should sacrifice for others when the benefit greatly outweighs the burden because, by doing so, we obtain a reputation as beneficent. Such a reputation encourages others to deal with us and to return the favour should we need help. It also brings gratitude. (*ME* 167) The benefit should be great to best enhance one's reputation. The burden should be small, because a large burden might outweigh the gains brought by reputation. If the agent happens to care about doing his duty or the welfare of those he helps, this is a further reason for helping. (*ME* 170)

Sidgwick does not think the appeal to indirect rational egoist considerations works. He notes that rational egoism best explains duties whose performance is likely to encourage beneficial reciprocal performance, and then only under conditions that do not always hold, such as equality of power and difficulty of deception. "[M]orality prescribes the performance of duties equally towards all," but on rational egoist grounds "we should exhibit our useful qualities chiefly towards the rich and powerful, and abstain from injuring those who can retaliate; while we may reasonably omit our duties to the poor and feeble, if we find a material advantage in so doing, unless they are able to excite the sympathy of persons who can harm us." (*ME* 168) Moreover, in the case at hand, one would not acquire a particularly good reputation if one helped only when the burden was small. As for a concern with duty or those we help, Sidgwick objects that many do not care enough about either to make large sacrifices reasonable. (*ME* 170–1, *LE* 56–8)

The point is not merely that utilitarianism generates common-sense dictates in more circumstances than rational egoism does. Sidgwick argues that common-sense *reasoning* about cases in which prudence and morality conflict is utilitarian rather than rational egoist.[73] Suppose I can help someone, where the benefit appears to outweigh the burden. The utilitarian asks herself questions such as "Could I help someone else more? Would helping encourage improvidence? Will the expecta-

---

73 Sidgwick summarises the utilitarian nature of common-sense reasoning about morality, rather than specifically about cases in which morality and prudence conflict, at *ME* 425–6.

tions of my friends and family be disappointed?" The rational egoist asks "Will anyone see? Do those I help, or those who see me help, have anything to offer me? Is the gain in reputation worth the sacrifice? Could I have the reputation without actually helping?" Since common-sense considerations are more utilitarian than rational egoist, this favours utilitarianism.[74]

Sidgwick might add a further argument. He thinks utilitarianism provides a good explanation of differences in common-sense morality over time, place, and occupation. For example, theft is venial where labour is unnecessary; private murder is accepted where state punishment is spotty; courage is more highly valued in soldiers than priests. (*ME* 454–5, *UG* 32) He also thinks utilitarianism can be seen as what common-sense morality is coming increasingly to approximate. (*ME* 455, 457, *UG* 32) This supports the conclusion that utilitarianism underlies common-sense morality. Sidgwick does not claim that rational egoism provides a poorer explanation or destination, and he has some reason not to do so: since rational egoists and utilitarians will usually make the same recommendations, the appeal to differences over time, place, and occupation may be insufficiently fine grained to reveal a winner. However, Sidgwick does record one change that favours utilitarianism. Rational egoism has difficulty explaining duties to those who cannot reciprocate. But such duties have become increasingly popular: Sidgwick notes the condemnation of exposing infants and the extension of aid for the sick and poor. (*ME* 455n) He might now add the concern with animal welfare. If so, utilitarianism better explains not just our verdicts and reasoning, but also changes in common sense.

Sidgwick gives the same treatment to another case in which morality and prudence conflict. Hobbes, he writes, held

> any aggression or breach of compact conducive to self-preservation to be lawful to the human individual or group, struggling to maintain its existence in the anarchy called a state of nature; but he justified this license on the ground that a member of such a "natural society" who may observe

74 Sidgwick cannot claim a clear victory for utilitarianism, since he argues that the utilitarian must sometimes ask "Will anyone hear?" A utilitarian should think about secrecy when considering whether some advice, beneficial when received by those in exceptional circumstances, would have bad effects when received by those in everyday circumstances. Sidgwick admits that common sense is opposed. (*ME* 489–90) He can still hold, however, in the case at hand, that utilitarianism defeats rational egoism. In other cases, he can add that rational egoism agrees with utilitarianism in holding, contrary to common sense, that "an action which would be bad if done openly [can be] rendered good by secrecy." (*ME* 490)

moral rules can have no reasonable expectation of reciprocal observance on the part of others, and must therefore merely "make himself a prey to others." In Hobbes' view . . . [the] obligation to realise [morality] in act is conditional on a reasonable expectation of reciprocity. This condition is, I think, with careful limitations and qualifications, sound. (*PE* 71)

He goes on to note international cases in which common sense demands reciprocity: We allow our diplomats to lie, if those of other nations do; we allow our government to break treaties, if those they break with themselves habitually break. (*PE* 75–6). Sidgwick thinks common sense agrees with Hobbes.

One might think this supports rational egoism: We require reciprocity because obeying moral constraints pays us only given reciprocity. Sidgwick disagrees. For he adds "limitations and qualifications" to what common sense accepts that resist the rational egoist explanation. Lying and promise breaking are not accepted by us in all cases in which the other party is guilty of the same nor in all cases where lying or promise breaking benefits one. They are accepted only where the other party lies or breaks first, lying or promise breaking is urgently needed for our self-protection, and no other means of protection is available. (*PE* 76, 79, 81) Sidgwick believes utilitarianism best explains these limitations. (*PE* 74, 81, 82) Again, his argument is that the limitations imposed and the reasoning employed are more easily explained by utilitarianism than rational egoism. The utilitarian imposes strict limitations on international lying and promise breaking in order to foster peace and cooperation; he mandates self-protection in order to discourage aggression. The rational egoist could, of course, agree – but since inequalities are greater, deception easier, and reputation less valuable at the international level, the rational egoist attempt to explain common sense looks even more forced. Rational egoism should give more licence to lie and break promises than common sense does. In addition, the rational egoist has difficulty explaining why common sense sometimes approves costly missions of international aid. (*PE* 80–1) Utilitarianism provides a better explanation.

Sidgwick does admit that

whatever difference exists between Utilitarian morality and that of Common Sense is of such a kind as to render the coincidence with Egoism still more improbable in the case of the former. For we have seen that Utilitarianism is more rigid than Common Sense in exacting the sacrifice of the agent's private interests where they are incompatible with the greatest happiness of the greatest number. (*ME* 499; also 87)

Sidgwick's point is that a rational egoist would face more difficulty capturing utilitarian demands than capturing the demands of common-sense morality. He does not, then, think his indirect considerations show that utilitarianism is no more demanding than common-sense morality. But it does not follow that common-sense morality supports rational egoism more than it supports utilitarianism, even when sacrifices alone are considered. For rational egoism is much *less* demanding than common-sense morality. Sidgwick can both make the quoted claim and say that common-sense morality supports utilitarianism over rational egoism. He can do so by holding that the departures rational egoism makes from common-sense morality, in the direction of being less demanding, are greater than the departures utilitarianism makes from common-sense morality, in the direction of being more demanding. Sidgwick is not, then, withdrawing his claim that common-sense morality supports utilitarianism over rational egoism.

This does, however, suggest a worry. It is quite plausible to think Sidgwick overestimates the force of his indirect utilitarian considerations. Utilitarianism is probably more demanding than he supposes.[75] It is less plausible, but still possible, that he underestimates the force of the indirect rational egoist considerations. If so, common-sense morality may be friendlier to rational egoism, and more hostile to utilitarianism, than has been argued. This, I think, shows the importance of Sidgwick's appeal to common-sense moral reasoning and to historical change. Provided these favour utilitarianism over rational egoism, Sidgwick might concede that, when attention is confined to the dictates of each theory regarding sacrifices, the case for choosing utilitarianism over rational egoism on the basis of common sense is inconclusive.

There is another worry. The common-sense belief about cases in which prudence and morality conflict shows compromise: morality should win where the moral gains *greatly* outweigh the prudential costs. Both the utilitarian and the rational egoist try to explain away the compromise by citing indirect considerations. But perhaps common sense holds the compromise position even where all indirect considerations are excluded. If so, examining common-sense beliefs about the relation

---

75 Note, however, that rational egoism is also quite demanding, at least in its maximising guise. Rational egoism is much less demanding than utilitarianism only given certain conditions: for example, if demandingness is measured against one's whole life rather than one's present inclinations, or if one does not have many other-regarding desires.

between morality and prudence would speak in favour of neither rational egoism nor utilitarianism. It would most favour a position Broad describes: "[I]t is fitting for A to desire to *some* degree the existence of *any* intrinsically good state of mind; but that, of equally good states of mind, one in himself and another in someone else, it is fitting for him to desire the existence of the former more intensely than that of the latter."[76] Although this prospect is still a defeat for rational egoism, it suggests a strategy for revival. Sidgwick admits that a philosopher "is allowed a certain divergence from Common Sense in his conclusions." (*ME* 373) If utilitarianism can win out over the compromise theory despite fitting more poorly with common-sense morality, then lack of fit with common-sense morality is not deadly, and rational egoism may be able to appeal to whatever factors there are, beyond fit with common-sense morality, that make utilitarianism superior to the compromise theory.

To decide between the compromise, rational egoist, and utilitarian interpretations of common sense, consider a series of cases in which there are no indirect gains of the sort the rational egoist notes – I shall never see the person helped again, and no one sees me helping. Add that all the indirect utilitarian considerations are also irrelevant. Consider:

> *Case One:* I have an opportunity to help someone. The benefit conferred outweighs the cost to me.

Here Sidgwick claims we hold the utilitarian position: "I think that a 'plain man' . . . if his conscience were fairly brought to consider the hypothetical question, whether it would be morally right for him to seek his own happiness on any occasion if it involved a certain sacrifice of the greater happiness of some other human being, – without any counterbalancing gain to any one else, – would answer unhesitatingly in the negative." (*ME* 382; also 327, 431, 436, UG 31–2) True, Sidgwick admits that utilitarianism and common-sense morality sometimes diverge. (*ME* 455–6, 463–7, 497) But his view is that they sometimes diverge in their practical recommendations, rather than in cases of the sort presented, in which indirect considerations are excluded. In these test cases, Sidgwick finds no disagreement.

If Sidgwick is right, this supports utilitarianism. But variations on *Case One* might lessen his confidence. At one point, Sidgwick describes a different general duty to help:

---

76 Broad, *Five Types*, pp. 243–4.

> *Case Two:* I have an opportunity to help someone. The benefit conferred greatly outweighs the cost to me. The cost is "not burdensome" and the benefit is great. Suppose, for example, I could save a drowning man by simply holding out my hand. (*ME* 437)

Perhaps common sense holds that we have a duty to help here, but not in all cases in which the benefit outweighs the burden. Consider the following cases.

> *Case Three:* I have the opportunity to slightly help each of a vast number of people by taking on a terrible burden. The total benefit slightly (or even greatly) outweighs the burden.

> *Case Four:* I have an opportunity to help. The benefit conferred greatly outweighs the cost to me. I am not told the cost.

Case Two supports utilitarianism or the compromise theory. In *Case Three*, many will say that I do not have a duty to bear the burden. This favours rational egoism or the compromise theory. In *Case Four*, many will refuse to decide until the burden is revealed. This supports the compromise theory. Taken together, these verdicts most support the compromise theory, and so question Sidgwick's verdict in *Case One*.

On the whole, perhaps common sense supports the compromise position rather than utilitarianism. It would not follow that utilitarianism is defeated. As noted in 3.1, Sidgwick thinks some of common-sense morality can be dismissed because it is based on cognitive error. But Sidgwick sees the unsystematic nature of common-sense morality as a much bigger defect. For Sidgwick it is a great virtue of utilitarianism that, in theory, it gives a clear and principled answer to the question "[W]hat do I have most reason to do?" Broad's compromise position reproduces the vagueness of common-sense morality: It does not say how much more intensely I should desire my good state of mind. More recent attempts to work out a compromise theory would leave Sidgwick equally unimpressed.[77] Utilitarianism might, then, withstand this disagreement with common sense. But if so, rational egoism might equally well survive, for it too gives a clear and principled answer.[78] (The point is not that the compromise theory should be replaced because it fails to give clear and principled answers. If one gave great

---

77 See Scheffler, *Rejection;* Susan Wolf, "Morality and Partiality," *Philosophical Perspectives* 6, 1992, pp. 243–60; Thomas Nagel, *The View from Nowhere* (New York: Oxford University Press, 1986), pp. 166–75. For the virtue of utilitarianism as systematising common-sense morality, see the summaries at *ME* 342–3, 425–6, 453–4, 496–7.
78 For a similar point, see Schneewind, *Victorian,* p. 359, and "First Principles," p. 155.

weight to fit with common-sense morality, this might count as a virtue, not a vice. Rather, the point is that *if* one values clear and principled answers sufficiently to make the compromise theory inadequate, then rational egoism may yet be the most desirable choice.)

The utilitarian can reply that giving a clear and principled answer is not the only reason for rejecting rivals such as the compromise theory and that the further reasons cannot be similarly co-opted to revive rational egoism. Consider two further problems for the compromise theory. First:

> *Case Five:* Suppose the compromise theory permits me to value my interest over the general interest provided the general interest does not exceed my interest by more than a factor of three. This permits me to avoid helping in some cases where common sense may agree that helping is not a duty. It also permits me to harm others provided the harm I inflict does not exceed my gain by more than a factor of three.

Common sense does not agree here.[79] This suggests that the cases considered above may not best support the compromise theory, but rather the compromise theory accompanied by a weighty distinction between doing and allowing.

Second, in each of the cases, the intuition may be that no one should fall below some minimal level of welfare. This is why the size of the sacrifice or benefit, rather than the total, is sometimes taken to be relevant. Call this the "minimum" theory. To decide between the minimum and compromise theories, consider:

> *Case Six:* I have an opportunity to help two people avoid falling below the minimum. I can do so only by falling below the minimum myself. All fall, or avoid falling, the same amount below the minimum.

The minimum theory says that I have a duty to help; the compromise theory can disagree. Some agree with the minimum theory, and so the compromise theory may not even be *part* of the correct interpretation of common sense.

These problems for the compromise theory do not obviously help utilitarianism. Instead, they seem to multiply opponents. They may, however, favour utilitarianism over rational egoism. In *Case Five*, utilitarianism, but not rational egoism, agrees with common sense. True, utilitarians cannot accommodate what may be the underlying intui-

---

79 I take this strategy from Shelly Kagan's treatment of Scheffler in "Does Consequentialism Demand Too Much?" *Philosophy and Public Affairs* 13, 1984, p. 251.

tion – a weighty distinction between doing and allowing. But here rational egoism does no better. In *Case Six,* utilitarianism, but not rational egoism, agrees with the minimum theory. And utilitarians can add an argument for preferring utilitarianism to the minimum theory.

> *Case Seven:* I have an opportunity to help many, many people live lives far, far above the minimum. I can do so only by falling slightly below the minimum myself. If I do not help, all will live at the minimum.

Rational egoists are not helped by *Case Seven.* They might reply with their own attacks on the minimum theory:

> *Case Eight:* I have an opportunity to help one other person live at the minimum. If I do not help, I live far, far above the minimum, and the other person lives slightly below the minimum.

But insofar as *Case Eight* aids the rational egoist, it also aids the utilitarian. A rational egoist attack on the minimum theory that does not also aid the utilitarian would rely on

> *Case Nine:* I have an opportunity to help many, many people live at the minimum. If I do not help, I live far, far above the minimum, and the others live slightly below the minimum, such that the harm to them exceeds my gain.

But since few will recommend not helping in *Case Nine,* rational egoism is less persuasive than utilitarianism against the minimum theory.

Thus, suppose some theory other than rational egoism or utilitarianism best models common sense, but that this other theory is to be rejected, not only because it fails to offer clear and principled answers, but for further reasons: the compromise theory, because of *Cases Five* and *Six;* the compromise theory accompanied by the distinction between doing and allowing, because of the dubiousness of the distinction and *Case Six;* the minimum theory, because of *Case Seven.* These reasons for rejection favour utilitarianism over rational egoism. And so, if one must choose either rational egoism or utilitarianism on the basis of common sense, one should choose utilitarianism.

There is a related strategy for reviving rational egoism that deserves mention. Suppose, again, that common sense favours the compromise theory even when indirect considerations are excluded. I have argued that if for various reasons the compromise theory is still to be rejected, the reasons for rejection favour utilitarianism over rational egoism. But the compromise theory might be employed to support rational egoism in a different way: Perhaps whatever rationale underlies the compromise theory's rejection of utilitarianism will provide a rationale for rational egoism.

Whether this strategy works depends on whether the needed rationale is discovered. In 4.6, I reject the one notable attempt to find a rationale underlying the compromise theory, proposed by Samuel Scheffler. But even without seeing the rationale, there is reason for thinking this strategy will be inconclusive. For the same strategy supports utilitarianism: Perhaps whatever rationale underlies the compromise theory's rejection of rational egoism will provide a rationale for utilitarianism. Indeed, if it is true that common sense is closer to utilitarianism than to rational egoism, then it is unlikely that the rationale supporting rational egoism will be more persuasive than the rationale supporting utilitarianism.

Suppose rational egoism is defeated here. There remain Sidgwick's various claims about its reasonableness. He need not jettison these. He notes that we sometimes "mistak[e] for an ultimate and independent axiom one that is really derivative and subordinate." (*ME* 341; also *EP* 106) And he argues, on indirect utilitarian grounds, that the general happiness is maximised by each person pursuing her own happiness (on most occasions). This suggests that the reasonableness of my pursuing my own happiness may derive, not from rational egoism, but from utilitarianism. "Common sense does not think it worth while to supply the individual with reasons for seeking his own interest," not because one's own interest is a reasonable ultimate goal, but because there is no need to bother. (*ME* 419) "[W]e need have no fear in urging men to be as unselfish as possible, since it is quite certain that they will always remain more than sufficiently selfish." (*LE* 186; also *ME* 428) Utilitarianism systematises rational egoism just as it does common-sense morality.[80]

I conclude that Schneewind and Sverdlik are right: The appeal to systematising common sense provides an argument against rational egoism. The appeal to arbitrariness suggests another such argument. And attempted defences of rational egoism, through considerations of self-evidence or the distinction between persons, at best defend rational egoism from one objection. In the next chapter, I turn to Sidgwick's argument from historical consensus.

80 For a similar argument, see Seth, "System," p. 184.

Chapter 4

From Hobbes to Bentham

W HEN Sidgwick was asked to defend the prominence he gave to rational egoism in the *Methods,* one of his replies was to note that there is "preponderant assent" to it in "the common sense of mankind" and "the history of ethical thought in England." (FC 483) Rational egoism has "wide acceptance" – Sidgwick even claims in the first edition of the *Methods* that "there seems to be more general agreement among re- flective persons as to the reasonableness of its fundamental principle, than exists in the case either of Intuitionism or of . . . Utilitarianism." (*ME* 119; *ME* [1] 107; also *ME* 95, *ME* [1] 388, 461) "It is not denied," by those who replied to Hobbes, "that the self-love which seeks the agent's greatest happiness is a rational principle of action." (UG 30; also *ME* 171n) In the *Methods* and the *Outlines of the History of Ethics,* he provides evidence for this claim, citing Hobbes, Shaftesbury, Butler, Hume, Paley, Bentham, and, more surprisingly, Cumberland, Samuel Clarke, Berke- ley, Reid, Stewart, Kant, and Comte as all admitting the ultimate reason- ableness of seeking one's own interest.[1] Given this heavyweight line- up, it is not surprising that Sidgwick found that "it is hardly going too far to say that common sense assumes that 'interested' actions, tending to promote the agent's happiness, are *prima facie* reasonable: and that the *onus probandi* lies with those who maintain that disinterested con- duct, as such, is reasonable." (*ME* 120; also xx, 7, 200, 386, 419)[2]

1 For Shaftesbury, Helvetius, Stewart, and Comte, see O 184–90, 196; 267–8; 232n; 268– 9. For Berkeley, see *ME* 120. For Cumberland, see UG 30. I discuss Hobbes, Clarke, Butler, Hume, Reid, Kant, Paley, and Bentham later in this chapter. Sidgwick, of course, held that, unlike the ancients, many of these figures also admitted the ultimate reasonableness of non-egoistic ends.
2 This claim concerning the onus is weaker than rational egoism, and so my strategy of showing little or misguided agreement to rational egoism will not show that there is little or misguided agreement about where the onus lies. I return to the onus claim in 4.10.

As the emphasis on social verification leads one to expect, Sidgwick would "rely less confidently" on his underlying axioms "if they did not appear . . . to be in substantial agreement . . . with the doctrines of those moralists who have been most in earnest in seeking among commonly received moral rules for genuine intuitions of the Practical Reason." (*ME* 384) The same goes for propositions of lesser certainty, such as rational egoism. It is important for Sidgwick to show "the wide acceptance of the principle that it is reasonable for a man to act in the manner most conducive to his own happiness." (*ME* 119) Disagreement inspires "distrust of Common Sense." (*ME* 466; also 214) When some reviewers of the *Methods* reject the dualism, sometimes by rejecting rational egoism, Sidgwick admits that this "shakes my confidence in the view." (FC 484) And so there is another way of attacking rational egoism: Sidgwick's confidence in rational egoism would be lessened if it turned out that there was much less agreement on rational egoism than he thought. (Similarly, he supposes Green's confidence in his moral ideal should be lessened if it turns out, as Sidgwick argues, that Green is largely mistaken in treating the Greeks as his predecessors. ([*LE* 80-99])

I shall consider Samuel Clarke, Butler, Hume, Reid, Kant, Paley, and Bentham, taking Sidgwick as my guide. I shall also consider Hobbes again, very briefly, to present Sidgwick's view of him, and John Clarke, a rational egoist overlooked by Sidgwick.

In Hobbes, Butler, Paley, and Bentham, Sidgwick sees support for rational egoism. In Samuel Clarke, Butler, Hume, Reid, and Kant, Sidgwick sees support for veto egoism – the view that contribution to self-interest is necessary for rational action. I shall argue that some of Sidgwick's figures did not endorse any sort of normative egoism and that those who did gave bad arguments for it. I close in 4.10 with more general worries.

One caveat is needed. Hobbes and John Clarke aside, my classification is somewhat artificial. Sidgwick often notes that Samuel Clarke, Butler, Reid, Kant, and Bentham view concern for oneself as a "rational" or "authoritative" or "governing" principle. This does not distinguish between treating contribution to self-interest as necessary for rational action (veto egoism) or as sufficient for rational action. And since most of the figures concerned hold that virtue always pays, they are not much interested in making precise their positions. I think veto egoism is usually the most plausible reading. But my main concern is with the arguments offered, rather than with imposing a foreign taxonomy. I sometimes, then, write of "egoism" without further distinctions, always intending the family of normative positions consisting of rational egoism, veto egoism, and the view that contribution to self-interest is sufficient (but not necessary) for rational action.

4.1 Hobbes

Sidgwick holds that Hobbes introduced rational egoism into modern moral thought. (*O* 163, *ME* xix, 86, 89) According to Hobbes, "since all the voluntary actions of men tend to their own preservation or pleasure, it cannot be reasonable to aim at anything else." (*O* 165) Later Sidgwick claims that Hobbes's "theoretical basis is the principle of egoism, – viz. that it is natural, and so reasonable, for each individual to aim solely at his own preservation or pleasure." (*O* 169) He also notes that Hobbes constructed his morality on the basis of rational egoism "on which alone, as he held, the social order could firmly rest, and escape the storms and convulsions with which it seemed to be menaced from the vagaries of the unenlightened conscience." (*ME* 89) But Sidgwick argues against both psychological egoism and any inference of rational egoism from psychological egoism. (*ME* 40–54) He also rejects the "quasi-theistic assumption that what is natural must be reasonable" and, presumably, the claim that only rational egoism brings stability. (*O* 192) I have, above, shown that Sidgwick rejects the argument from systematisation he sometimes ascribes to Hobbes. (*ME* 103n, *PE* 71) As a result, he cannot take Hobbes's adherence to rational egoism as providing much support for the position. (Sidgwick uses a similar strategy against Green: If those areas where Aristotle does anticipate Green are also those areas where Aristotle is unsatisfactory, Green's position is not improved by citing Aristotle's anticipation of it. ([e.g., *LE* 87–8])

4.2 Samuel Clarke

Samuel Clarke gives an influential account of obligation that tries to explain how one can be bound rationally, without conceding anything to motivation.

> [T]he Judgement and Conscience of a Man's own Mind, concerning the Reasonableness and Fitness of the thing, that his Actions should be conformed to such or such a Rule or Law; is the truest and formallest *Obligation;* even more properly and strictly so, than any . . . Regard he may have to its Sanction by Rewards and Punishments. . . . [This] Sanction . . . however indeed absolutely necessary to the Government of frail and fallible Creatures . . . is yet really in itself, only a *secondary* and *additional* Obligation, or *Inforcement* of the first. The original *Obligation* of all . . . is

the eternal *Reason* of Things. . . . So far therefore as Men are conscious of what is right and wrong, so far they *Are* under an *Obligation* to act accordingly.[3]

But he is not content. In a passage noted by John Clarke, he adds that "[v]irtue is unquestionably *worthy to be chosen for its own sake,* even without any expectation of Reward; yet it does not follow that it is therefore intirely *Self-sufficient,* and able to support a Man under all kind of Sufferings, and even Death itself, for its sake; without any prospect of future recompence."[4] One might think Samuel Clarke is making a claim about motivation, not justification. He is criticising the Stoics for offering an ideal few can attain: "[T]he general Practice of Virtue in the World, can never be supported upon this Foot."[5] But for two further passages, noted by John Clarke and Sidgwick, this interpretation is not plausible:

> Men never will generally, and indeed '*tis not very reasonable to be expected they should,* part with all the Comforts of Life, and even Life itself; without expectation of any future Recompence.

> [It is] neither possible *nor truly reasonable,* that Men by adhering to Virtue should part with their Lives, if thereby they eternally deprived themselves of all possibility of receiving any Advantage from that adherence.[6]

One might ask why Clarke adds this.

Sidgwick offers an insidious explanation. Samuel Clarke aims to "prove the 'reasonableness and certainty' of the Christian revelation"; when his account of virtue and obligation threatens to make God irrelevant, he introduces veto egoism and so finds God and an afterlife a role, as the guarantee that virtue is reasonable. (*O* 179, 183) If Samuel Clarke were not under pressure to find some work for God to do, he would not have introduced veto egoism. This fits the egoist passages: All occur in the course of arguing for an afterlife. Here religious belief operates not

---

3   Samuel Clarke, *Discourse Concerning the Unalterable Obligations of Natural Religion,* in Samuel Clarke, *Works* (London: 1738), p. 614; see also pp. 596, 618, 626–9. Butler and Price propose similar sanction-independent accounts. See Joseph Butler, *Fifteen Sermons Preached at the Rolls Chapel,* in *The Works of Bishop Butler,* ed. J. H. Bernard (London: Macmillan, 1900), vol. 1, pref. 27, 3.5; Richard Price, *A Review of the Principal Questions in Morals,* in Selby-Bigge, *British Moralists,* vol. 2, pp. 129n, 130–2, 155–65.
4   S. Clarke, *Discourse,* p. 629; J. Clarke, *The Foundation of Morality in Theory and Practice* (York: T. Gent, 1726), p. 28.
5   S. Clarke, *Discourse,* p. 646.
6   S. Clarke, *Discourse,* pp. 630, 646, all italics added; J. Clarke, *Foundation,* pp. 28–9; UG 30–1, *ME* 120, *O* 183.

only by removing any conflict between veto egoism and, say, utilitarianism, but also by motivating veto egoism itself.

If Sidgwick is right about Samuel Clarke, he should not put much stock in Clarke's agreement with him about veto egoism. For on Sidgwick's interpretation, Clarke's reason for endorsing veto egoism is disreputable. It is not an explanation that gives credibility to the veto. Clarke may, of course, take the veto to be self-evident, and so hold that little argument can be given for it. His adoption of the veto may be motivated by this, rather than its "convenient" provision of an argument for an afterlife. (*O* 183) He may even be excused of inconsistency, if his apparently anti-Hobbesian claims about obligation are understood (surprisingly) as concerning only situations where self-interest is silent. Virtue

> truly deserves to be chosen for its own sake, and [vice] ought by all means to be avoided, though a Man was sure for his own particular, neither to gain nor lose any thing by the practice of either. . . . But the Case does not stand thus. The question Now in the general practice of the World . . . will not be, whether a Man would choose Virtue for *its own sake*, and avoid Vice; But the practice of Vice, is accompanied with great Temptations and Allurements of Pleasure and Profit; and the practice of Virtue is often threatened with great Calamities, Losses, and sometimes even with Death itself. And this alters the Question, and destroys the practice of that which appears so reasonable.[7]

But even then, Clarke is not a happy ally: His argument for the axiom of rational benevolence, cited with approval by Sidgwick as an ancestor of his own, is certainly more impressive than the bare assumption of veto egoism now countenanced. (*ME* 385) Sidgwick admits as much: after writing that among intuitionists "there is no one who shows more earnestness in the effort to penetrate to really self-evident principles than Clarke," he concedes that "the reasonableness of Prudence or Self-love is only recognised by Clarke indirectly," in the passages quoted above. (*ME* 384, 384n4)

4.3 John Clarke

Sidgwick does not mention John Clarke. He is worth presenting, however. For Clarke is much clearer than Hobbes in both his psychological and rational egoism – no doubt because he is criticising the anti-Hobbes-

---

7   S. Clarke, *Discourse*, p. 629; *O* 182–3.

ian efforts of Samuel Clarke and Hutcheson on just these points. He is also the perfect victim for Sidgwick's attack on the inference from psychological to rational egoism, noted at the start of Chapter 3.

Clarke offers various arguments for rational egoism. The first appeals to ordinary language:

> The terms *reasonable* and *fit*, in [Samuel Clarke's] way of using them, seem altogether . . . unintelligible. . . . For what can possibly be meant by them, when . . . all Respect to any thing of Benefit or Advantage, either present or future, to be reaped by the Practice of Moral Rules is excluded; nay, Pain and Misery only supposed to attend it, I know not. . . . Those terms, when applied to Human Actions, have always, I think, a final Reference to some real Advantage of the Agent, upon account of their Tendency to which, they are denominated reasonable and fit for him. Does it not sound very strangely to say, it is reasonable and fit for a Man to make himself extremely miserable in this Life, tho' he is to receive no Benefit or Advantage by so doing hereafter? What agreeable Sense can there be, in saying it is reasonable and fit for a Man to destroy himself for nothing?
>
> [N]othing can be said to be reasonable or fit for him, that is not proper to promote his welfare.[8]

Clarke gives a similar argument for "obligation": To be "under an obligation" is to be positioned such that the "consequence of behaving otherwise, would be some way or other prejudicial to our Interest." This is the only sense in which there can be a "Bond upon the Mind." It follows that "upon the Supposition, that the observation of moral Rules should be attended with nothing but Pain and Misery, Men would be so far from being obliged to the Observation, that they would be obliged on the contrary to the Breach and Violation of them."[9] But Clarke is aware that ordinary usage is not decisive: although no one would call a sacrifice "for nothing" reasonable, one might find a sacrifice for the happiness of others reasonable.

Against this, Clarke has a second argument. "The only seeming Reason that can be alleged [for sacrifice], is that such an Adherence to Virtue, tho' attended with nothing but Pain and Misery to a Man's Self, may yet be good for others. . . . Very true, but what then? this can be . . . no Reason, no Motive to a man to act at all."[10] It is "no reason," Clarke

---

8 J. Clarke, *Foundation*, pp. 12–13; also 11, 14–15, 21–2. Since this part of *Foundation* is hard to find, I quote liberally. Where possible, I cite the portion reprinted in Selby-Bigge's *British Moralists*, vol. 2.

9 J. Clarke, *Foundation*, pp. 10–11.

10 Ibid., p. 22.

holds, *because* it is "no motive." It is not "reasonable or fit for him absolutely to postpone the Consideration of his own Happiness to their Advantage, for that seems in the nature of the thing utterly impossible. . . . I deny [sacrifice] to be Fit or Reasonable, whatever the meaning of those Terms, because it appears indeed to be impossible."[11] The same argument handles obligation: "What then shall oblige a Man? Shall the Fitness or Tendency of Justice to the Good of others? . . . But if so, then, a Man must be obliged to prefer the Good of others before his own, [which is] utterly and absolutely impossible."[12] Clarke moves repeatedly from psychological to rational egoism. The agent's happiness, being "the highest Reason, the strongest Motive possible for Action, it is most apparently very reasonable and fit" to pursue only one's happiness.[13] Benefit to the agent is "absolutely necessary to dispose the Mind" to virtue, "and render the Practice thereof reasonable and fit," since "it seems impossible for the mind, to divest itself of the great and powerful Principle of Self-Love, by absolutely preferring the Good of others before its own."[14] "[I]f Virtue be not . . . able to support a Man under all kind of Sufferings for its sake . . . the Practice of Virtue, where it is attended with such Sufferings, upon the Supposition of no future Recompense, would not be fit or reasonable."[15] The "Foundation of Morality in Practice, is the Tendency thereof to the private Happiness of the Practicer, that only being able to support it."[16]

Clarke, then, assumes that it is reasonable to pursue one's own happiness and wields psychological egoism to make any rival claim to reasonableness otiose. If asked why we should believe that it is reasonable to pursue one's own happiness, Clarke's reply would seem to be that it is reasonable because unavoidable or that this is what "reasonable" should be taken to mean, once confusion about the possibility of non-self-interested action is removed.[17] Only once does Clarke suggest anything more:

11   Ibid., pp. 23–4.
12   Ibid., pp. 36–7.
13   Ibid., p. 13.
14   Ibid., pp. 39–40.
15   Ibid., p. 28.
16   Ibid., p. 31.
17   The latter suggestion is that J. Clarke offers a "reforming" definition in the sense employed by C. L. Stevenson and Richard Brandt. See Stevenson, "The Emotive Meaning of Ethical Terms," *Mind* 46, 1937, pp. 14–15; and Brandt, *Theory*, pp. 10–16, 126–9.

Since my Reason can be of no Value or Account to me, any further than it serves to conduct me to . . . happiness, which I find my self obliged, by the very Nature of my Mind, to pursue, and cannot help it; such a Conduct as is most proper to promote that End, even the Violation of Moral Rules . . . must best deserve the Denominations of *reasonable* and *fit*.[18]

The point of being able to reason must be to show me how to be happy, since such ability could play no practical role by showing me anything else, and it must have *some* practical role. Clarke does not make the appeal to God's design explicit here. But when considering the moral sense, he does not hesitate to ask "for what End the Moral Sense could be given us," and to argue that Hutcheson cannot explain "what it is good for" or God's "Intention in bestowing the Moral Sense."[19]

Sidgwick's (correct) replies have been noted: If Clarke intends maximising psychological egoism, there is no room for guidance; Clarke has no defence for the inference from the unavoidable to the reasonable, apart from a possible appeal to God's design; and, in any case, all varieties of psychological egoism are false.

4.4 Butler

Sidgwick often cites three passages from Butler. One is the famous "cool hour" passage. He takes it to show that Butler gives self-love "theoretical priority" over conscience. (*ME* 200; also 119–20, 366, *O* 196) This is a misreading.

The passage runs as follows: "Let it be allowed, though virtue or moral rectitude does indeed consist in affection to and pursuit of what is right and good, as such; yet, that when we sit down in a cool hour, we can neither justify to ourselves this or any other pursuit, till we are convinced that it will be for our happiness, or at least not contrary to it."[20] This does seem to favour a rational egoist reading. But Butler's rationale is made clear by the context. Making "all possible concessions" to self-love, Butler writes that

> there can no access be had to the understanding, but by convincing men, that the course of life we would persuade them to is not contrary to their interest. It may be allowed, without any prejudice to the cause of virtue and religion, that our ideas of happiness and misery are of all our ideas

18   J. Clarke, *Foundation*, p. 14.
19   Ibid., in *British Moralists*, pp. 241–2; also pp. 243–4.
20   Butler, *Sermons*, 11.20.

the nearest and most important to us; that they will, nay, if you please, that they ought to prevail over those of order, and beauty, and harmony, and proportion, if there should ever be, as it is impossible there ever should be, any inconsistence between them.

Immediately after the cool hour passage, Butler adds that "so far as the interests of virtue depend upon the theory of it being secured from open scorn, so far its very being in the world depends upon its appearing to have no contrariety to private interest and self-love."[21] Rational egoism "may be allowed" since it does no harm to do so, and showing that virtue pays does some good, by allowing "access . . . to the understanding" that might otherwise "scorn" virtue. Were Butler to admit the conflict between virtue and self-interest that he finds "impossible," we would remain "under the strictest moral obligations, whatever their opinion be concerning the happiness of virtue. . . . [T]hough a man should doubt of everything else, yet . . . he would still remain under the nearest and most certain obligation to the practice of virtue, an obligation implied in the very idea of virtue."[22] Butler implies that showing virtue pays is useful but strictly unnecessary: Were virtue not to pay, fewer would be virtuous,[23] but the same obligations would remain.[24]

Sidgwick's other passages appear to support veto rather than ra-

21 Ibid., 11.3, 20–1.
22 Ibid., pref. 27.
23 I write "fewer" because Butler holds, contrary to the allowance made in the quoted passages, that conscience can motivate. See Alan R. White, "Conscience and Self-Love in Butler's Sermons," *Philosophy* 27, 1952, pp. 334–5. White also notes that Butler is following Shaftesbury's claim that "though the habit of selfishness and the multiplicity of interested views are of little improvement to real merit or virtue; yet there is a necessity for the preservation of virtue, that it should be thought to have no quarrel with true interest and self-enjoyment." (337) See Anthony Earl of Shaftesbury, *Characteristics of Men, Manners, Opinions, Times, etc.*, ed. John M. Robertson (Gloucester: Peter Smith, 1963), vol. 1, p. 274.
24 For more evidence in favour of this interpretation, see White, "Conscience"; Darwall, *Internal*, p. 265n38; Broad, *Five Types*, p. 80; A. E. Taylor, "Some Features of Butler's Ethics," in *Philosophical Studies*, pp. 321–9; Austin Duncan-Jones, *Butler's Moral Philosophy* (Harmondsworth: Penguin Books, 1952), pp. 113–15; and Terence Penelhum, *Butler* (London: Routledge & Kegan Paul, 1985), pp. 73–6. John Kleinig gives what may seem like the same interpretation. But at times he takes Butler to be distinguishing between what makes an action right and what makes performing an action justified to an agent. He sees self-interest as relevant to the latter but not the former. This differs from my interpretation and that of White (and others), according to which the rightness of an action makes performance justified, and self-interest enters strictly as a motive. See John Kleinig, "Butler in a Cool Hour," *Journal of the History of Philosophy* 7, 1969, pp. 399–411.

tional egoism. "[I]nterest, one's own happiness, is a manifest obligation. . . . Reasonable self-love and conscience are the chief or superior
principles in the nature of man, because an action may be suitable to
this nature, though all other principles be violated; but becomes unsuitable, if either of those are."[25] There are two issues here: whether Butler
believes in the "dualism of practical reason," as Sidgwick thinks, and
whether Butler has a good argument in favour of the authority of self-
love.

In many places, Butler claims that conscience is supreme. It has
"authority over all the rest, and claims the absolute direction of them
all."[26] His assertion that one's own happiness is "a manifest obligation"
does not conflict with this claim, for he holds that conscience demands
that we pursue our own happiness.[27]

Sidgwick's final passage is more difficult. There Butler seems to give
self-love a veto over conscience: An action is unsuitable should either
conscience or self-love oppose it. Broad thinks this is "simply an inconsistency."[28] But there is an alternative. Butler follows the quoted sentence by writing that "[c]onscience and self-love, if we understand our
true happiness, always lead us the same way."[29] He does not, then,
intend to give self-love a veto that can be exercised. Rather, he is sum-
marising two earlier claims: (a) conscience aside, following a particular
passion condemned by self-love is unsuitable; and (b) following a particular passion condemned by conscience is unsuitable. These two cases
are the reference of Butler's "if either [are violated]." He is illustrating
the point that some principles "are in nature and kind superior to
others."[30] If so, nothing follows about a case where self-love and conscience conflict; in particular, it does not follow that an action would be
unsuitable were conscience to recommend and self-love to condemn
it.[31]

Admittedly, this interpretation is strained, but it seems the best way
to save Butler's repeated insistence that conscience is supreme. The

---

25 Butler, *Sermons*, pref. 26, 3.9. Sidgwick notes pref. 26 at *ME* xiii, xx, 7, 386, *O* 199. He
    notes 3.9 at *ME* xiii, xx, 206, SE 411, UG 31, *O* 196.
26 Ibid., pref. 24; also pref. 25, 2.8, 2.13–15, 3.5.
27 Butler, *Sermons*, pref. 39, 12.14–19; "A Dissertation of the Nature of Virtue," in *Works*,
    vol. 2, paragraphs 6–7. See ME 176n, 327, 366; and Taylor, "Some Features," pp. 308–
    9.
28 Broad, *Five Types*, p. 80.
29 Butler, *Sermons*, 3.9; also 1.4, 1.6, 3.8.
30 Ibid., 3.9.
31 For this interpretation, see White, "Conscience," pp. 332–3.

alternatives are unpalatable. Some argue – implausibly – that self-love and conscience are identical or that conscience adds nothing to self-love.[32] Sidgwick tries a different gambit. He attempts to reconcile his dualist reading with the supremacy of conscience by arguing that Butler takes conscience to have "practical" supremacy: "A man knows certainly, [Butler] says, what he ought to do: but he does not certainly know what will lead to his happiness." (*ME* 200) Sidgwick is relying on Butler's claim that

> the natural authority of the principle of reflection is an obligation the most near and intimate, the most certain and known; whereas the contrary obligation [on the side of interest] can at the utmost appear no more than probable, since no man can be *certain* in any circumstances that vice is his interest in the present world, much less can he be certain against another; and thus the certain obligation would entirely supersede and destroy the uncertain one.[33]

Conscience is supreme, not because it has greater authority than self-love, but because its instructions are known more certainly than those of self-love. The problem is that this does not appear to be *Butler's* argument for, or understanding of, the supremacy of conscience. Butler offers the epistemic argument to one who thinks self-love and conscience have equal authority and conflict. It is premised on thinking that an "obligation from . . . interest on the side of vice remain[s]," even in the face of conscience.[34] This is surely not Butler's own argument for, or understanding of, the supremacy of conscience, which is put consistently in terms of the supreme authority or "right" of conscience.[35] When arguing from his own premises, Butler does not seem to make the supremacy of conscience conditional on our greater certainty of its pronouncements. It is, instead, conditional on the "claim" of conscience

---

32 T. H. McPherson, "The Development of Bishop Butler's Ethics," *Philosophy* 23, 1948, pp. 317–31 and 24, 1949, pp. 3-22; Nicholas L. Sturgeon, "Nature and Conscience in Butler's Ethics," *Philosophical Review* 85, 1976, pp. 316–56. McPherson – who gives a rational egoist interpretation of the *Sermons* but not the *Analogy* – is well-criticised by White, "Conscience"; Kleinig, "Cool Hour"; and Raphael, "Bishop Butler's View of Conscience," *Philosophy* 24, 1949, pp. 236–7. Sturgeon is well-criticised by Penelhum, *Butler*, pp. 61–70, and Darwall, *Internal*, pp. 249–61. (Hayward also takes Butler to be a rational egoist: See *Ethical Philosophy*, pp. 7–8, 35–6, 44, 123n1, 124.)

33 Butler, *Sermons*, pref. 26.

34 Ibid., pref. 26.

35 Ibid., 2.14, 2.15.

to be superior, combined with (I shall argue) a theological guarantee that the claim is genuine.[36]

I conclude that Butler is probably best read, not as a dualist or rational egoist, but as giving conscience supremacy (in both theory and practice).

Now consider whether Butler has a good argument in favour of the authority of self-love. In the course of explaining the notion of "natural supremacy" or "authority," he asks one to suppose

> a brute creature by any bait to be allured into a snare by which he is destroyed. He plainly followed the bent of his nature, leading him to gratify his appetite; there is an entire correspondence between his whole nature and such an action – such an action therefore is natural. But suppose a man, foreseeing the same danger of certain ruin, should rush into it for the sake of a present gratification; he in this instance would follow his strongest desire, as did the brute creature, but there would be [a] manifest . . . disproportion between the nature of a man and such an action. . . . Now what is it which renders such a rash action unnatural? Is it that he went against the principle of reasonable and cool self-love considered *merely* as a part of his nature? No; for if he had acted the contrary way, he would equally have gone against a principle or part of his nature, namely, passion or appetite. . . . [I]t necessarily follows that there must be some other difference or distinction to be made between these two principles, passion and cool self-love, than what I have yet taken notice of. And this difference, not being a difference in strength or degree, I call a difference in *nature* and in *kind*. And since, in the instance still before us, if passion prevails over self-love, the consequent action is unnatural; but if self-love prevails over passion, the action is natural; it is manifest that self-love is in human nature a superior principle to passion. . . . [I]f we will act conformably to the economy of man's nature, reasonable self-love must govern.[37]

It is, presumably, with this argument in mind that Sidgwick comments that "it is upon [its] generality and comprehensiveness that the 'authority' and 'reasonableness' attributed to Self-love in Butler's system are founded." (*ME* 93)

Butler offers this argument "without particular consideration of conscience." He is trying to show that there is "natural superiority, quite

---

36 Ibid., pref. 24, 2.8, 2.14, 3.5. For a similar reply to Sidgwick, see Kleinig, "Cool Hour," pp. 403–4.
37 Butler, *Sermons*, 2.10–11.

distinct from degrees of strength and prevalency."[38] This forestalls anyone who rejects Butler's claim that conscience has authority by rejecting
the notion of authority itself. But since conscience is put aside, the
argument cannot show that self-love and conscience have equal authority. For all that Butler has said, it may be that we find any action resulting from the prevalence of self-love over conscience unnatural.

Butler is not keen on such a case. As noted above, he does not think
self-love and conscience conflict. But, this aside, perhaps one can con-
struct an argument for the equality of conscience and self-love that
parallels the argument for the superiority of self-love over particular
passions. Butler thinks it natural for the animal to follow the particular
passion because he assumes the animal contains no further principle
judging the pursuit of the particular passions. It is unnatural for a
person to follow the particular passion because persons contain a further principle, self-love, that does judge such pursuit. An action is unnatural when it is condemned by a principle the agent contains. People,
however, have two principles that play the same roles – both self-love
and conscience judge the pursuit of the particular passions and each
other. For an action to be natural, then, it must not be condemned by
either self-love or conscience. Provided there is no difference in the
roles of self-love and conscience, Butler has an argument for their
equality.

Butler must explain, however, why the judging roles of self-love and
conscience give them authority. A critic might admit that self-love condemns entering the trap, yet deny that self-love has authority. There are,
the critic might say, simply two principles that conflict; that one principle condemns the other does not by itself show that it is superior.

Butler could give two replies. (Since Reid makes the same replies, I
reserve some discussion of them for later.) Butler might argue that he
does not rely on the judging role of self-love. Instead, he relies on our
agreement with its judgements. I do not think this would be Butler's
defence: It makes no use of the distinction between the principles found
in the animal and in the person, upon which the initial argument turns.
But if it were, the argument for the authority of self-love would be
endangered. For we might well approve of acting on a particular passion, even when doing so is condemned by self-love. Suppose the particular passion of benevolence leads me to "certain ruin" in an attempt

38 Ibid., 2.11.

122

to help someone I love or a large number of people.[39] Many will side with benevolence. Butler might reply that benevolence is approved here only because it is approved by the other judging principle, conscience. But even those who deny the authority of conscience might approve of benevolence. And if conscience *is* responsible for the approval of benevolence over self-love, the case for the equality of self-love and conscience, based on our approvals, has been lost. Conscience has been made superior, at least in this instance.

It is more likely that Butler takes the judging roles of self-love and conscience to be evidence of God's design. We, unlike the animal, find ourselves with two principles that judge both particular passions and each other. God would not have given us these principles unless He intended us to follow them:

> [E]very particular thing . . . is for some use or purpose out of and beyond itself.

> If the real nature of any creature leads him and is adapted to such and such purposes only, or more than to any other, this is a reason to believe the Author of that nature intended it for those purposes.

> Every one of our passions and affections hath its natural stint and bound.[40]

Thus the presence of self-love is an "indicatio[n] . . . that we were intended to take care of our own life and health," just as conscience "was placed within to be our proper governor," as "the guide assigned us by the Author of our nature."[41] The authority of self-love and conscience derives from God, and their equal authority from their similar roles.

---

39 Butler usually treats benevolence as a particular passion – a passion whose object is external to one's self. Just as the object of hunger is food, the object of benevolence is the happiness of others. (*Sermons*, pref. 39, 1.6, 3.8, 11.11–13, 11.16–19) On occasion, he seems to treat benevolence as a principle of the same sort as self-love. (For a list of passages, with discussion, see Raphael, "View," pp. 237–8.) If the latter reading were adopted, I could replace benevolence, in my example, with compassion, or love of society, or love of one's neighbour, all of which Butler views unequivocally as particular passions. (pref. 35, 3.8, 5.2, 6.3, 6.6; 1.7; 11.7, 11.11, 11.16, 11.17)

40 Butler, *Sermons*, pref. 14, 2.1, 11.9.

41 Ibid., 1.5, 2.15, 3.5. See also 1.6–9, 1.15; and, for this interpretation, Alan Millar, "Following Nature," *Philosophical Quarterly* 38, 1988, pp. 165–85; Wendell O'Brien, "Butler and the Authority of Conscience," *History of Philosophy Quarterly* 8, 1991, pp. 43–57. Butler's teleology is even clearer when he considers resentment and compassion. See *Sermons*, 8.1, 8.3, 8.6, 8.8, 8.13–14, 8.17, 9.1, 9.6–9. 5.1, 6.1, 6.3, 6.6.

This construal of Butler's argument, however, could not appeal to Sidgwick or any secular theorist. When considering Reid, I shall consider whether evolution might successfully replace God.

4.5 Hume

Sidgwick writes that in the *Treatise* Hume "agrees broadly with Hobbes as to the original connection of Justice with Self-interest." The *Enquiry* concurs: There, "the sphere of justice [is] limited by its indirect relation to self-interest, – e.g. [Hume] expressly says that we should not, properly speaking, lie under any restraint of justice with regard to rational beings who were so much weaker than ourselves that we had no reason to fear their resentment." (*O* 205–6n) This suggests that Sidgwick sees Hume as a veto egoist with respect to justice. Later he notes that Hume recognises no "'obligation' to virtue, except that of the agent's interest or happiness. He attempts . . . to show, in a summary way, that all the duties which his theory of morals recommends are also 'the true interest of the individual.'" (*O* 212) This suggests that Sidgwick sees Hume as a veto egoist with respect to all the virtues. I shall argue that Hume is not, and has no reason to be, a veto egoist. I take the cited passages in turn.

The weaker beings passage runs as follows:

> Were there a species of creatures intermingled with men, which, though rational, were possessed of such inferior strength, both of body and mind, that they were incapable of all resistance, and could never, upon the highest provocation, make us feel the effects of their resentment; the necessary consequence, I think, is that we should be bound by the laws of humanity to give gentle usage to these creatures, but should not, properly speaking, lie under any restraint of justice with regard to them, nor could they possess any right or property, exclusive of such arbitrary lords. . . . [A]s no inconvenience ever results from the exercise of a power, so firmly established in nature, the restraints of justice and property, being totally *useless*, would never have place in so unequal a confederacy.[42]

Sidgwick, along with many others, takes the passage to support veto egoism. Justice should not be introduced because doing so would not profit both parties. In particular, it would not profit the superior party.[43]

42 Hume, *Enquiry Concerning Morals*, pp. 190–1.
43 For other examples of the veto egoist interpretation, see James Balfour, *A Delineation of the Nature and Obligation of Morality, with Reflexions upon Mr. Hume's Book, intitled,*

There is, however, reason to think that Hume would reject the claim that justice ought to be introduced only where it is mutually advantageous. Hume notes that we approve of virtuous acts performed "in very distant ages and remote countries" and where we "never so much as enquire in what age and country the person lived."[44] We approve of qualities useful to their possessors, such as discretion and riches, without considering whether we gain anything from them.[45] We even approve of virtuous acts performed "by an adversary," although the consequences of the virtuous act "may be acknowledged prejudicial to our particular interest."[46] In all these cases, our approvals outstrip our self-love. Hume concludes that our approvals are explained by a "fellow-feeling with others" and that this fellow-feeling is "one great source of moral distinctions."[47] Given this, it would be surprising if Hume were to say that mutual advantage is needed for justice to be properly endorsed. That we might, for example, be hurt by treating animals better should not prevent us from approving of better treatment for animals, given that our approvals are not tied to our self-love in other cases.

The point can be put differently. According to the interpretation of Hume given in 2.2, a systematisation of our approvals is not simply part of a psychological investigation. Our approvals establish the correct normative principles. Since our approvals outstrip self-love, rational egoism cannot, for Hume, be the correct normative theory.

The oddity of insisting on mutual advantage as necessary for introducing justice can be seen in another way. When Hume reflects on his overall project, he supposes that justice is approved (even "solely") because of its usefulness to others.[48] If so, the textually preferable interpretation will take him to be arguing that, because justice is not useful to others, it ought not to be introduced.

Hume writes that, when inferior creatures are intermingled with

An Inquiry concerning the Principles of Morals (Edinburgh: 1753), p. 46; Reid, *Active Powers*, p. 660; Barry, *Theories*, pp. 161–2; and David Gauthier, "David Hume, Contractarian," *Philosophical Review* 89, 1979, pp. 19–21.

44 Hume, *Enquiry Concerning Morals*, pp. 215–6; also pp. 218, 219, 230, 273, 274, and *Treatise*, p. 499.

45 Hume, *Enquiry Concerning Morals*, pp. 234, 243–4, 246.

46 Hume, *Enquiry Concerning Morals*, p. 216; also pp. 217, 218, 219, and *Treatise*, pp. 582–3.

47 Hume, *Enquiry Concerning Morals*, pp. 219n, 218.

48 Ibid., p. 277; also pp. 269, 280–2. At p. 238, Hume notes that "*[h]onesty, fidelity, truth*" are also praised because they are useful to their possessor, but he sees this as derivative from their usefulness to others.

superior ones, it is a "necessary consequence" that the inferior be given "gentle usage." The point seems to be that humanity, rather than justice, is approved here. Elsewhere, when considering relations between un-equals, Hume consistently notes the importance of virtues such as "Generosity, Humanity, Affability, and Charity," but not justice.[49] This preference for humanity requires defence. The controversial passage does not explain: It states only that humanity rather than justice applies between superior and inferior. I suggest that Hume is thinking of justice as precisely that virtue that sometimes stands in the way of humanity. Elsewhere, Hume stresses its "inflexible" nature and blindness to "the characters, situations, and connexions of the person concerned, or any particular consequences which may result." With justice, "it is impossi-ble . . . to prevent all particular hardships, or make beneficial conse-quences result from every individual case."[50] Justice requires that "a profligate debauchee," who "wou'd rather receive harm than benefit from large possessions," be given those possessions anyway.[51] Justice "put[s] into the hands of the vicious the means of harming both them-selves and others."[52] In these cases, Hume holds that in the long term, humanity is served by permitting people to "combine"; any arrange-ment other than justice would not suffice to keep the combination to-gether.[53] But no such arrangement is necessary in the case of inferior creatures. When my dog reduces his bone to a stump he can easily swallow or picks up a razor blade on the street, I do not suppose that we should leave him with it, on the ground that this is humane in the long run because it is needed to maintain the combination of canine and human. In order to combine with inferior creatures, justice is not needed, since the inferior creatures cannot tear apart the combination should they dislike what we do. This is not an egoist thought: The point is not that justice is misplaced because it fails to advantage both parties, but rather that nothing so insensitive to the particularities of the case as justice is needed for the parties to combine. Suppose my dog continued

49 Hume, *Essays*, p. 546; also pp. 132–3, 383–6, 397.
50 Hume, *Enquiry Concerning Morals*, p. 305. Thus Barry notes, in contrasting humanity and justice, that "the crucial characteristic of justice is that the obligation to make the transfers required by it does not depend upon the use made of them by the recip-ient." See Brian Barry, "Humanity and Justice in Global Perspective," in *Nomos XXIV: Ethics, Economics, and the Law*, ed. J. R. Pennock and J. W. Chapman (New York: New York University Press, 1982), p. 248.
51 Hume, *Treatise*, p. 482.
52 Hume, *Treatise*, p. 579; also p. 532, and *Enquiry Concerning Morals*, p. 305.
53 Hume, *Enquiry Concerning Morals*, p. 307, also *Treatise*, p. 532.

to swallow stumpy bones and razor blades, but gained sufficient strength to become my equal. In this case, I could not so easily help him by taking the bone, since he could resist. Justice might well enter, to prevent endless fighting – but it would enter as second best. It would be better for my dog were I able to give and take the bone as circumstances dictate. It is this freedom to decide on a case-by-case basis that separates humanity from justice.

The defence of Hume's preference for humanity has proceeded by arguing that the superior may be able to help the inferior more by means other than rigidly respecting property rights. This is especially true in the case Hume considers, in which superior and inferior are "intermingled." Suppose Stronger (S) and Weaker (W) begin with equal and legitimate holdings. S soon improves his holdings, so that in any competition for customers between S and W, S wins. In time, W is broke. Humean justice does nothing to help W, but humanity would – by, for example, giving aid to W or by putting restrictions on the ways in which S might employ W.

I conclude that the weaker creatures passage is most plausibly inter-preted in a way that does not support Sidgwick's attribution of veto egoism.

The second egoistic passages noted by Sidgwick run as follows:

> Having explained the moral *approbation* attending merit or virtue, there remains nothing but briefly to consider our interested *obligation* to it, and to inquire whether every man, who has any regard to his own happiness and welfare, will not best find his account in the practice of every moral duty.

> [W]hat theory of morals can ever serve any useful purpose, unless it can show, by a particular detail, that all the duties which it recommends, are also the true interest of each individual?[54]

These passages suggest veto egoism.[55] And again, the passages are surprising in the context of the *Enquiry:* In addition to arguing against an egoistic explanation of our approvals, Hume has, directly before the passages, claimed that we must take up the general viewpoint and

---

54 Hume, *Enquiry Concerning Morals*, pp. 278, 280.
55 Again, Sidgwick is not alone in thinking this. See Frankena, "Concepts of Rational Action" p. 188; Nicholas Capaldi, *Hume's Place in Moral Philosophy* (New York: Peter Lang, 1989), pp. 256, 260; Christine Korsgaard, *The Sources of Normativity* (New York: Cambridge University Press, 1996), pp. 55–66.

explained how the sentiment of humanity can overcome self-love.[56] The passages require explanation.

I think the best explanation comes from comparing Hume and Butler in the cool hour passage. Like Hume, Butler rejects psychological egoism yet seems to suggest rational egoism. In Butler's case, the best interpretation is that showing virtue pays is useful but strictly unnecessary, in the sense that failure to show that virtue pays would not change what Butler takes to be our obligations. The same is true of Hume. After first noting the turn to considering "interested obligation," Hume writes that, if virtue pays, "we shall have the satisfaction to reflect, that we have advanced principles, which . . . may contribute to the amendment of men's lives, and their improvement in morality and social virtue."[57] Before claiming that any theory of morals must show that virtue pays, Hume asks "what hopes can we ever have of engaging mankind to a practice which we confess full of austerity and rigour?" Showing that virtue pays is needed for a theory to "ever serve any useful purpose."[58] Showing that virtue pays, then, is desirable because it would motivate many people to adopt the Humean virtues. It is not necessary, in that doing so is irrelevant to the correct account of the virtues. Hume supposes that, if it turns out that virtue does not pay, he would still have "advanced principles, which . . . will stand the test of reasoning and inquiry. . . . The philosophical truth of any proposition by no means depends on its tendency to promote the interests of society."[59] This is why he considers interested obligation "briefly," *after* confessing that "I cannot, *at present*, be more assured of any truth, which I learn from reasoning and argument, than that personal merit consists entirely in the usefulness or agreeableness of qualities to the person himself possessed of them, or to others, who have any intercourse with him."[60]

The *Treatise* shows the same pattern. Before arguing that Humean virtues "may interest every principle in our nature," Hume has concluded that "I am hopeful that nothing is wanting to an accurate proof of this system of ethics."[61] It is not necessary for "an accurate proof" to show that the possession of Humean virtues pays. Hume does go on to

---

56 Hume, *Enquiry Concerning Morals*, pp. 271–6.
57 Ibid., p. 279.
58 Ibid., p. 280.
59 Ibid., p. 279.
60 Ibid., p. 278.
61 Hume, *Treatise*, pp. 620, 618.

try to show that Humean virtue pays. But this attempt lies in a section that begins as follows: "Were it proper . . . to bribe the readers assent, or employ any thing but solid argument, we are here abundantly supplied with topics to engage the affections."[62] The demonstration of interested obligation is a "bribe" rather than solid argument. And it is a rather half-hearted bribe at that: After noting "that a mind will never be able to bear its own survey, that has been wanting in its part to mankind and society," Hume stops: "I forbear insisting on this subject. Such reflexions require a work a-part, very different from the genius of the present. The anatomist ought never to emulate the painter."[63] Again, it is unnecessary to show that virtue "interest[s] every principle of our nature."

It is true that those who "dig up the pestilence from the pit in which it is buried" show "a bad grace," and we will "sink them, at least, in eternal silence and oblivion." A theory "full of austerity and rigour" has no hope of "engaging mankind."[64] This explains why Hume turns to interested obligation soon after his attack on the "monkish virtues."[65] In context, the problematic passages are a rather hopeful overstatement of the vast difference between, on one side, the "engaging charms" and "play, frolic, and gaiety" of Humean virtue, and on the other, the "dismal dress" of "useless austerities and rigours, suffering and self-denial."[66] Hume is actually content with less than veto egoism to separate himself from the monks: "It is sufficient, if the whole plan or scheme be necessary to the support of civil society, and if the balance of good, in the main, do thereby preponderate much above that of evil."[67]

I turn to objections to the Butlerian interpretation. The objections rely on Hume's views concerning justice and the practicality of morality. In both cases, the worry is that other commitments require Hume to take his apparent statements of veto egoism at face value.

One might object that, since Hume holds that morality must be practical, showing that it engages us cannot be strictly unnecessary. With the added claim that we are often extremely partial to ourselves, our families, and our friends, this objection also suggests that at least *most* of our duties must lie within these interests, and so would put a check on the duties prescribed from the general survey.

---

62 Ibid., p. 619.
63 Ibid., p. 620.
64 Hume, *Enquiry Concerning Morals*, pp. 279, 280.
65 Ibid., p. 270.
66 Ibid., p. 279.
67 Ibid., p. 305.

Hume does write that moral speculations must "set in motion the active powers of men" and have an "influence on conduct and behaviour."[68] Yet, as some have noted, Hume does not think that morality often motivates more than speech-acts.[69] He is usually careful to claim that morality motivates only when other passions are silent.[70] And morality is usually practical by influencing our approbations and our resulting speech-acts. The "general survey" is often a method of correcting not our "stubborn" sentiments, but our "language" and "abstract notions."[71] Sympathy often serves "only to excite sentiments of complacency or censure."[72] Hume is content to conclude that "the principles of humanity . . . have *some* authority over our sentiments," that they "make some distinction" and are "sufficient, at least, for discourse, serv[ing] all our purposes in company, in the pulpit, on the theatre, and in the schools."[73] "Let these generous sentiments be supposed . . . insufficient to move even a hand or finger of our body, they must still direct the determination of our mind, and where everything else is equal, produce a cool preference of what is useful and serviceable to mankind."[74] The "accurate proof of this system of ethics," from which "nothing is wanting," shows that sympathy "has force sufficient to give us the strongest sentiments of approbation" and that sympathy "is the chief source of moral distinctions."[75] This sympathy "is too weak to countroul our Passions; but has sufficient Force to influence our Taste, and give us the Sentiments of Approbation or Blame."[76] It is because of this emphasis on approbation that Hume – unlike, say, Kavka – can "ente[r] not into that vulgar dispute concerning the *degrees* of benevolence or self-love, which prevail in human nature," where this dispute is understood to concern motivation.[77]

---

68   Ibid., p. 172; also pp. 274, 294, and *Treatise*, pp. 457–8, 462, 465.
69   Balfour complains that "virtue is represented as a subject of talk and declamation, but of very little force to influence the heart and life." (*Delineation*, p. 123) For a similar point put sympathetically, see Baier, *Progress*, pp. 183–5; and David Miller, *Philosophy and Ideology in Hume's Political Thought* (New York: Oxford University Press, 1981), pp. 42, 56.
70   See, for example, Hume, *Enquiry Concerning Morals*, pp. 226, 227, 230.
71   Hume, *Treatise*, pp. 582, 585, and *Enquiry Concerning Morals*, pp. 275–6.
72   Hume, *Enquiry Concerning Morals*, p. 234n; also *Treatise*, p. 586.
73   Hume, *Enquiry Concerning Morals*, pp. 226, 229; also *Treatise*, pp. 583, 603.
74   Hume, *Enquiry Concerning Morals*, p. 271.
75   Hume, *Treatise*, p. 618.
76   Ibid., p. 500, var. p. 670.
77   Hume, *Enquiry Concerning Morals*, p. 270.

Hume's practicality objection to rationalism, then, is not that the rationalist's reason fails to produce more than speech-acts. The moral sentiment often fails here as well. Rather, his objection is that this reason "is not alone sufficient to produce any moral blame or approbation," and so cannot even produce the speech-acts that sustain morality. Practicality, then, demands only that moral distinctions influence our approbations. This is the sense in which it must engage us. This is what is necessary. Now Hume argues at length that our approbations cannot be explained on grounds of self-love. Neither veto egoism nor the weaker requirement that most of our duties be in our self-interest is a constraint on moral approbation, and so both remain unnecessary.

Some critics suppose that Hume's apparent veto egoism is motivated, not by appeal to practicality, but by his account of the original motive to be just.[78] Hume does argue that *"self-interest is the original motive to the* establishment *of justice."*[79] But this does not motivate veto egoism. Hume aims to show that the original motivation to be just stems from post-convention self-interest, rather than from promise, a sense of duty, reason, public benevolence, private benevolence, preconvention self-interest, or instinct. To do this, he must show that post-convention self-interest explains what the rival explanations do not – "the manner, in which the rules of justice are established."[80] And to do this, he need not show that, as one critic puts it, post-convention self-interest "explain[s] how someone is motivated to be just on *every* occasion." He need not show "that the path of justice *all the time* is a 'wiser' path."[81] He need only show that the rival explanations fail and that his explanation would explain the establishment of justice – two claims the critics rarely attack.[82]

To show that post-convention self-interest does explain the establish-

---

78 See David Gauthier, "Artificial Virtues and the Sensible Knave," *Hume Studies* 18, 1993, pp. 401–28; Stroud, *Hume,* pp. 205–18; Gerald Postema, "Hume's Reply to the Sensible Knave," *History of Philosophy Quarterly* 5, 1988, pp. 23–5; Stephen Buckle, *Natural Law and the Theory of Property* (New York: Oxford University Press [Clarendon], 1991), pp. 291–5; Marcia Baron, "Hume's Noble Lie: An Account of His Artificial Virtues," *Canadian Journal of Philosophy* 12, 1982, pp. 539–55.
79 Hume, *Treatise,* p. 499.
80 Ibid., p. 484.
81 Stroud, *Hume,* pp. 210, 215; second italics added. See also pp. 208, 214.
82 Thus Baron admits that self-interest "frequently does explain our motivation." Stroud admits that "[i]t should not be supposed that there are many people" whose justice is not explained by self-interest, and that self-interest will "often" recommend justice. (Baron, "Lie," p. 547n9; Stroud, *Hume,* pp. 206, 207)

ment of justice, Hume might argue that, in the small societies in question, justice always pays.[83] Cheating would be hard, and perhaps Hume holds that, before later artifices change us, we would not be interested in cheating anyway. In larger societies, with artifices such as promises, cheating is possible and attractive for some. But here Hume does not rely on self-interest alone. He adds moral education.[84] If this interpretation is correct, one could allow that justice must pay in the initial societies, without allowing that it must pay in any later societies.[85] But Hume need not say even this. For even if some *always* profit from injustice, it does not follow that justice will not be established. Those who do not profit from injustice could establish it, and those who gain from cheating will help, wherever helping is needed to keep the system intact. Hume need not show that everyone has a motive to be just to show that justice will be established.[86]

This defence of Hume would fail if, as one critic supposes, "the same reasoning which led Hume to deny that there is a natural motive to act justly forces him to reject his account of justice as an artificial virtue." The reasoning noted proceeds by showing that the motive up for evaluation "will not always direct us to act justly."[87] But this is wrong. For Hume does not show the superiority of his artifice account simply by showing that, for each rival account, there are possible cases in which no motive is to be found. This is *one* of his reasons for rejecting public benevolence.[88] (It is not the reason emphasised later, when the stress is on the uselessness of justice given public benevolence.[89]) He rejects promises, instinct, duty, and reason without relying on the possible case argument.[90] Pre-convention benevolence, private benevolence, and pre-convention or unrestrained self-interest are rejected, not because they

83 Hume, *Treatise*, p. 499.
84 Ibid., pp. 499–501.
85 For the effect of later artifices on our interests, see Annette Baier, *Progress*, pp. 235–6, 246–8, and "Artificial Virtues and the Equally Sensible Nonknaves: A Response to Gauthier," in *Hume Studies* 18, 1993, pp. 429–40. For stress on moral education, see Frederick G. Whelan, *Order and Artifice in Hume's Political Philosophy* (Princeton, NJ: Princeton University Press, 1985), pp. 275–92.
86 For a similar interpretation, see Páll Árdal, *Passion and Value in Hume's Treatise* (Edinburgh: Edinburgh University Press, 1989), pp. 172, 182; and Mackie, *Theory*, p. 87.
87 Baron, "Lie," pp. 546, 541.
88 Hume, *Treatise*, p. 481.
89 Hume, *Treatise*, pp. 494–6, 529, and *Enquiry Concerning Morals*, pp. 184–5.
90 Hume, *Treatise*, p. 490; *Treatise*, pp. 527–9; *Enquiry Concerning Morals*, pp. 201–3; *Treatise*, pp. 477–80; *Treatise*, p. 496.

fail in a few cases, but because they fail "so often" and in "most" cases.[91] Thus Hume can retain his own account, even given a few cases in which injustice pays, without giving up his criticisms of rival accounts.

My interpretation has the advantage of explaining Hume's treatment of a popular objection. Many see the key text for the evaluation of Hume's account of justice to be the reply to the sensible knave, where Hume explicitly asks whether justice pays. Hume worries that "*honesty is the best policy,* may be a good general rule, but is liable to many exceptions; and he, it may perhaps be thought, conducts himself with most wisdom, who observes the general rule, and takes advantage of all the exceptions."[92] He goes on to give a much-criticised reply, stressing the pleasure of watching knaves get caught and, as in the *Treatise,* the superiority of "peaceful reflection on one's own conduct" to "worthless toys and gewgaws."[93] At best, this shows it to be false that *everyone* "conducts himself with most wisdom" through knavery, since the honest would not. It shows the honest that they should not convert to knavery rather than showing the knave that he should convert to honesty.[94] The point is to "fortify that [honest] temper and furnish it with views, by which it may entertain and nourish itself."[95] And so the critics conclude that the account of the original motive to be just either fails or needs a "noble lie." The reply to the knave is part of a cover-up intended to discourage a "practice dangerous and pernicious."[96]

91 Hume, *Treatise,* pp. 483, 579, *Enquiry Concerning Morals,* pp. 306, 309n. For pre-convention benevolence, see Hume, *Treatise,* pp. 532, 579, *Enquiry Concerning Morals,* p. 306. For private benevolence, see Hume, *Treatise,* pp. 482–3, 532, *Enquiry Concerning Morals,* p. 309n. For pre-convention self-interest, see Hume, *Treatise,* pp. 497, 532, *Enquiry Concerning Morals,* p. 306. For unrestrained self-interest, see Hume, *Treatise,* p. 480.
92 Hume, *Enquiry Concerning Morals,* pp. 282–3.
93 Ibid., pp. 283–4. For criticisms of the reply to the knave, see, for example, David Gauthier, "Artificial Virtues," "David Hume, Contractarian," p. 26, and "Three Against Justice: The Foole, the Sensible Knave, and the Lydian Shepherd," *Midwest Studies in Philosophy* 7, 1982, p. 22; Postema, "Reply"; Stroud, *Hume,* pp. 215–16; Baron, "Lie," pp. 552–3; Barry, *Theories of Justice,* pp. 167–8; Donald T. Siebert, *The Moral Animus of David Hume* (Newark: University of Delaware Press, 1990), pp. 181–2; Whelan, *Order,* p. 266; and Hampton, "Two Faces," p. 40.
94 Hume's argument to show that humanity pays, given directly before the knave is introduced, has the same limitation. See Hume, *Enquiry Concerning Morals,* p. 281; and Butler, *Sermons,* XI.12–19, from which the argument is taken. For a similar view of the reply to the knave, see Baier, "Artificial Virtues"; and Michael J. Costa, "Why Be Just?: Hume's Response in the *Inquiry,*" *Southern Journal of Philosophy* 22, 1984, p. 471.
95 Hume, *Essays,* p. 177n.
96 Hume, *Enquiry Concerning Morals,* p. 279.

On my view, Hume need not give a convincing answer to the knave. Since showing that justice pays is a concession to "engaging," separate from justification, failure can be permitted. Massive failure is not permitted. But Hume can argue that, even if there are many knaves, there cannot be many of them practicing at any one time. Each must be careful to avoid the "considerable breach in the social union and confederacy" that would occur were too many "pushe[d] forward . . . by imitation" of successful knavery or were too many to adopt knavery to avoid being cullies of their integrity.[97] Hence most of the time, and for most people, self-interest is served by justice, even if these people are convinced that *"honesty is the best policy"* is "liable to many exceptions."[98]

Thus Hume treats the problem of replying to the knave "in a summary way." The knave's argument is "a little difficult" to rebut, *"if* a man think that this reasoning much requires an answer."[99] In "The Sceptic," after presenting another knave, Hume writes that

> [f]or my part, I know not how I should address myself to such a one, or by what arguments I should endeavour to reform him. Should I tell him of the inward satisfaction which results from laudable and humane actions, the delicate pleasure of disinterested love and friendship, the lasting enjoyments of a good name and an established character, he might still reply, that these were, perhaps, pleasures to such as were susceptible of them; but that, for his part, he finds himself of a quite different turn and disposition. I must repeat it; my philosophy affords no remedy in such a case.[100]

Hume even admits that "[s]ome extraordinary circumstances may happen, in which a man finds his interests to be more promoted by fraud or rapine, than hurt by the breach which his injustice makes in the social union."[101] Where Hume speaks of "a little difficulty," his critics see a crushing counter-example and a cover-up. But this hardly fits "The Sceptic," with its repeated avowals of failure. A more charitable explanation is that Hume supposes it is not so important to show that justice pays.

The critics might object that Hume still must convince the knave, in order to preserve his account of the original motive to be just. As one

---

97 Hume, *Enquiry Concerning Morals*, p. 282, *Treatise*, p. 535.
98 Hume, *Enquiry Concerning Morals*, p. 282.
99 Ibid., p. 283, italics added.
100 Hume, *Essays*, pp. 169–70.
101 Ibid., p. 38.

puts it, "[i]f the knave's challenge cannot be answered, Hume's project fails on its own criteria of success."[102] But Hume does not present the knave as an objection to his account of the original motive to be just. The knave comes at the end of a review of all the Humean virtues. The critics find Hume disingenuous for not noting that the knave undercuts the earlier account of the motive to be just. But if the earlier account is not jeopardised by stray cases in which injustice pays, this would explain why Hume does not make the connection between it and the knave.

I conclude that Hume should not be read as a veto egoist.[103]

4.6 Reid

Sidgwick notes that Reid takes "regard for one's good on the whole" as a "governing" and "rational" principle. (*O* 228) This is true. Reid wants to show three things concerning one's good on the whole: This good requires reason to be conceived; this good, when conceived, motivates; and this good is a "leading and governing" end that "ought" to govern.[104] Only the third claim helps establish veto egoism. In its support, Reid writes that

> [t]o prefer a greater good, though distant, to a less that is present; to choose a present evil, in order to avoid a greater evil, or to obtain a greater good, is, in the judgement of all men, wise and reasonable conduct; and when a man acts the contrary part, all men will acknowledge that he acts foolishly and unreasonably. . . . That . . . the rational principle ought to prevail, and the animal to be subordinate, is too evident to need, or to admit of proof. Thus . . . it appears, that to pursue what is good upon the whole, and to avoid what is ill upon the whole, is a rational principle of action grounded upon our constitution as reasonable creatures.[105]

Reid may seem to assert temporal irrelevance rather than any brand of normative egoism. But in the context, the references to good and evil are to one's own good and evil. Reid's point is that it is reasonable to prefer one's good on the whole to the satisfaction of the "animal principles"

102 Postema, "Reply," p. 23.
103 For further consideration of these passages, see my "Hume's Self-Interest Requirement," *Canadian Journal of Philosophy* 17, 1994, pp. 1-17, and (with Joyce Jenkins) "Mr. Hobbes Could Have Said No More," forthcoming in the Hume volume for Penn State's *Rereading the Canon* series, ed. Anne Jaap Jacobson.
104 Reid, *Active Powers*, p. 580; also p. 598.
105 Ibid., p. 581.

that "do not suppose any exercise of judgement or reason; and are most of them to be found in some brute animals, as well as in man."[106]

This argument is unsuccessful. It relies on "the judgement of all men." As noted against Butler, all do not find it reasonable to prefer their good on the whole to any animal principle. Consider various sacrifices of my good on the whole, each motivated by an animal principle: I risk or deprive myself to feed, help, or defend my mate, my children, my group, or the distressed.[107] Many find these choices reasonable. Reid himself notes that "[w]e cannot, without pleasure, observe the timid ewe, who never shewed the least degree of courage in her own defence, become valiant and intrepid in defence of her lamb, and boldly assault those enemies, the very sight of whom was wont to put her to flight."[108] Reid might reply that these choices are reasonable *qua* his second rational principle – that one ought to do one's duty – and not *qua* animal principle. This seems wrong: As Reid stresses, I might, like the ewe, make these sacrifices out of non-rational affection rather than duty.[109] Worse, the reply does not give Reid what he wants. He would hold the position most ascribe to Butler: The rational principle that I ought to do my duty overrules the rational principle that I ought to pursue my good on the whole.[110] Reid might object that we find these choices reasonable only because we think it is reasonable to do one's duty *and* think these choices are really for our good on the whole. Yet this is false: Many find these actions reasonable even when they believe their good on the whole to suffer.

Reid appears to deny this. Anyone acting against their good on the whole is a "fool." Every action for our good on the whole

> is accompanied with self-approbation and the approbation of mankind. The contrary actions are accompanied with shame and self-condemnation in the agent, and with contempt in the spectator, as foolish and unreasonable. . . . We cannot help disapproving the man that acts con-

---

106 Ibid., p. 551.
107 For parental affection, compassion, love between the sexes, and public spirit as animal principles, see ibid., pp. 560–4.
108 Ibid., p. 565.
109 Ibid., p. 561.
110 At one point, Reid seems to agree. He claims that only conscience has authority. But he immediately turns to discuss possible conflicts between our "two regulating or leading principles – a regard to what is best for us upon the whole, and a regard to duty." See ibid., pp. 597–8.

trary to [his own greatest good], as deserving to lose the good which he wantonly threw away.[111]

Reid is not thinking about conflicts between one's good on the whole and duty here; he is thinking of "wanton" imprudence, imprudence not intended to benefit anyone. The reason is that, like Butler, he supposes one's good on the whole and duty cannot conflict: "While the world is under a wise and benevolent administration, it is impossible that any man should, in the issue, be a loser by doing his duty."[112] This assumption undercuts my counter-examples and so vindicates egoism. But it is not a vindication to console Sidgwick, since he rejects the assumption.

At times, Reid suggests a different argument – the theological argument that Butler gives. In explaining why it is wrong to think that concern for duty should extinguish concern for one's good on the whole, he writes that "there is no active principle which God hath planted in our nature that is vicious in itself, or that ought to be eradicated. . . . They are all useful and necessary in our present state. The perfection of human nature consists, not in extinguishing, but in restraining them within their proper bounds."[113] *Any* active principle has some authority. Given the theological assumption, this is a plausible defence against one who wants concern for duty to replace other concerns. It does not, however, privilege the concern for one's own good on the whole over animal principles. To do this, Reid appeals to our design rather than to our agreement about our design. Although his argument concerns conscience rather than one's good on the whole, he must intend it for the latter as well.

The argument would run as follows. Our various parts are "in-

---

111 Ibid., pp. 598, 584, 638.
112 Ibid., p. 598. This is a very standard refrain. To cite but three other examples: John Clarke notes that it "would have been . . . downright Cruelty" and "a barbarous piece of Tyranny" for God "to have enjoyned Men to adhere to Virtue in all Times, and in all Cases, even where it would expose them to the greatest Sufferings and Misery, without proposing to reward them hereafter for it." (Clarke, *Foundation*, pp. 18–19; also pp. 30–1) Stewart writes that "I never could conceive that an all-wise, just, and benevolent Being would . . . make that to be our duty which is not, upon the whole, and generally speaking, (even without consideration of a future state) our interest likewise." (quoted in Frankena, "History of Ethical Dualism," p. 189) The Unitarian Thomas Belsham agrees: "It is incredible that, under the government of God, any of his creatures should be ultimately losers by any sacrifice which they can make to the happiness of others." (quoted in Schneewind, *Victorian*, p. 128)
113 Reid, *Active Powers*, p. 598.

tended" to achieve specific ends. Our hearts, for example, are intended to circulate blood. The point is not merely that circulating blood is one beneficial effect of having a heart. Hearts may have other beneficial effects that are not part of their intention – perhaps cannibals find them particularly tasty. Circulating blood is the intention because circulating blood, not tasting good, forms part of the explanation of why we have hearts and of why they have the properties they do. Similarly, our concern for our good on the whole is intended to govern our animal principles. Our concern for our good on the whole naturally judges our animal principles. And we suppose judging our animal principles forms part of the explanation of why we have a concern for our good on the whole and of why this concern has the properties it does.[114]

This argument can take both theological and secular forms, in two ways. First, one might wonder how circulating blood forms part of the explanation of why we have hearts and of why they have the properties they do. This is important to establish, since Reid wants a particular role for one's good on the whole to be vindicated. It is the *governing* role that must be vindicated, rather than simply any effects whatever of having concern for one's good on the whole. One explanation cites God's design: God decided that we should survive, in part, through circulating blood and chose hearts as the means of circulation. Another explanation is evolutionary: crudely, random mutation creates various arrangements; those arranged to survive, in part, by circulating blood by means of hearts have survived and reproduced; those with alternative arrangements have not. Similarly, governing animal principles can form part of the explanation of why we have concern for our good on the whole and why this concern has the properties it does, in two ways. God decided that we should survive and prosper, in part, through governed animal principles and chose concern for one's good on the whole as the means of government. Or perhaps those with ungoverned animal principles, or animal principles badly governed by other means, have not survived to reproduce.

Second, suppose one admits that hearts are intended to circulate blood, but does not see why this makes hearts good. This challenge could be met by arguing that God designed us and is good. It could also be met by noting the benefits of circulating blood. Similarly, one might admit that concern for one's good on the whole is intended to govern animal principles, but ask why this shows that concern for one's good on the whole has authority. The challenge could be met by arguing that

114 Ibid., pp. 543, 597.

God designed us and is good or by noting the benefits of governed animal principles.

I shall leave aside the theological readings. They could not appeal to Sidgwick. But nor should the secular versions. Consider the proposed evolutionary explanation. For the sake of argument, grant that governed animal principles increase the chances of survival and that the capacity for governing animal principles can be inherited. It does not follow that the government must be either constant or exercised by concern for one's good on the whole. One can survive, and even prosper, with a great deal of imprudence – particularly if one need only survive long enough to reproduce. And imprudent animal principles can often be restrained by rival animal principles or, as Reid notes, by duty.[115] Reid even holds that "the happy man . . . is not he whose happiness is his only care, but he who, with perfect resignation, leaves the care of his happiness to him who made him, while he pursues with ardour the road of his duty."[116] Although concern for one's good on the whole should govern animal principles, it should not be consulted: Duty is the active governor.

The same point could be made concerning the benefits brought by governed animal principles: The governing need not be performed by concern for one's good on the whole. Here, however, this objection is insufficient, for one might hold, against Reid, that I will benefit most by letting my concern for my good on the whole be the active governor. This is particularly plausible if one gives God no role. Grant, then, that any challenge to the authority of my good on the whole is to be met by noting that concern with this good brings me the greatest benefits. The problem is that this presupposes, rather than establishes, veto egoism. A challenge to the authority of my good on the whole from, say, duty is not rebutted by noting that doing my duty does not benefit me; that duty must always benefit me is what needs to be argued. Here Reid could fall back on his appeal to agreement – but that argument is unsatisfactory.

Although Reid's arguments fail, this does not hurt what may be his main project. Both directly before and during the discussion of one's good on the whole, Reid notes that some, and Hume in particular, "think it no part of the office of reason to determine the ends we ought to pursue."[117] Reid disagrees. The quoted part of his treatment of one's

115 Ibid., p. 584.
116 Ibid., p. 586.
117 Ibid., pp. 580, 581.

good on the whole reads like an attack on Hume: we *do* think some preferences are reasonable and some unreasonable. My criticisms do not endanger this conclusion, for they attack only the specific end Reid finds reasonable. They are compatible with concluding, against Hume, that one who sacrifices a greater to a lesser good for himself, with no counterbalancing gain to others, acts unreasonably or that one who thinks the time at which a good comes is by itself relevant to its worth is unreasonable.

This does not exhaust Reid's discussion of one's good on the whole. For he repeats that "[w]e ought to prefer a greater good, though more distant, to a less; and a less evil to a greater," not as a rational principle distinct from duty, but rather as one of the self-evident first principles of morals. For defence, he refers one to his epistemic tests.[118] A proposition p is a self-evident first principle requiring no further proof if (1) propositions that contradict p are absurd or have absurd consequences; (2) p has "the consent of ages and nations"; (3) we believe p "before we could reason, and before we could learn it by instruction"; (4) p is "so necessary in the conduct of life, that without the belief of it, a man must be led into a thousand absurdities in practice."[119] Although he does not explicitly apply these tests to the proposition that we ought to prefer our good on the whole, the considerations noted above can be seen as applications of some of these tests. Reid might think it absurd, as in test (1), to prefer an animal passion to one's good on the whole. The appeal to agreement is test (2). But Reid cannot derive support from test (3): He stresses that the preference for one's good on the whole requires that reason "is so far advanced that [one] can seriously reflect upon the past, and take a prospect of the future part of his existence."[120] Whether test (4) helps is unclear: Reid might think that acting on an animal passion against one's good on the whole is a practical absurdity – yet since he thinks we should in practice appeal to our duty, rather than our good on the whole, the proposition that one ought to prefer one's own good does not seem necessary for practice at all.

I leave aside the question of why the proposition is a principle of morals as well as a non-moral rational principle. Reid does not offer separate arguments for the principle in its moral guise.[121] Instead, he

---

118 Reid, *Active Powers*, p. 637, also *Intellectual Powers*, p. 480.
119 Reid, *Intellectual Powers*, pp. 439–41, 233–4.
120 Reid, *Active Powers*, p. 581.
121 Reid perhaps implies that concern for our good on the whole acquires its status as a first moral principle in the same way as it becomes a rational principle: "A regard to

refers to the epistemic tests, which apply in both moral and non-moral cases. I have argued that the proposition does not pass the consent and absurdity tests and that Reid believes it does only because he believes one's good on the whole and duty can never conflict. Like Sidgwick, Reid notes that consent does not count in favour of a proposition when "we can show some prejudice, as universal as that consent is, which might be the cause of it."[122] The belief that God makes conflict between one's good on the whole and duty impossible seems an excellent candidate for such a prejudice. Reid notes of his first principles that "the best moral reasonings of authors I am acquainted with [are] grounded upon one or more of them."[123] That we would now not make this claim, where the principle at issue is that one ought to prefer one's good on the whole, attests to the power of the idea that God makes one's good on the whole and duty coincide. When the idea goes, so in many cases does the principle.

(The role of God can be stressed in another way, by considering a contemporary example. Samuel Scheffler looks for a rationale for "agent-centred prerogatives" – roughly, Broad's compromise theory. He notes that since, like Broad, he does not say how much one may favour one's own interests, rational egoism could be construed as one version of an agent-centred prerogative theory.[124] He also notes that the rationale for agent-centred prerogatives is not meant to rest on the intuition that utilitarianism is too demanding.[125] The rationale runs as follows: My personal point of view is "independent," in that I *"naturally"* give more weight to my interests than an impersonal, utilitarian point of view would dictate;

> if, as Rawls has said, "the correct regulative principle for anything depends on the nature of that thing," we must surely reject any regulative principle for persons which ignores the independence of the personal point of view. To have an independent point of view is part of the nature of a person if anything is. [Thus] there is . . . a motivation for an agent-centred prerogative. . . . [f]or by incorporating a plausible prerogative which allows agents to devote energy and attention to their projects and

our own good, though we had no conscience, dictates this principle," since we disapprove of those who sacrifice their good on the whole. For the majority of his discussion, he stresses that prudence supports every moral duty and that "its force is felt by the most ignorant, and even by the most abandoned." See ibid., p. 638.

122 Reid, *Intellectual Powers*, p. 233; also p. 440.
123 Reid, *Active Powers*, p. 640.
124 Scheffler, *Rejection*, p. 69.
125 Ibid., pp. 52–5, 112.

commitments *out of* proportion to the weight from the impersonal standpoint of their doing so, hybrid theories recognize and mirror the independence of the personal point of view.[126]

Scheffler goes on to consider how utilitarians might "recognize and
mirror" or "make a rational response to" the independence of the personal point of view.[127] But the real issue is elsewhere. Scheffler infers
that the independence of the personal point of view needs to be recognised and mirrored by claiming that it is "natural" or part of "the nature
of a person." If "the nature of a person" simply denotes truths about us,
then it is unclear why these truths need to be recognised and mirrored
in a moral theory – a rational response to our thoughtless cruelty would
be condemnation, not approval. Perhaps "the nature of a person"
denotes *essential* truths about us, and thoughtless cruelty is not an essential trait – although Scheffler offers no argument to this effect, and
admits that one *can,* though we do not "typically," take up the impersonal point of view.[128] Still, it remains unclear why even essential traits
ought not to be attacked by education or channelled into better direc-
tions rather than recognised and mirrored. The point is that Scheffler's
appeal to our natures carries no normative significance without further
argument. Butler and Reid give the further argument – but they appeal
to God, not Rawls.[129])

4.7 Kant

Sidgwick writes that in his account of the Highest Good, Kant

recognises by implication the reasonableness of the individual's regard
for his private happiness: only, in Kant's view, it is not happiness simply

126 Ibid., pp. 56, 57–8. Elsewhere, Scheffler writes that he "takes account of the natural
independence of the personal point of view precisely by granting it moral independence. . . . [A] moral view gives sufficient weight to ['the natural fact of personal
independence'] only if it *reflects* it. . . . [A]gent-centred prerogative[s] give more
weight than consequentialism does to the nature of a person as a being with a
naturally independent point of view." (pp. 62, 64) For further mention of the natu-
ralness of the independence, see pp. 67, 79, 92, 113, 125.
127 For the latter formulation, see ibid., pp. 64–5, 67, 79, 92, 98, 113.
128 Ibid., p. 62; pp. 21–2, 96–7.
129 For this strategy against appeals to nature, see ME 80–3; and, especially, Mill,
"Nature," in *Collected Works,* vol. 10. Mill adds that God does not help: If God is
benevolent, he is obviously not omnipotent, given the state of the world, and so one
cannot read God's intentions off the world. For a similar objection to Scheffler, see
Kagan, "Consequentialism," p. 253.

which a truly reasonable self-love seeks, but happiness under the condition of being morally worthy of it. Though duty is to be done for duty's sake, and not as a means to the agent's happiness, still, Kant holds, we could not rationally do it if we did not hope thereby to attain happiness: since the highest good for man is neither virtue nor happiness alone, but a moral world in which happiness is duly proportioned to merit. And Kant holds that we are bound by reason to conceive ourselves as necessarily belonging to such a world under the government of a wise author and ruler; since without such a world, 'the glorious ideas of morality would be indeed objects of applause and admiration, but not springs of purpose and action.' (*O* 276)

Even in Kant, Sidgwick finds support for veto egoism.

He should not. It is true that, in the passage Sidgwick quotes, Kant seems to claim that we cannot do our duty without the hope of happiness.[130] This would make Kant resemble Hobbes. Kant seems to make this claim in various places. A virtuous atheist will find it hard "to continue to adhere to the call of his own inner moral vocation," and his respect for the moral law will be "weakened."[131] Disbelief in immortality "hinder[s]" and makes "practically impossible" the performance of duty.[132] It causes "inability to comply."[133] Belief in God is a "means to promoting" and one of the "necessary conditions" for obedience.[134] Belief is necessary for us to "apply our forces."[135] Kant even makes the un-Kantian suggestion that "the moral laws could not be [commands] if they did not connect *a priori* suitable consequences with their rules, and thus carry with them *promises* and *threats*." God is needed to give "effect" to the moral law.[136] Call this the "practicality argument."

I do not think the practicality argument is Kant's considered position. But even if it were, it need not betray sympathy for any sort of normative egoism. Kant might, like Bentham, hold that duty must be in the interest of the agent, without adding that the interest of the agent is relevant to the grounds of duty. He might, that is, view the need for

---

130   Immanuel Kant, *Critique of Pure Reason* (New York: St. Martin's, 1965), trans. Norman Kemp Smith, Ak. A813/B841.

131   Immanuel Kant, *Critique of Judgement* (Indianapolis: Hackett, 1987), trans. Werner S. Pluhar, Ak. 452.

132   Immanuel Kant, *Critique of Practical Reason* (Indianapolis: Bobbs-Merrill, 1956), trans. Lewis White Beck, Ak. 123, 143.

133   Kant, *Judgement*, Ak. 456.

134   Kant, *Practical Reason*, Ak. 146, 132.

135   Kant, *Judgement*, Ak. 455.

136   Kant, *Pure Reason*, Ak. A811/B839, A818/B846.

motivation as demanding institutions that make duty pay, rather than as demanding that duty be cut to fit motivation. Indeed, God *is* just such an institution.

But Kant would not follow Bentham. For the practicality argument is not his intended argument. The obvious problem with it is that Kant thinks reason alone can motivate. If so, the hope of happiness is not necessary for motivation. In various discussions of the highest good, he disavows the practicality argument. For example,

> everything remains disinterested and based only on duty, without being based on fear or hope as incentives. . . . The moral law commands us to make the highest possible good in a world the final object of all our conduct. This I cannot hope to effect except through the agreement of my will with that of a holy and beneficent Author of the world. And although my own happiness is included in the concept of the highest good . . . still it is not happiness but the moral law . . . which is proved to be the ground determining the will to further the highest good.[137]

> [M]orality . . . stands in need neither of the idea of another Being . . . nor of an incentive other than the law itself, for [one] to do his duty. . . . [M]orality does not need religion . . . as regards ability [to act]. . . . [M]orality requires . . . no end . . . to impel the performance of duty. . . . All men could have sufficient incentive if (as they should) they adhered solely to the dictation of pure reason in the law.[138]

> The need to assume a *highest good* . . . is not a need deriving from a deficiency in moral motives.[139]

Kant must intend a different argument.

One suggestion is that, again like Hobbes, Kant relies on the principle that "ought implies can." The argument would be that, since we ought to realise the highest good, it must be possible to do so. Now, Kant sometimes describes his argument in these terms. He initially describes it as concluding that "*something is* . . . because *something ought to happen.*" Since "reason commands that such actions should take place, it must be possible for them to take place."[140] Similarly, "we

---

137 Kant, *Practical Reason*, Ak. 129–30; also 109–10.

138 Immanuel Kant, *Religion Within the Limits of Reason Alone* (New York: Harper & Row, 1960), trans. T. M. Greene and H. H. Hudson, pp. 3, 6n.

139 Immanuel Kant, "On the proverb: That may be true in theory, but is of no practical use," in *Perpetual Peace and other essays* (Indianapolis: Hackett, 1983), trans. Ted Humphrey, Ak. 279n.

140 Kant, *Pure Reason*, Ak. A806/B834, A807/B835.

should seek to further the highest good (which therefore must be at least possible)."[141] And he explicitly subscribes to "ought implies can."[142]

But again, I do not think this is Kant's intended argument. The worry is that if I cannot convince myself that God exists, then "ought implies can" dictates that I ought not to promote the highest good. Kant sometimes draws just this conclusion.[143] But his considered view is that the moral law is not hostage to our beliefs about God. The argument

> is not trying to say that it is as necessary to assume that God exists as it is to acknowledge that the moral law is valid, so that anyone who cannot convince himself that God exists may judge himself released from the obligations that the moral law imposes. No! All we would have to give up is our *aiming* at that final purpose that we are to achieve in the world by complying with the moral law.[144]

This passage suggests what Kant's argument should be: One cannot rationally aim at the highest good without believing that it can be realised. It is the "intention," the setting of a purpose, that would be given up without God.[145]

This argument has the advantage of neither conflicting with Kant's view that reason can motivate nor threatening the moral law. It is a variation on neither Hobbesian arguments from practicality nor Butlerian hopes for motivation. One might ask whether, as Sidgwick thinks, it nevertheless "recognises by implication the reasonableness of the individual's regard for his private happiness." It does not. For Kant's point is not that the agent must believe it possible that *he* will derive happiness from doing his duty. Rather, the agent must believe that happiness will be proportioned to virtue in *all* cases. The virtuous atheist Kant describes "does not require that complying with [the] law should bring him an advantage, either in this world or in another; rather, he is unselfish and wants only to bring about the good to which that sacred law directs all his forces."[146] He may even see "himself in danger of paying in his own person a heavy price in happiness – it being possible that he might not be adequate to the demands of the [highest good]."[147] Since

---

141 Kant, *Practical Reason*, Ak. 125.
142 For example, see Kant, "To Perpetual Peace: A Philosophical Sketch," in *Perpetual Peace*, Ak. 370.
143 Kant, *Pure Reason*, Ak. A811/B839, A828/B856, *Practical Reason*, Ak. 114, 122.
144 Kant, *Judgement*, Ak. 450–1.
145 Kant, *Practical Reason*, Ak. 143; *Judgement*, Ak. 450. See also Kant, *Religion*, pp. 4–7.
146 Kant, *Judgement*, Ak. 452.
147 Kant, *Religion*, p. 5.

the highest good is happiness in proportion to virtue, a duty to promote the highest good is not evidence for "the reasonableness of the individual's regard for his private happiness." (*O* 276) As Kant notes,

> the motive contained in the idea of the highest possible good . . . is not the happiness he intends for himself, but only this idea as an end in itself and of his pursuit of it as his duty. For it does not straightforwardly include the prospect of happiness, but includes it only as a function of a proportion between happiness and the subject's worthiness of it, whatever that may be. But a determination of the will that in itself and in its intention is restricted to the condition of belonging to such a totality is *not selfish*.[148]

At best, the duty to pursue the highest good shows that Kant finds happiness (sometimes) valuable. This admission fails to reveal support for rational egoism, even were the "sometimes" omitted; valuing happiness might just as well reveal support for utilitarianism.[149]

4.8 Paley

Sidgwick notes that Paley takes rational egoism as self-evident. (*ME* 121) Since Paley neither doubts nor argues for rational egoism, this is probably correct. But it is worth seeing whether some further argument might be discovered.

Paley found that "[w]hen I first turned my thoughts to moral speculations, an air of mystery seemed to hang over the whole subject" of moral obligation. To be obliged morally was taken to be "very different from being *induced* only" and "quite another thing, and of another kind, than the obligation which a soldier is under to obey his officer, a servant his master, or any of the civil and ordinary obligations of human life."[150] To clear the mystery, Paley asks "Why am I *obliged* to keep my word?" He replies that it is right, or fit, or beneficial to the public, or required by God to do so. But these answers "leave the matter short; for, the inquirer may turn round upon his teacher with a second question

---

148 Kant, "Theory and Practice," Ak. 28on.

149 There is an extensive literature on the highest good. I have benefited most from Allen W. Wood, *Kant's Moral Religion* (Ithaca, NY: Cornell University Press, 1970), chs. 1–4; R. Z. Friedman, "The Importance and Function of Kant's Highest Good," *Journal of the History of Philosophy* 22, 1984, pp. 325–42; and Andrews Reath, "Two Conceptions of the Highest Good in Kant," *Journal of the History of Philosophy* 26, 1988, pp. 593–619.

150 William Paley, *The Principles of Moral and Political Philosophy* (New York: Garland, 1978), p. 52.

. . . namely, *why* am I obliged to do what is right; to act agreeably to the fitness of things; . . . to promote the public good, or obey the will of God?"[151] The reply here is that

> we can be obliged to nothing, but what we ourselves are to gain or lose something by. . . . As we should not be obliged to obey the laws, or the magistrate, unless rewards or punishments, pleasure or pain, some how or other depended upon our obedience; neither could we, without the same reason, be obliged to practice virtue, obey the commands of God, do what is right, or to any thing else.[152]

The upshot is that "moral obligation is like all other obligations; and . . . all *obligation* is nothing more than an *inducement* of sufficient strength, and resulting, in some way, from the command of another."[153] Moral obligation is special only in that "we consider also what we shall gain or lose in the world to come." Paley does not say why the distinction between inducements in this world and inducements in the next is important. He continues, however, by noting that "[t]hose who would establish a system of morality, independent of a future state, must look out for some different idea of moral obligation; unless they can shew that virtue conducts the possessor to certain happiness in this world, or to a much greater share of it, than he could attain by a different behaviour."[154] This implies that reference to another world is important because it allows for conclusive inducements.

Paley's view of obligation suggests an argument for rational egoism. Suppose psychological egoism is true. Suppose also that moral obligation – or normativity more generally – is mysterious unless its binding force is understood in terms of motivation. I "must" do what it is my duty to do in the sense that something forces me to do it. Given psychological egoism, only the prospect of my pleasure or pain can so force me. Rational egoism arises from conjoining psychological egoism with a view of how normative status is acquired.

It is worth noting that Paley's view is common. Sidgwick cites John Gay as the obvious influence. (*O* 237) Gay defines "obligation" as

> the necessity of doing or omitting any action in order to be happy: i.e. when there is such a relation between an Agent and an action that the Agent cannot be happy without doing or omitting that action, then the

151 Ibid., pp. 47–9.
152 Ibid., pp. 50–1.
153 Ibid., p. 52.
154 Ibid., p. 53; also pp. 17, 56.

agent is said to be obliged to do or omit that action. So that obligation is evidently founded upon the prospect of happiness, and arises from that necessary influence which any action has upon present or future happiness or misery.[155]

The reason for this odd definition is made clear later. Gay argues that those who drop God and make

the immediate criterion of virtue to be the good of mankind; must either allow that virtue is not in all cases obligatory . . . or they must say that the good of mankind is a sufficient obligation. But how can the good of mankind be any obligation to me, when perhaps in particular cases, such as laying down my life, or the like, it is contrary to my happiness?[156]

The obligatory must be necessary, and the only way of ensuring that some act is necessary is for that act to be a necessary means to an end one cannot but pursue. Similar claims are made by John Clarke and Locke.[157] For all, the "mystery" of normativity is cleared, and "empty sounds" avoided, by treating normative claims as descriptions of the consequences of performing certain actions, where the consideration of these consequences will motivate the agent. This is another use of the internalism noted in 2.1.[158]

Yet Paley's argument for rational egoism fails, even given psychological egoism. To see why, consider the claim that consideration of the consequences will motivate the agent. Paley would qualify this: Consideration of the consequences will motivate the agent *provided the agent is rational*. The qualification is needed for two reasons. First, the model of obligation used to understand moral obligation is not one where motivation is always secured. Soldiers sometimes disobey their officers, servants their masters, and citizens the law. Second, our free will cannot be impugned; it must be possible to disobey. (Thus John Clarke writes that men "have it generally in their Power, to determine themselves to the Pursuit of a [smaller] present or [larger] future Happiness, without being invincibly or irresistibly attached to either; . . . herein lies their

155 Gay, *Principle*, p. 273.
156 Ibid., p. 275.
157 Clarke, *Foundation*, p. 8; John Locke, "Of Ethick in General," in Lord King, *The Life and Letters of John Locke* (New York: Burt Franklin, 1972), pp. 309–12.
158 See Darwall, "Internalism," esp. pp. 162–5, "Motive and Obligation," pp. 140–2, and *Internal*, pp. 9–15, 58–60, 85–91.

Freedom, which is sufficient for all the Ends and Purposes of Religion."[159] Gay follows his definition of "obligation" by noting that "no greater obligation can be supposed to be laid upon any free agent without an express contradiction."[160]) An "inducement of sufficient strength," then, is not an inducement that always secures motivation. It is enough to show that "virtue conducts the possessor to certain happiness;" the agent might fail to act as conducted. An inducement is "sufficient" in that it secures motivation among rational agents.[161]

The "rational agent" concession poses a problem for internalism. Internalists separate themselves from externalists by claiming that the connection between the truth of a moral claim and motivation is the distinctive feature of normative claims, without which we cannot understand normativity. But, in addition, internalists require a separate account of what makes one claim a reason for another. This account is not explicated by the connection with motivation. Rather, the connection to motivation is tacked on to the account. And the account of proper reasoning is itself normative: It is the practical equivalent of other normative accounts – accounts to which one is not tempted to require a connection to motivation, such as the rules of logic, or Mill's methods.[162] The addition concerning motivation does not help us to understand normativity, but instead takes an understanding of normativity for granted. If so, there seems no reason for requiring a connection to motivation in order to understand normativity.[163] Even if true, psychological egoism becomes irrelevant.

If Paley is read as suggesting an internalist understanding of normativity, his project fails. But there is an alternative interpretation. Paley takes the obligation to obey a superior officer or a magistrate as clear – one is obliged because of the cost of disobedience – and proceeds by treating moral obligation in the same way. If so, it is unfair to protest that no non-normative explanation of normativity has been given. Perhaps none was ever intended. Perhaps, that is, mystification is directed

159 Clarke, *Foundation*, p. 26.
160 Gay, *Principle*, p. 273.
161 See Darwall, "Internalism," pp. 164, 165, and *Internal*, p. 107. For a contemporary statement of the point, see Korsgaard, "Skepticism."
162 See Kurt Baier, *The Rational and the Moral Order* (La Salle: Open Court, 1995), p. 90; Korsgaard, "Skepticism," p. 17.
163 This is Sidgwick's objection to the naturalist, internalist proposal. See *ME* 112; and my "Sidgwick's False Friends," *Ethics* 107, 1997, pp. 314–20.

not at normativity in general, but at accounts of practical normativity other than the instrumental.[164]

Two positions should be distinguished. Paley wants to explain moral norms by understanding them as instrumental norms. Instrumental norms are preferable in some way. They may be preferable because one thinks they can in turn be understood as non-normative claims, concerning (say) the motivation that follows reflection on the consequences of disobedience. Or they may be preferable for some other reason. I have criticised the first reason. The second reason for preferring instrumental norms remains open. But this is to abandon the internalist suggestion under consideration, for the arguments of 2.1.

4.9 Bentham

Bentham is, of course, usually taken to be a utilitarian; sometimes he is taken to be a psychological egoist; rarely is he taken to be a rational egoist. Sidgwick, however, cites several passages to show that Bentham holds rational egoism along with his utilitarianism. Sidgwick often quotes the first sentence of this passage from Bentham's *Memoirs*:

> 2. Constantly proper end of action on the part of any individual at the moment of action, his real greatest happiness from that moment to the end of his life. See Deontology, private. 3. Constantly proper end of action on the part of every individual, considered as a trustee for the community of which he is considered a member, the greatest happiness of that same community, in so far as depends upon the interest which forms the bond of union between its members. 4. Constantly proper end of action on the part of an individual, having a share in the power of legislation in and for an independent community, termed a political state, the greatest happiness of the greatest number of its members.[165]

He also cites the *Deontology*, intended to tell "each man on each occasion what course of conduct promises to be in the highest degree conducive to his happiness: to his own happiness, first and last," and the discussion of "private ethics," which "teaches us how each man may dispose

---

164 At one point, Darwall makes a similar suggestion: The puzzling claim is that "there exist requirements or *demands* that are binding on all rational persons, even though the conduct demanded may lack any necessary connection to the good of the person obligated." This is a much narrower puzzle than a puzzle about normativity in general (and it is a puzzle "resolved," by rational egoists and instrumentalists, by denying the phenomenon to be explained). See Darwall, *Internal*, p. 2.

165 Bentham, *Memoirs*, in Bowring, *Works*, vol. 10, p. 560.

himself to pursue the course most conducive to his own happiness, by means of such motives as offer of themselves."[166] Sidgwick concludes that Bentham admits two ultimate ends, the general happiness and the individual's happiness. (*ME* 10, 88, 119, *O* 244, BB 166, *PE* 65, 246)

Sidgwick is sometimes tempted to explain away the appearance of rational egoism. He suggests that in the *Deontology*, Bentham is doing what can be done, outside of legislation, to convince people to do what utilitarianism demands. Given Bentham's psychological or predominant egoism, the only route is to show that what utilitarianism asks lies in the self-interest of the agent: "By no other means with any rational prospect of success can you endeavour to cause a man to do so and so, otherwise than by shewing him that it is, or making it to be, his interest so to do."[167] Appeal is made to self-interest as a way of motivating virtuous action, rather than as an ultimate end or necessary condition of its own. (BB 166–8, *O* 243–4, 268, *ME* 84–5)[168] This is the interpretation I assumed in 1.1. But the passage from the *Memoirs* does not seem to suggest this, and so Sidgwick's preferred interpretation is different: Bentham combined utilitarianism and rational egoism by supposing that "it is always the individual's true interest, even from a purely mundane point of view, to act in the manner most conducive to the general happiness." (*ME* 88; also *O* 244)[169]

I shall not assess Sidgwick's interpretation. For recently it has been revived, amid controversy, by David Lyons.[170] Lyons differs from Sidgwick in some ways. In particular, he thinks Bentham's non-egoistic standard is "parochial" – the happiness of the community, rather than

---

166 Bentham, *Deontology*, ed. Amnon Goldworth (Oxford: Oxford University Press [Clarendon], 1992), p. 123, *Introduction to the Principles of Morals and Legislation*, ed. J. H. Burns and H. L. A. Hart, (London: Athlone, 1970), 17.20.

167 Bentham, *Deontology*, p. 128, quoted in John Dinwiddy, "Bentham on Private Ethics and the Principle of Utility," *Revue Internationale de Philosophie* 36, 1982, p. 296.

168 For the same interpretation, see Harrison, *Bentham*, pp. 268–76; J. Brenton Stearns, "Bentham on Public and Private Ethics," *Canadian Journal of Philosophy* 5, 1975, pp. 583–94; Dinwiddy, *Bentham*, pp. 31–2, and "Private Ethics."

169 Sidgwick makes the same point at BB 167. But there he has doubts, noting that Bentham claims in the *Constitutional Code* that the interests of rulers and ruled disagree. Rather than claim an inconsistency between the *Deontology* and the *Constitutional Code*, he suggests that Bowring, who assembled the *Deontology*, may have overstated the harmony of interests. Sidgwick does not explain how Bentham could then hold his two standards.

170 See David Lyons, *In the Interest of the Governed* (Oxford: Oxford University Press [Clarendon], 1991) (revised edition). The works by Stearns, Harrison, and Dinwiddy just cited argue, convincingly, that Lyons is wrong about the text.

the general happiness. But he agrees with Sidgwick's imputation of rational egoism, and even finds a justification in Bentham for it. I turn to this justification, assuming – contrary, I think, to fact – that Lyons is right about the interpretation of Bentham.

Lyons argues that Bentham's starting point is the "fundamental normative idea that government should serve the interests of those being governed."[171] Rational egoism is derived by noting that one governs oneself; parochial utilitarianism is derived by noting that some govern others.

I think neither Sidgwick nor anyone else should be attracted to this position. Sidgwick's condemnation of "national egoism" and of any end between the happiness of the individual and the happiness of every sentient being suggests that he could not accept Bentham's starting point. And as Lyons notes, the starting point seems to have odd consequences, of two sorts.

First, suppose I govern others. Two standards then apply to me. They would seem to offer conflicting prescriptions in some cases: For example, when considering whether to take a bribe for political favours, self-government may favour accepting while my role in governing others may favour rejecting. Lyons replies that Bentham does not, at least early in his career, believe these cases arise.[172] But then Bentham gives a poor defence against the inconsistency worry, one that Sidgwick could not accept.

Lyons also seems to find this a poor defence. He suggests two other defences against the charge of inconsistency: The two standards are not logically inconsistent, since they issue inconsistent prescriptions only given a further empirical fact; and there is no objection to inconsistent prescriptions, provided the prescriptions do not each add that they are the only prescription.[173] These defences may be adequate to show that Bentham could plausibly hold the view Lyons ascribes to him. But they cannot content anyone who, like Sidgwick, wants to know what one ought to do given the empirical facts.

The second odd consequence arises from considering various cases. Suppose I lead a powerful nation. Another nation has a resource my nation wants. I contemplate taking it by force. Or suppose, again, I lead a nation. A citizen of another nation is about to suffer, and I can prevent the suffering very easily – perhaps she is bringing a candle into a room

171   Lyons, *Interest*, p. 32.
172   Ibid., pp. 42–3, 54–5, 59; see also pp. 15, 18.
173   Ibid., p. 100; pp. 15–16, 38–43.

filled with gunpowder. Or suppose I am a private citizen, and I see that I can profit by murder. In deciding what to do in the first two cases, I consult the interests of those I govern – myself and the citizens of my nation. The interests of the citizens of the other nation enter indirectly, if at all. (But should I learn that the candle-bearer is a citizen of my nation, the case changes dramatically: I acquire a fundamental obligation to prevent her suffering.) In the third case, I consult only my own interest – not that of my potential victim. These results require more to support them than the undefended claim that government should serve the interests of the governed.

Lyons agrees. He thinks Bentham handles the third case by positing a harmony of interests within a nation. This is unsatisfactory: Again, rational egoism (or the normative idea it is deduced from) is protected from unpalatable results by assuming a harmony of interests. Lyons suggests three replies for the international cases: (a) "[P]arochialism neither exhausts the whole of Bentham's position nor represents a basic principle for him"; (b) "Bentham most likely considered his political standard as applying only to domestic or internal matters"; (c) Bentham believed in a harmony of interests between nations.[174] None of these replies is persuasive. Reply (a) is irrelevant, since what is added to parochialism – the principle that government should serve the interests of the governed, and rational egoism – does not change the cases. Reply (b) leaves Bentham's "fundamental normative idea" silent where one ought not to be silent. And reply (c), as Lyons admits, seems false.

There is a further reason for dissatisfaction with Bentham's starting point. That government should serve the interests of the governed is not derived from considering what would maximise the general happiness. "[I]t is not implausible to suppose that, in a political context, the obligation to act in the interest of those under one's governance . . . is more basic than an obligation to promote happiness."[175] The starting point specifies a fundamental obligation, an obligation that can conflict with the maximisation of happiness. In these features, it resembles the many obligations offered by the intuitionists so scorned by Bentham and Mill. An intuitionist might ask: Why is *this* obligation fundamental, and not, say, an obligation to keep promises? The traditional utilitarian defence of an obligation is to argue that only happiness is good; hence happiness should be maximised; hence certain actions, maximising happiness, are obligatory. But this answer is not open to Bentham.

174 Ibid., pp. 26, 80; 86; 103–4.
175 Ibid., p. xvi.

Bentham might give a contractarian reply. At one point, he notes that government should serve the interests of the governed because "[t]his is the end which individuals will unite in approving, if they approve of any."[176] Suppose the justification comes from the uniting, rather than from an approval-independent perception that happiness alone is good. Suppose also that no other duties, restricting maximisation of the happiness of those concerned, would be approved. Bentham might then have a plausible argument for parochial utilitarianism, provided divisions into different communities are taken as given. He does not, however, have a plausible argument for rational egoism. For rational egoism, the point would be that an individual "unites" with himself only by holding that he should pursue his own interest. It is unclear that this makes sense. Worse, the possible rationales for looking to unity in approval are unhelpful in the rational egoist case. One might, like later Rawls, look to unity in approval on practical political grounds – agreement, not an argument for the true view of the good, is what is needed to bring people together in peace. Where only one person is considered, this rationale disappears.

4.10 Conclusion

I close with four more general points about Sidgwick's history.

(1) At one point, Sidgwick suggests a general reason for thinking many hold both rational or veto egoism and some other theory. He notes that few explicitly state both, but infers "a wider implicit acceptance of the dualism from the importance attached by dogmatic moralists generally to the conception of a moral government of the world, and from the efforts of empirical utilitarians to prove – as in Bentham's posthumous treatise – that action conducive to greatest happiness generally is always also conducive to the agent's greatest happiness." (FC 484) There is, however, an alternative explanation, which Sidgwick himself offers in the case of Bentham. Moralists, whether utilitarian or not, want people to be motivated to do what the moralists take to be right. Most moralists are psychological or predominant egoists. As a result, they insist that doing what is right brings happiness to the agent.

---

176 Jeremy Bentham, *Principles of International Law,* in Bowring, *Works,* vol. 2, p. 537. For contractarian interpretations of Bentham's argument for utilitarianism, see Lyons, *Interest,* p. 102; Harrison, *Bentham,* pp. 183–94; Stephen Darwall, "Hume and the Invention of Utilitarianism," in *Hume and Hume's Connexions,* ed. M. A. Stewart and John P. Wright (University Park: Pennsylvania State University Press, 1995), pp. 74–5.

They do not hold that there are two "rational or governing principles" of equal normative weight; there is one normative standpoint, which requires virtue to pay to become practical. (FC 484) Considerations of what pays can be seen, in Sidgwick's own words, "as bearing on the Sanctions of morality, not Morality itself; that is not on the theory of what duty is, but on the practical question how a man is to be made to do his duty." (UG 29) I have argued that this fits the Butler of the cool hour passage. It fits Samuel Clarke, Hume, and Kant, in places. Others have argued, against Lyons, that it fits Bentham. (Leslie Stephen even argues, implausibly, that it fits Sidgwick.[177])

(2) Sidgwick wants the agreement of experts, of those "most in earnest." (ME 384) If there is reason to believe that many moralists require that virtue must pay without careful reflection on this requirement, then agreement with them counts for less. There is such reason. Suppose I assert that virtue must pay. Suppose, in addition, I am a religious moralist, in the sense that I believe God will ensure that virtue pays. In this case, requiring that virtue must pay costs me nothing. Indeed, if – like Samuel Clarke and perhaps Reid and Kant – it is part of my project to show the necessity of belief in God, I will be all too eager to add that virtue must pay.[178] Now suppose I do not believe that God will ensure that virtue pays. Sidgwick notes that no moralist "in the present age" claims that virtue always pays "taking only mundane considerations into account." (LE 188) If I add that virtue must pay, I have a problem – Sidgwick's dualism. The problem forces me to reflect carefully on my position and, in particular, on my addition that virtue must pay.[179] Religious moralists – the great majority of moralists – may have kept the addition because they were not forced to think so carefully.

(3) Sidgwick notes that failure with respect to social verification hurts only "if I have no more reason to suspect error in the other mind than in my own." (ME 342; also LK 464) If I can show that the other mind employs bad arguments, whereas I cannot find a problem with my

177 See Hayward, *Ethical Philosophy*, pp. 95–6, 99. Hayward, with equal plausibility, argues that Sidgwick is best read as a rational egoist. See pp. 96–7, 107, 123.
178 For a similar point concerning the need to give God a job in morality, see J. B. Schneewind, "Voluntarism and the Foundations of Ethics," *Proceedings and Addresses of the A.P.A.* 70, 1996, pp. 25–41, particularly pp. 27, 32–4.
179 I might, of course, reflect on other things. Hayward and Hastings Rashdall react to Sidgwick by abandoning hedonism. See Hayward, *Ethical Philosophy*, pp. 243, 246; and Hastings Rashdall, *The Theory of Good and Evil* (Oxford: Oxford University Press [Clarendon], 1907), vol. 1, pp. 57–79. For a recent survey of choices, see Brink, "Puzzle."

argument, then I have more reason to suspect error in the other mind. In this case, disagreement with the other mind need not lessen my confidence.

I have argued that defenders of rational and veto egoism employ various bad arguments. Often, they defend both from objections by citing a harmony of interests or they appeal to God's design.[180] Sidgwick agrees that these arguments are bad. He also attacks, as I have, the various Hobbesian arguments.

There is a further common mistake that he might have noted. Sidgwick writes that

> most of the practical principles that have been seriously put forward are more or less satisfactory to the common sense of mankind, so long as they have the field to themselves. . . . When I am asked, 'Do you not consider it ultimately reasonable to seek pleasure and avoid pain for yourself? . . . Do you not acknowledge the general happiness to be a paramount end?' I answer 'yes.' (*ME* 14)

The claim "that it is reasonable for each individual to seek his own happiness" is "scarcely questioned" when "present[ed] singly." (*ME* [1] 388) Butler and Reid can be seen as arguing for egoism by considering cases in which it has the field to itself – others are not involved. Reid, at least, concludes that egoism is true and must be reconciled with other principles. This is an error, in two ways: In cases in which others are not involved, utilitarianism is supported as much as egoism; and even if egoism were uniquely supported by considering cases in which others are not involved, it would not follow that egoism remains supported in any case in which others are involved.[181]

Sidgwick himself may be guilty of a similar error. Consider his claim that, to common sense, "'interested' actions, tending to promote the agent's happiness, are *prima facie* reasonable: and that the *onus probandi* lies with those who maintain that disinterested conduct, as such, is reasonable." (*ME* 120) No doubt common sense views actions that benefit the agent as prima facie reasonable. Their claim to reasonableness is muddied, however, once effects on others are introduced. Say, for example, many others are hurt greatly and the agent reaps a tiny gain. But

---

180 They also appeal to Scripture. John Clarke claims that when Paul says that "if the dead rise not, let us eat and drink, for to morrow we die," he means "that Men must be allowed to pursue and prefer their own Advantage or Happiness, before all other Considerations." See *Foundation*, p. 24; also pp. 25, 107, 111; Selby-Bigge, *British Moralists*, p. 222.

181 For the first error, see Parfit, *Reasons and Persons*, p. 130.

similarly, common sense views actions that benefit others as prima facie reasonable. To use Hume's example: We think it reasonable to avoid stepping on the gouty toes of a stranger, where our self-interest is unconcerned.[182] And again, the claim to reasonableness is muddied once effects on the agent are introduced: Say the action hurts the agent greatly and provides a tiny gain to many others. Sidgwick may think common sense places the onus on disinterested action because he compares interested action, considered without thinking of its effects on others, with disinterested action, considered as involving some sacrifice to the agent.[183] (Alternatively, Sidgwick usually thinks of "disinterested action," not as action directed at the pleasure of others, but rather as action simply not directed at the pleasure of the agent. [*ME* xxi, 57, 136, 367] He would find the onus against disinterested action described in this way, since, as a hedonist, he suspects ends other than pleasure (such as promise keeping or knowing the truth). But this argument for placing the onus supports hedonistic rational egoism over non-hedonist positions, rather than hedonistic rational egoism over hedonistic utilitarianism.)

(4) Sidgwick admits that some – Whewell and John Stuart Mill – explicitly reject egoism. (*O* 245, 233, *ME* xx) He sometimes adds Kant and might have added that most uncompromising of utilitarians, Godwin. (*ME* xx, *O* 233) In other cases – Wollaston and Price – he does not find egoism, though he does find inclusion of prudence as a duty. Sidgwick may think this reveals sympathy for egoism. But as W. K. Frankena notes, the inference would be illegitimate, since prudence may be a duty on non-egoist grounds.[184] Some, then, reject egoism.

After Sidgwick, more reject it, perhaps in part because he showed so well the cost of maintaining rational or veto egoism without God. In *Ethics,* Moore finds it simply self-evident that rational egoism is mistaken and that "it must always be our duty to do what will produce the best effects *upon the whole,* no matter how bad the effects upon ourselves may be and no matter how much good we ourselves may lose by it." In *Principia Ethica,* he finds rational egoism not mistaken, but incoherent.[185] Prichard rules out rational egoism by assuming that no appeal to

---

182 Hume, *Enquiry Concerning Morals,* p. 226; also p. 235.
183 For this use of "disinterested," see *ME* 138.
184 See Frankena, "History of Ethical Dualism," pp. 178–9, 181, 187.
185 Moore, *Ethics* (New York: Oxford University Press, 1965), p. 100, *Principia Ethica,* pp. 96–105.

consequences (or, indeed, no appeal to anything other than "direct apprehension") can justify an ought-claim.[186] And Russell gives a very quick version of Sidgwick's arbitrariness argument against rational egoism.[187]

Unfortunately, none of these arguments is convincing or, in Russell's case, developed. And until very recently, this century has not seen much serious work on egoism. Nor has much been done in the way of arguing for, rather than elaborating, the instrumental theory. No doubt this is due, in part, to the fascination with metaethics and, in part, to the habit of dismissing rational egoism as not a "moral" theory. But whatever the reason, this inattention has made it easier to think of egoism, or the instrumental theory, as a "default" position. When exposed, neither deserves such a privilege.

186 H. A. Prichard, "Does Moral Philosophy Rest on a Mistake?" in *Moral Obligation* (Oxford: Oxford University Press [Clarendon], 1949), pp. 3–5.
187 Bertrand Russell, "The Elements of Ethics," in *Philosophical Essays* (London: Allen & Unwin, 1966), pp. 50–1.

Index

Index

Farrell, Daniel, 36 n80
Fogelin, Robert, 51 n49
Foot, Philippa, 43–4, 45 n27
Frankena, W. K., 1 n4, 8 n3, 12 n17, 39 n2,
  78 n39, 127 n55, 137 n112, 157
Friedman, R. Z., 146 n149
Fumerton, Richard, 40

Gay, John, 10 n11, 147–8, 149
Gauthier, David, 3, 6 n1 and n2, 7, 11
  n13, 31 n65 and n67, 58 n75, 124 n43,
  131 n78, 133 n93; arguments for instru-
  mentalism, 46–7
Gert, Bernard, 37 n83
Giere, Richard, 41 n6
Gizycki, Georg von, 75 n28, 76 n30, 83
God, 4, 16, 113, 117, 123, 124,
  137–9, 141–2, 143–5, 146–7, 148, 155,
  156, 157
Godwin, William, 157
Goldie, Mark, 26 n52, 36 n79
Goldman, Alan, 11 n13
Goldsmith, M. M., 6 n2
Goodman, Nelson, 54
Green, T. H., 88, 111, 112
Grote, George, 38 n84
Grotius, Hugo, 5, 36–7; on self-defence,
  21, 23, 24–7, 28 n59, 30

Hampton, Jean, 6 n2, 7, 16, 16 n29, 26
  n52, 30, 31, 31 n65 and n67, 32 n68, 33,
  37, 45 n29, 49 n41, 50 n43, 57 n72, 133
  n93
Hare, R. M., 57 n72, 71, 72–3
Harman, Gilbert, 40
Harris, Arthur, 30
Harrison, Jonathan, 51 n49, 52 n50
Harrison, Ross, 9 n4 and n5, 151 n168
  and n170, 154 n176
Harsanyi, John, 40
Hayward, F. H., 71 n19, 73 n23, 75 n28,
  83 n48, 87 n55, 89 n60, 120 n32, 155
  n177 and n179
hedonism, 2, 4, 47, 61, 74, 88 n59, 92, 155
  n179, 157
Hill, Thomas E., 48 n39, 49 n41
Hobbes, Thomas, 4, 10, 12, 14, 36 n80,
  114, 143, 144; on agreement, 21–2; in
  historical context, 35–7; and instrumen-

talism, 31–3, 34; and peace, 36–8; a rational egoist, 1, 6– 7, 35–8, 110, 111,
  112; arguments for rational egoism, 3,
  16, 33–4; on self-defence, 17–21, 23–4,
  25 n50, 26, 27, 28, 29–30, 34–5
Homer, 54
Hospers, John, 28 n59
Hubin, Don, 57 n73
Hume, David, 14, 139–40, 157; as an egoist, 4, 5, 110, 111, 124–35, 155; and instrumentalism, 3, 5, 40, 47, 50–3, 56; on
  justice, 124–7, 129, 131–5; on norms,
  53– 6; on practicality, 129–31
Hutcheson, Francis, 4, 115, 117

imperatives, categorical, 40, 43, 44–5, 47,
  48, 56–7; hypothetical, 5, 40, 45, 47–50,
  56–7
instrumental theory, 2, 3, 5, 7, 13–14, 39,
  94, 150, 158; argument against, 56–8,
  60–1; arguments for, 40–50; in Hobbes,
  31–3, 34; in Hume, 50–3; Sidgwick on,
  57 n72, 58, 60–1, 94
internalism, 42–3, 148–50

Jenkins, Joyce, 135 n103
just war theory, 27–8

Kagan, Shelly, 107 n79, 142 n129
Kant, Immanuel, 6, 7, 44; as an egoist, 4,
  5, 110, 111, 142–3, 146, 155, 157; on the
  highest good, 142–6; arguments for hypothetical imperatives, 5, 47–50; on
  "ought" implies "can," 144–5; on practicality, 143–4
Kavka, Gregory, 2 n6, 4 n10, 6 n1, 7, 16,
  20, 27 n58, 28 n59, 30, 31 n67, 35 n76,
  38 n84, 130; on "ought" implies "can,"
  11–14; practicality argument for rational egoism, 8–14, 34
Kleinig, John, 118 n24, 120 n32, 121 n36
Korsgaard, Christine, 42 n14, 45 n29, 127
  n55, 149 n161 and n162

Lacey, A. R., 96 n68
Lackey, Douglas, 27 n58
Laudan, Larry, 3, 40–2
Little, Daniel, 71 n19

160